The Creative Curriculum® for Preschool, Sixth Edition

Volume 5: Science and Technology, Social Studies & the Arts

Heather Baker and Kai-leé Berke

TeachingStrategies® · Bethesda, MD

The publisher and the authors cannot be held responsible for injury, mishap, or damages incurred during the use of or because of the information in this book. The authors recommend appropriate and reasonable supervision at all times based on the age and capability of each child.

Editorial: Kimberly Maxwell and Dana Wood
Layout/production: Jeff Cross and Abner Nieves
Illustrations: Jennifer Barrett O'Connell
Cover design: Abner Nieves

Teaching Strategies, LLC
4500 East West Highway, Suite 300
Bethesda, MD 20814

www.TeachingStrategies.com

978-1-60617-702-0

Library of Congress Control Number: 2016934452

Printed and bound in the United States of America.

2020 2019 2018 2017 2016

11 10 9 8 7 6 5 4 3 2

Contents

How to Use This Book vi

Chapter 1. Components of Science and Technology 2
- Science and Technology 3
- Components of Science and Technology 5
- Physical Science 5
- Life Science 10
- Earth and the Environment 14
- Awareness of Technology 17
- Basic Operations and Concepts 20
- Tools and Equipment 23
- People and Technology 26
- Studies: Simple Machines 29

Chapter 2. Science and Technology Learning in Interest Areas and Outdoors 36
- Science and Technology Learning in Interest Areas and Outdoors 37
- The Discovery Area: The Hub of Science and Technology Learning 38
- Science and Technology in the:
  - Toys and Games Area 42
  - Block Area 46
  - Dramatic Play Area 50
  - Art Area 54
  - Library Area 57
  - Sand and Water Area 61
  - Music and Movement Area 64
  - Cooking Area 67
  - Technology Area 71
- Science and Technology Outdoors 74

Chapter 3. Planning Your Science and Technology Program...... 78
Planning Your Science and Technology Program 79
Objectives for Science and Technology Development and Learning 80
Guiding Children's Science and Technology Learning 81
Creating a Scientifically and Technologically Rich Physical Environment 82
Integrating Science and Technology Throughout the Day 84

Chapter 4. Components of Social Studies 92
Social Studies 93
Components of Social Studies 95
People and How They Live 95
People and the Environment 99
People and the Past 103
Spaces and Geography 107
Studies: Reduce, Reuse, Recycle 111

Chapter 5. Social Studies Learning in Interest Areas and Outdoors 118
Social Studies Learning in Interest Areas and Outdoors 119
The Library Area: The Hub of Social Studies Learning 119
Social Studies in the:
- Toys and Games Area 122
- Block Area 125
- Dramatic Play Area 128
- Discovery Area 131
- Art Area 134
- Sand and Water Area 137
- Cooking Area 140
- Technology Area 143
- Music and Movement Area 145

Social Studies and the Outdoors 148

Chapter 6. Planning Your Social Studies Program 152
Guiding Children's Social Studies Learning 153
Creating an Environment for Social Studies Learning 153
Integrating Social Studies Throughout the Day 155

Chapter 7. Components of the Arts 160

The Arts 161
Components of the Arts 163
Visual Arts 163
Music 166
Dance 169
Drama 173
Studies: Music Making 177

Chapter 8. Learning the Arts in Interest Areas and the Outdoors 184

Learning in the Interest Areas and the Outdoors 185
The Arts in the:
- Library Area 186
- Art Area 189
- Discovery Area 192
- Toys and Games Area 195
- Cooking Area 198
- Block Area 201
- Technology Area 203
- Dramatic Play Area 205
- Sand and Water Area 208
- Music and Movement Area 210

The Arts and the Outdoors 213

Chapter 9. Planning Your Arts Program 217

Guiding Children's Learning of the Arts 219
Creating an Environment for Learning the Arts 220
Integrating the Arts Throughout the Day 221

References 226

Index. 231

How to Use This Book

A good preschool prepares children for the future. It prepares them for success in school, and it prepares them for life beyond the classroom. While math and literacy curricula are prevalent in early childhood education, they don't cover areas of learning that address concepts found in every interaction, every task, and any creative thought and achievement. Roy, Baker, and Hamilton stress how important it is for teachers to ensure that the children in their classrooms are able to experience all the different ways children experience the world. These "diverse ways of understanding" reflect the diverse nature of children's individual "capabilities and dispositions," for "human endeavor is multifaceted, not just verbal and mathematical" (2012).

The content areas of science and technology, social studies, and the arts are often overlooked as being frivolous and are pushed aside for the more "academic" pursuits of literacy and math. But research continues to show how children use the arts and technology to refine their inquiry skills to explore and learn about the world, for these topics of discovery both complement and build upon other content subjects (Cohen & Stupiansky, 2013). In particular, children's learning around the subject of the arts encourages children to "use all their senses to develop a sense of wonder and appreciation" of the world (Koster, 2012). For young children, this artistic sense of wonder and aesthetic joy in the arts "inform(s) children's navigation of the world and their experiences" (Bentley, 2013).

The Creative Curriculum® for Preschool, Volume 5: Science and Technology, Social Studies & the Arts takes these critical ideas one step further by providing detailed guidance for including content learning as part of everyday preschool learning experiences. This volume expands on information provided in *The Creative Curriculum® for Preschool, Volume 1: The Foundation*, showing in detail the ways that the classroom can be a rich environment for the areas of science and technology, social studies, and the arts. It discusses how to make these subject areas a part of children's everyday learning through in-depth investigations, teacher-child interactions, changes to the interest areas, and family and community involvement.

This volume shows you how to make science and technology, social studies, and the arts both naturally occurring and fascinating concepts found in the classroom. It is an invaluable resource for teachers planning project-based investigations through studies of science and technology and social studies and arts topics. There are so many ways to plan for teacher-guided experiences with these areas and to follow children's lead and interests to determine what children might investigate and discover next!

Chapters 1–3: Science and Technology

These chapters address the science and technology learning that takes place in your classroom. They explain the components of, the research behind, and the role the teacher plays in promoting awareness of physical science, earth science, life science, and technology concepts. These chapters also give examples of how science and technology are part of everyday classroom experiences as well as key components of studies related to these topics. An in-depth look at how these content areas can be explored in the interest areas and ideas for incorporating science and technology throughout your day give you the tools you need to support children's love of learning and exploration.

Chapters 4–6: Social Studies

These chapters introduce the areas of social studies including people and how they live, people and the environment, people and the past, and spaces and geography. In this section you will find strategies for planning studies, incorporating social studies concepts into your daily experiences, and including families and community members in support of children's learning. You will be guided through the interest areas, with particular focus on dramatic play, to explore and examine the many ways that children investigate social studies concepts in the classroom. Additional research and prompts to reflect on your own teaching practices will give you a solid foundation of social studies to share with the children you teach.

Chapters 7–9: The Arts

These chapters invite you to explore the arts beyond the play dough on the table and the paints at the easel. Here you will find information about visual arts, drama, music, and dance that can help you transform your art experiences with children. These chapters focus on the research behind the importance of the arts in a preschool setting and how to plan for both teacher- and child-led art exploration. You will gain a better understanding of the ways that the arts can fit into each part of your day, and you will read about how to make interest areas an integral part of the art experiences you offer to children.

Meeting the Needs of All Children

All children should have opportunities to be actively engaged in science and technology, socials studies, and art experiences that are challenging yet achievable. Chapter 1 in *Volume 1: The Foundation* explains similarities and differences between children and how those characteristics affect their learning. This chapter also includes detailed information about how to support all learners in your program. When introducing content, asking questions, and supporting children as they begin a study, you may find that some children are eager to jump in while others may hang back and observe. Studies serve the great purpose of providing open-ended experiences that children can work together on or decide to investigate on their own. In *The Creative Curriculum*® classroom, the teacher's role is to determine what individual supports a child needs in order to participate fully. It is important to observe children carefully and continually to see whether the current supports are effective and to make any changes as necessary. Below are suggestions for ways to modify the environment and your interactions with children to meet the needs of all children with regard to English-language learners, advanced learners, and children with disabilities.

Supporting English-Language Learners

The teacher's role is to provide an environment that is welcoming and reassuring. When planning experiences related to science and technology, social studies, and the arts, teachers can incorporate ideas and modifications that will help support English-language learners and ensure opportunities for full participation. Fortunately, learning experiences in these content areas open so many possibilities for including English-language learners and their families, their languages, and their cultures. In addition to the suggestions found in the other resources of *The Creative Curriculum® for Preschool*, here are a few examples of how to ensure inclusiveness when sharing learning experiences in the areas of of science and technology, social studies, and the arts:

- Show and talk (e.g., when examining the physical properties of objects, encourage children to look at, touch, smell, and/or listen to the object by modeling the action as you describe it).
- Let children respond in nonverbal ways (e.g., pointing to a photo on the job chart and then picking up the watering can to water the plant).
- Include bilingual audio books and videos for children to enjoy.
- Pose questions that you know children can confidently answer, either in English or in their home languages.
- Encourage children who speak the same language to work together (e.g., planning and setting up the Dramatic Play area as a grocery store).
- Use gestures and physical actions along with speech. For example, dancing to music requires no verbal explanation.
- Learn and speak a few words and phrases in the child's home language (e.g., review your current *Teaching Guide* for vocabulary and select words relevant to the topic).
- Add cooking experiences that include foods from the cultures represented in your classroom.
- Sing or listen to music in the children's home languages.
- Help them incorporate others' ideas during experiences such as when making a list of materials needed to transform the Dramatic Play area.
- Give children an opportunity to use technology in new ways. Encourage them to think of other uses for classroom technology devices.
- Pose critical thinking questions when interacting with children during choice time.

Supporting Children With Disabilities

Supporting the active participation of a child with a disability may mean adapting the environment or materials and modifying instructions. Again, the open-ended learning that takes place when pursuing science and technology, social studies, and art concepts allows for a great deal of modification to support these learners. In addition to reviewing your daily plans and assessing your displays and materials in the interest areas, talk with families, colleagues, and specialists who can help determine how to best meet the needs of the children in your class as they explore these concepts. As children's interests change, your interest areas change and your studies evolve; periodically reevaluate your efforts to support all children to ensure that each child can enjoy the rich experiences associated with science and technology, social studies, and the arts. Here are some examples of adaptations and modifications that may help further support children with disabilities:

- Introduce technology that enables children to see, hear, and touch things while the technology devices are used in different ways.
- Provide a range of artifacts for a study topic that are accessible to all children.
- Preview activities and learning experiences with children such as beginning a new study or introducing new materials to an interest area.
- Introduce and reinforce relevant vocabulary during investigations.
- Think about the ease with which materials can be handled during experiments.
- Include a wide range of art materials so that all children can create in the Art area.
- Invite families to share their experiences from home when learning about a topic.
- Think outside the box when adding building materials to interest areas. Make space for very large or very small structures.
- Look around the room for objects that can be used as musical instruments. Encourage children to think of how they can use them to make sounds.
- Take children outdoors and gather natural items for them to explore.
- Add a classroom pet or plant for children to look at closely at children's eye level.
- Use pictures to explain science and social studies concepts such as a plant's life cycle or the tools used for a specific job.
- Use the sand and water table to introduce a variety of sensory materials for exploration.
- Provide children with gloves when exploring new objects with different textures.
- Plan a variety of ways for children to investigate and experiment together (e.g., large groups, small groups, one-on-one, and individually).
- Add materials to interest areas that reflect children's experiences and backgrounds (e.g., food items in Dramatic Play or bilingual books in the Library).
- Work with children to generate ideas for classroom rules, study topics, and celebrations to foster a strong classroom community.
- Provide nonverbal ways for children to participate (e.g., dancing, playing instruments, and exploring natural items outdoors).

- Encourage children to bring familiar items from home to add to relevant interest areas and to further the study in Dramatic Play.
- Refer to your *Teaching Guide* for call-out boxes that offer suggestions for supporting children.
- Foster partnerships with families by including them in classroom investigations and experiments.
- Send home books and learning materials such as *LearningGames*® to help connect the classroom learning experiences with family experiences at home.

Supporting Advanced Learners

Interacting with children during experiences related to science and technology, social studies, and the arts gives children a chance to explore a wide range of subjects using a variety of methods. Teachers can observe these investigations and experiments to help determine how to best support advanced learners by offering more support or challenges. Here are a few examples of how teachers can support these learners:

- Give students a range of options to choose from when exploring (e.g., mixed media for art creations or a variety of tools for tinkering).
- Support children who wish to further investigate a science or social studies concept (e.g., following up after a study has finished to help a child find out more).
- Notice which ideas and experiments are interesting to children and then group children according to their interests during investigations.
- Challenge children to plan and implement an effective way to share information with families about a study topic.
- Be aware of the strengths of advanced learners and understand how to help them grow in all areas of development.
- Encourage children to work together during different learning experiences (e.g., forming a musical band, practicing retelling a story using props, etc.).
- Support children to expand the scope of their experiences to avoid repetition (e.g., using a wide variety of materials and techniques to create a mural).
- Invite children to share their interests and think of ways to learn more about a topic (e.g., a child notices small hairs on a flower stem and decides to find out their purpose and which plants have them).

1

Components of Science and Technology

Science and Technology 3

Components of Science and Technology 5

Physical Science 5

Life Science 10

Earth and the Environment 14

Awareness of Technology 17

Basic Operations and Concepts 20

Tools and Equipment 23

People and Technology 26

Studies: Simple Machines 29

Science and Technology

Science is a natural part of children's everyday experiences. Because they are inherently interested in their surroundings, children continually observe and analyze what they see, hear, smell, taste, and touch. A 1-year-old might get excited when he sees a squirrel scamper across the playground and up a tree. Two-year-olds might try different tools at the water table: watering cans, cups of different sizes, funnels, scoops, sponges, and basters. Three-year-olds might carefully feed the fish in the fishbowl and then watch them swim to the surface to eat. Four-year-olds might use a magnifying glass to compare the characteristics of different rocks. Five-year-olds might explain to their families why recycling is important after visiting a recycling center.

Technology is found in many places in our everyday lives. In the classroom, children use and see adults model the use of a variety of tools, electronics, and other materials that help us work more efficiently. When children experiment with technology, they are able to understand real-life scenarios and how technology tools support us. When children turn up the volume on an e-reader, use two fingers to zoom in on a picture on a tablet, or use an electric mixer during a cooking experience, they are gaining an understanding of the many ways that we depend on technology in a preschool classroom.

Research shows that children's inquiry skills are best supported through hands-on, project-based investigations. Starting with what children already know, teachers and children work together to develop questions, investigate to find answers, ask follow-up questions, and reflect on what they've learned. A preschool classroom is the ideal setting for this type of learning. When children show some knowledge and interest in a scientific topic, teachers can encourage children's deeper learning using scientific inquiry skills and experimentation. As children explore more science topics, they can apply their knowledge and skills to more in-depth learning.

As an early childhood teacher, you play an important role in bridging children's informal understanding of science concepts with more formal, investigative practices. You design the learning environment by purposely including natural materials, investigative tools, and physical objects in interest areas for child-initiated explorations. You intentionally introduce activities with a scientific and technological focus. You observe and listen as children interact with materials and with their peers, and then you use scientific and technology vocabulary to describe their actions and thinking, for verbal language skills are related to children's understanding of this terminology. You ask questions that children investigate. You include science and technology activities as part of the everyday routine.

Standards in technology outline the skills, understandings, knowledge, and attitudes that children in preschool through grade 12 should acquire. The standards focus on both the basics of using computers and the uses of technology to communicate, learn new information, solve problems, and create. Equally important, the standards also stress social skills, such as working cooperatively with peers and using technology responsibly (ISTE, 2007).

What Does Research Say?

Research from *The Progress of Education Reform: Science in the Early Years* shows that science learning "improved children's readiness in science and non-science domains including approaches to learning, creative arts, language and literacy, and early math." "Children's school readiness in science and social science has been found to predict science achievement at grade 5, in addition to math and reading achievement at grade 5, even more strongly than reading readiness does" (Brenneman, 2014).

Creativity, even in the sciences, is an important way of discovering new worlds, new ways of doing things, and new ideas that no one else has had. Teachers can build upon young children's learning when they actively inspire children's natural investigative skills of "observing, wondering, and questioning" (Bentley, 2013).

There are numerous links between mathematics and science, including the development of reasoning, ability to classify and identify patterns, problem solve, and make predictions (Brenneman, 2014).

The science objectives for development and learning in *The Creative Curriculum® for Preschool* are:

24. Uses scientific inquiry skills

25. Demonstrates knowledge of the characteristics of living things

26. Demonstrates knowledge of the physical properties of objects and materials

27. Demonstrates knowledge of Earth's environment

Technology is represented in:

28. Uses tools and other technology to perform tasks

Objectives 24–27 encompass the important areas of physical science, earth science, and life science. For technology concepts, there are four components of technology standards that apply to preschool children: awareness of technology; basic operations and concepts; tools and equipment; and people and technology. This chapter discusses each area and each component in more detail, relating research to the teacher's role and to assessment strategies. With a clear understanding of the components of science and technology, teachers will be able to observe children, analyze and evaluate their scientific learning, and plan experiences to expand each child's knowledge of science and technology concepts.

Components of Science and Technology

Thinking about the scientific interests of the children in your classroom is a great first step in determining which science concepts you want to introduce and focus on. Pay particular attention to how children's interests fall within the following categories (National Research Council, 2012):

- physical science
- life science
- Earth and the environment

Four components of technology standards apply to preschool children:

- awareness of technology
- basic operations and concepts
- tools and equipment
- people and technology

Although young children naturally begin to develop some informal understandings of science and technology, many more opportunities to learn about them need to be provided. The teacher's role is critical to that development. Generally, teachers should identify everyday situations that involve science and technology concepts, and intentionally share those concepts with children through daily routines, choice-time activities, and investigative studies. Many teaching strategies contribute to children's development of understanding of science and technology.

Physical Science

Physical science refers to the properties that make up objects. Children can explore physical science by observing the size, color, or weight of objects. They can explore changes to an object's properties. When children stack hollow objects on top of solid ones, use a potato masher to mash a banana, or add wheels to their block construction to make it roll, they are experimenting with physical science concepts. Support children's learning by asking questions such as:

- What is this made of? Is it hard or soft? …rough or smooth? …heavy or light?
- What does this smell like? Why do you think it smells that way?
- What does this taste like?
- What sound does this make? How does it make that sound?
- What texture does this have? What else feels the same way?
- How can we move this easily?
- What can we do to change this into something else?

Instead of planning specific science experiments for children, use your planning time to reflect on ways to create learning opportunities based on available materials and children's interests.

What Does Research Say?

It is through their active participation in experiential learning – learning through doing – that young children become familiar with science and gain science skills. To encourage children's full engagement with science (e.g., children's exploration and investigation of science activities and materials), teachers should be intentional in their classroom approach to science. By intentionally setting up the classroom to engage children in science experiences, children are able to "question, explore, investigate, make meaning, and construct explanations and organize knowledge" as they take part in various science activities in the classroom (NSTA, 2014).

Children are natural scientists, natural investigators, who from an early age use "scientific inquiry" to explore. Their natural desire to better understand all that is around them, inspires children to interact with and closely examine all the objects that make up their world (Moomaw, 2012).

When the classroom is purposely set up to encourage children to investigate and ask questions, it gives children the opportunity to further their explorations and to begin making the connections between language and what they are encountering as they explore (Brenneman, 2014).

There should be numerous opportunities in the classroom and at home for children to be "science explorers and discoverers" (NAEYC, 2013).

Through interacting with the various objects they encounter, from blocks to baby dolls, and moving their own bodies, children demonstrate how they learn as "natural 'manipulators'" of the world around them (Kneas & Perry, 2011).

Classroom science activities (e.g., having children experiment with inclined planes) allow children to investigate a variety of scientific principles (e.g., force and motion) that lay the foundation for young children's science knowledge and their inquiry skills (Zan & Geiken, 2010).

The Teacher's Role in Promoting Understanding of Physical Science

As adults, it is sometimes easy to overlook the everyday objects that are used and manipulated in the classroom. But it is the everyday materials that children come in contact with that often provide the most meaningful and engaging physical science experiences. Promoting understanding of physical science does not require a site visit to a science center. It can be as simple as talking about how to stack the chairs so they don't fall over or why it's easier to pull a wagon along the sidewalk instead of through the grass. Remember to keep it simple so that children can easily observe the physical characteristics of objects and look closely at how they work. As you take a moment to look around the classroom and notice how you might use different materials to interact with children and discuss physical science concepts, consider the following ideas:

Provide tools for exploration.
Offering tools such as magnets, magnifying glasses, balance scales, pulleys, and mirrors to encourage children's explorations helps them learn about common objects through observation and manipulation.

Ask open-ended questions.
You can extend children's investigations by asking questions that prompt them to think more critically as they explore (e.g., *Why does the paint come off when we rub sandpaper over it?*).

Describe observable physical changes.
As children notice changes to physical objects, describing what they see can help them to better understand what is happening and why (e.g., *When we hold the play dough in our hands it gets softer. It also feels warmer when we touch it.*).

Include a variety of materials for children to use for experimentation.
Designate a *makerspace* in the classroom for children to work with a variety of materials as they experiment to learn how things work, how things fit together, and what else they can be used for. Describe what you notice as you see children working with the new objects.

Discuss children's constructions.
Ask questions as children build to help them think about why some materials are better for building structures than others. Encourage them to experiment with different materials and compare the outcomes.

Observing Children's Understanding

To assess children's understanding of physical science, observe children consistently and regularly. Here are a few examples of what you might notice taking place in your classroom:

- Building a marble run out of cardboard tubes
- Adding another block to the base of a tower to make it sturdier
- Using a knife as a wedge to cut fruit
- Saying, "I glued the paper together and now it's really strong! It won't rip at all."

As children explore physical objects or work together to investigate a physical science study topic, ask the following questions:

What do you notice about this?

What did you discover? Why do you think that happened?

Where can you find out more about that?

How did you do that? What will you do next?

What happens when...? How does it change?

How does it work?

What did you observe? How can you record your findings?

How does it compare with...?

How can you make it move differently?

Can you make it bigger? Heavier? Smoother? Slower?

Your Teaching Practice

Look around the room at the materials you currently have in your interest areas. Do they encourage physical science exploration? What small changes can you make that will invite children to think more about the properties of and changes to the objects they use each day?

As children pay attention to your words and actions throughout the day, do you point out physical characteristics of materials and talk about how they can be used?

Tips to Share With Families

- Read books about science. Together, talk about the objects in the book and how they are used or made and how they work.
- Give your child plenty of time to explore new and familiar objects. Ask questions about the object to encourage your child to describe it.
- Help your child use different materials at home to build. Talk about what you see your child doing.
- Ask your child to help you make minor repairs around the house. Talk about what you're fixing and why. Show your child what is broken and ask her for ideas about how to fix it.
- Encourage your child to use his five senses when exploring objects. Give him new words to describe what he notices. For example, if he says the sponge is wet and heavy, you can tell him it's "saturated."
- Point out and talk about how things move. Ask your child to help you move things around the house and talk about the easiest way to move items of different shapes, sizes, and weights.

Life Science

Life science refers to the science of living things. Plants and animals provide the easiest source of learning life science in a preschool classroom. Teachers can easily use their immediate environment and community to find interesting resources for teaching and learning. For example, a preschool in Monterey, California might observe and investigate sea otters, while children in Raleigh, North Carolina can look more closely at carnivorous pitcher plants. The following questions may help you introduce life science concepts to children using the plants and animals in your area:

- What do living things eat? How do they find food?
- What do plants and animals need to survive?
- How do plants and animals live together? How do they help each other?
- What changes do we see in living things?
- What plants and animals can we find in our community?

Learning about our bodies and how to take care of them also explores life science concepts. The following questions may help children think critically about how their bodies work and change:

- How are our bodies different from when we were babies?
- What do we use our eyes, ears, noses, hands, and mouths for?
- What types of foods help our bodies grow strong?

What Does Research Say?

The National Science Teachers Association (NSTA) affirms that learning science practices in the early years can foster children's curiosity and enjoyment in exploring the world around them (NSTA, 2014).

When children learn about the natural world at an early age, they develop both an "appreciation of and respect for the environment." By taking part in the care of animals and plants, children learn that living things have basic needs that need to be met for them to survive and thrive (Center for Information Science Education at the Florida Museum of Natural History/University of Florida, 2004, 2010).

Young children's curiosity and fascination with the outdoors and nature can contribute to their science learning and scientific skills as children "increase their observational skills" and "develop sensory, physical, emotional, intellectual, and social skills." When children explore nature and the outdoors, they also gain "a greater appreciation and understanding of the natural world" (Dominguez, McDonald, Kalajian, & Stafford, 2013).

Observing and interacting with the natural world gives children the chance to engage in scientific thinking as they "describe, compare, and classify the things they encounter" (Center for Information Science Education at the Florida Museum of Natural History/University of Florida, 2004, 2010).

Through play, children can gain an understanding of scientific inquiry and of various science concepts, such as "the diversity and interdependence of life" (Hamlin & Wisneski, 2012).

As children learn and explore how their bodies work, they are gaining the scientific knowledge and skills that lead to having the "positive attitudes needed to make healthy lifestyle choices" (Carraway-Stage, Henson, Dipper, Spangler, Ash, & Goodell, 2014).

The Teacher's Role in Promoting Understanding of Life Science

Life science refers to the exploration of living things, their life cycles, and their habitats. For preschool children, their classroom explorations could be of a class pet, wildlife found outdoors, or a plant they observe and care for daily. Paying attention to children's interests can help you focus their investigations within the broad area of life science.

There are so many opportunities to share life science concepts with children. Below are just a few of the ways that life science can be an integral part of your everyday classroom experiences:

Include living things in your classroom environment.
Plants and pets provide daily opportunities for children to observe and care for living things. Depending on your interest level, you can choose a plant or pet that requires a great deal of care or very little. Including children in the care of living things gives them a chance to gain firsthand experience and learn responsibility as well.

Provide materials for observing and documenting.
Make sure that the area near a classroom pet or plant encourages observation and recording. Provide drawing and writing materials so children can document their observations and any changes they see in plants or animals.

Discuss a variety of animal homes.
Brainstorm with children all of the types of animal homes you can think of such as dens, squirrel nests, spider webs, etc. Look for these animal homes outdoors or research them to find out more information about how different animals live.

Explore plant and animal life cycles.
Animals such as butterflies and frogs have fascinating life cycles with easily observable stages. Help children discover what happens during these life cycles and make comparisons to the life cycles of other animals.

Help children learn about how their bodies work.
Look for opportunities each day to talk about health and how children can take care of their bodies (e.g., *Can you feel that your cheeks are warm? That's because you were running fast.* and, *These tasty apples are sweet and delicious. They give you energy and help you grow.*).

Learn more about the animals that live in your community.
Children achieve a better understanding of life science if they can observe plants and animals firsthand. Find out what animals are native to your area and encourage children to learn more about them.

Observing Children's Understanding

Children are naturally fascinated with living things. They might show some anxiety or fear of animals, so allow them to observe at their own pace and from a safe distance. You might see children show understanding of life science when they are:

- Commenting, "Our plant is always droopy when it doesn't get watered."
- Drinking water to cool down after running
- Noticing that the baby rabbit in the classroom is getting bigger

As children explore plants and animals or work together to investigate a life science study topic, ask the following questions:

What does it need in order to grow?

Where does it live?

What does it eat? How does it get food?

How can we take care of it?

Why do our bodies move that way?

What changes do you see?

How is that animal different from...?

What do you notice about it?

What if it got too much water? Not enough?

Where does it sleep?

Your Teaching Practice

Think about the following questions as you prepare for life science experiences in your classroom:

- How do I feel about animals?
- How do I talk about animals (including insects and reptiles) during classroom experiences?
- Am I modeling respect for all living things?
- Are there easy ways to include more life science investigations for children?
- What do I enjoy the most about life science? What do I enjoy the least?

Tips to Share With Families

- Ask your child to help care for a plant or animal at home. As you care for it together, talk about why it needs care and how to take care of it.
- Talk about the changes you notice in your child as she grows.
- Read books about animals and help your child learn more information about the animals that interest him most.
- Walk outside with your child and look for animals such as birds or insects. Encourage your child to draw what she sees.
- Model how to care for your body and support your child to care for his. For example, model and talk about drinking water, exercising, and getting plenty of sleep.
- Ask your child to notice small details in the plants and animals she sees by asking her to observe and make comparisons.

Earth and the Environment

Environmental and earth science refers to science concepts that children can explore in their natural environment. Children can easily get firsthand experience exploring their environment, and because of this, it is easy to make the Earth and the environment very relevant to children's learning. Consider the following questions when introducing science concepts related to the Earth and the environment:

- What do you notice about the area where we live? Is the ground the same everywhere you go? What do you see on the ground?
- What do you notice in the sky? What happens when the sun rises and sets? How does that change what we see?
- What is our weather like today? What are all of the different types of weather we experience in our community?
- What should we do to take care of our community and the Earth?

What Does Research Say?

Children's environmental education during the early childhood years should be based on children's life experiences and help children gain and/or further develop their positive attitude towards the environment. When children's "natural sense of wonder" and "appreciation for the beauty and mystery" of the world is encouraged through thoughtful and intentional experiences provided by teachers, this "interest and appreciation in the world" furthers their science skills and knowledge and their attitude towards learning (Kara, Aydoes, & Aydun, 2015).

By creating a "climate of curiosity" for children in the classroom, teachers can use the learning environment to encourage children's observations, explorations, ideas, and questions as they participate in "spontaneous investigations" (Brenneman, 2014).

As children observe, they are able to start making connections about the world around them, which leads to "creating knowledge" (Hamlin & Wisneski, 2012).

Everyday life is rich with science experiences, but these experiences can best contribute to science learning when an adult prepares the environment for science exploration, focuses on children's observations, and provides time to talk about what was done and seen (NAEYC, 2013).

One way to encourage children's interest in Earth science is to have children experiment at the sensory table with water (e.g., how does the force of the currents and the flow of the water influence the ways items move?) and sand (e.g., how does sand move when compared to water?) (Moomaw, 2012).

Research has shown that young children are able to develop a "rich knowledge of the Earth and environmental issues" that "nurtures hopefulness and is future directed" (Engdahl & Rabušicová, 2011).

The Teacher's Role in Promoting Understanding of Earth and the Environment

Children become familiar with the science of Earth and the environment by exploring the properties of the world around them, noticing changes, and making predictions. Regardless of the time of year or local climate, children can investigate a variety of concepts related to Earth and the environment. There are many ways you can encourage this type of investigation:

Relate concepts such as "day" and "night" to children's experiences.
Lead a discussion about things that are done during the day and things that are done at night. Encourage children to use vocabulary related to understanding day and night as they talk about their school and home lives.

Use water to demonstrate simple environmental changes.
Use paintbrushes and water outdoors on a hot day, or freeze ice cubes and leave them outside to melt in the sun.

Talk about seasons.
Depending on where you live, the change of seasons might be drastic or very minimal. Regardless, talk about the seasons as children notice environmental changes (e.g., *I know that it is springtime because the flowers in our garden are blooming.*).

Talk about the weather every day.
You can easily find times to discuss the weather each day and make it relevant to children's experiences. When children come into the classroom at the beginning of the day, when they are preparing to go outdoors, and at the end of the day, you can talk about the weather and how to dress appropriately for it (e.g., *Tran, it feels very warm outside now. Will you need to wear the jacket you wore to school this morning?*).

Include discussions about sunlight.
Draw children's attention to the light and warmth of the sun on a clear day, and talk about the changes on a cloudy day. Remind children about how to play safely in the sun, (e.g., wearing a hat, sunglasses, or sunscreen and not looking directly at the sun).

Observing Children's Understanding

Children may demonstrate understanding of Earth and the environment in subtle ways as they go through their daily routines and experiences without realizing what exactly they are observing or investigating. Draw their attention to these concepts whenever possible, such as when they are:

- Using chalk to trace the movement of shadows
- Drawing the objects they see in the sky
- Using wet sand to build a mountain in the sand box
- Feeling the water that has warmed up in the watering can after sitting outside in the sun

As children make observations and test their predictions about Earth and the environment, ask the following questions:

What does it feel like outside today?

What is making that shadow?

Where is the sun in the sky right now?

How many sunny/cloudy days have we had this week?

How can we find out which way the wind is blowing?

What happens when we leave this outside?

How can we measure the rain?

What should we wear on the playground today? Why?

What different types of (leaves, pine cones, acorns, flowers, etc.) can you find?

What can we see in the sky today?

Your Teaching Practice

Avoid limiting your children's seasonal experiences to theme-based activities. If you're not sure how to make seasonal experiences more investigative and meaningful, think about the changes you make at home at the beginning or end of each new season and how you might adapt those changes for the classroom. Encourage children to reflect on the changes they make and see at home.

Tips to Share With Families

- Encourage your child to evaluate the weather each day and decide what clothes to wear. Talk about the different choices and why they may or may not be best.
- Go outdoors with your child and look for rocks and other natural materials. Categorize what you find and talk about their similarities and differences.
- Play shadow games with your child and talk about what makes a shadow and how the shadow changes.
- Talk about changes in the seasons and what you do during each season.
- Read books with your child about the Earth, seasons, and the environment.
- Encourage your child to make observations throughout the day of the changing light outside and the position of the sun.
- Look at the night sky together and talk about what you see.

Awareness of Technology

Preschool children often enter school with working knowledge of technology. Often at home, children are exposed to different technology tools. Because of this they are familiar with technology but may have a limited scope of how it is used outside of the home. You can increase children's understanding by pointing out when technology is used in the classroom and outdoors. On site visits, look for opportunities to share new or unusual tools with children. Talk about how various tasks are done with and without technology.

What Does Research Say?

When preschoolers are intentionally encouraged to explore various digital technology productions in the classroom – audio and video clips and photos on the tablet – teachers are motivating children to see technology as "building blocks for … creativity" (PBS Parents, 2015).

When children engage with technology in the classroom, it is important for teachers to remember that children do not become "digital learners" by simply interacting and navigating various technology tools. Teachers should model these digital interactions, explaining what they are doing to children and answering any questions from children. "If we want children to understand that digital media technologies can be used for art making, learning, and communication," all of these possibilities should be explored and shown with children. "Technology integration" in the classroom should always encourage children to be inquiry-based learners (Rogow, 2015).

As children share and together navigate an app or game on the tablet, they become partners in learning. Often the use of technology will highlight their "technology knowledge, skills, and determination and persistence as engaged problem solvers" (Sharapan, 2015).

The Teacher's Role in Promoting Awareness of Technology

Gaining awareness of technology means being mindful of the tools and equipment used to find information, communicate with others, and create and complete projects.

Technology learning is not restricted to the Technology area. Most preschool classrooms offer ample opportunities to support children's awareness of technology, through both daily tasks and play. In *The Creative Curriculum®*, teachers make learning about technology an appropriate part of the preschool program. Here are a few examples:

Offer both real and pretend technology tools.
Children may already be familiar with a range of electronic devices, but offering toy technology tools allows them to explore freely and imitate the adults they see who use these devices daily.

Look for opportunities to broaden children's understanding of technology.
While children may be used to seeing adults at home and in the classroom using a variety of technology tools, there are still many opportunities to introduce technology use in ways that are new to children. Talk with children about the tools they encounter (e.g., *The machine quickly counts the money at the bank so that the bank teller doesn't have to do it.*).

Create audio and video recordings of children's play.
Technology now allows us to take photos and digital videos and share them instantly with children and families. After taking video of children playing, share the videos with children and their families. Talk about how it can be helpful to create a recording.

Talk about how technology helps us.
When using technology in the classroom, talk about how it helps with a specific task. Explain another way to do the same task without technology (e.g., *This projector makes the words big enough on the screen so that we can all see it. We would have to all sit very close if we couldn't see the words on the screen.*).

Use technology only as needed.
It is easy to use technology when there are so many devices available. Remember to use technology to enhance learning and not simply because it's there.

Observing Children's Understanding

Because children are exposed to technology daily, they are often accustomed to its uses at home and in the classroom. Notice ways that children demonstrate awareness of technology. A few examples are:

- Pretending to talk on a cell phone
- Taking a picture of a block structure
- Asking questions about an electronic scale in the produce section of the grocery store

As children develop their awareness of technology, ask the following questions:

Where can we find more information about that?

What is this used for?

How can we use this to send a message?

What can we create from these options on the screen?

How can we use this?

Where have you seen this used? How was it used?

What tool can we use to record what we're saying?

Your Teaching Practice

Take a few moments to think about all of the ways you use technology each day. Are there technology tools that you use without even thinking about it? How can you make children more aware of the tools used in the classroom and in the community?

Tips to Share With Families

- Use technology with your child and talk about how and why you're using it.
- When you're out in the community, look for technology tools together. Encourage your child to ask questions about what she sees.
- Think of new ways to use technology at home for communicating with others. Invite your child to use the technology tools with you.
- Ask your child to help you find information using technology. Talk together about the best ways to look for information.

Basic Operations and Concepts

Children are able to gain experience with the basic operations and concepts of technology any time they use technology at school and at home. For example, if children are using a tablet, they need to know how to turn the tablet off and on, use their finger to tap or swipe gently on the screen, and how to navigate through the content. If they are interacting with a smart board, they need to know which icons to touch and how to move in and out of different apps. The Technology area chapter of *The Creative Curriculum® for Preschool, Volume 2: Interest Areas* explains in detail how to introduce children to various technology tools.

What Does Research Say?

The "essentials" for early childhood learning, "that children learn best in active environments when they are engaged in meaningful, interactive, and social contexts," remain constant even in this digital age. Technology learning in the classroom is further encouraged when teachers consider and understand children's use of various technology tools in the "context of the child's family, home environment, community, culture, language, and experience" (Fred Rogers Center, 2012).

Digital learning and understanding in the classroom should "seamlessly integrate inquiry and technology learning." Children should be encouraged to use various technology tools to document and record their observations and interests throughout the day and to also engage in explanation and back-and-forth discussion on how they plan to use the classroom computer or smart board (Rogow, 2015).

Technology devices in the classroom are not isolating children as was often expected. "Teachers are finding that children ... are engaged in cooperative play, encouraging each other, exploring, discovering, and problem-solving ... and discovering together" (Sharapan, 2015).

"Sharing" and "learning together" (children, families, and teachers) creates "meaningful communication, experiences, and participation" with technology in the classroom and in children's home environments. In fact, "children will often be leading parents and educators in these digital lessons." Technology in the classroom is not just a child playing with a tablet during choice time but includes how teachers engage and partner with children and their families from "diverse linguistic, cultural, and economic backgrounds" (Kaldor, 2015).

The Teacher's Role in Promoting Understanding of Basic Operations and Concepts

A foundation of basic technology skills is fundamental to using technology to create and perform tasks. Many of the steps of using technology tools are consistent across digital devices, which helps reinforce the concepts for children who use them. By integrating technology learning into the day, children also learn to correctly name tools and communicate about technology. Here are a few examples of simple ways to incorporate these skills and concepts into your teaching:

Show children how to use the technology tools in your classroom.
Although many children may already be familiar with how to operate common types of technology, you can still take the opportunity to introduce terms, review ways of handling equipment safely, and demonstrate how to use the tools efficiently and effectively.

Teach children about the icons that help them navigate the apps they use for learning.
Once children have a basic understanding of how to operate the mobile digital devices, tablets, and computers, show them how they can get the most from the tools they are using. Talk about the icons they see, what they mean, and how they can be used.

Use correct terminology when talking about technology terms.
Although it might seem easier to simplify technology terms, it's important to use correct terminology to expand children's understanding of technology tools. For example, you can use proper terminology when showing children how to navigate on a table (e.g., *I can use two fingers to swipe and see what other apps I have open.*).

Teach children how to properly handle and store technology tools.
In the same way that we want children to practice self-sufficiency during the day, we also want to encourage them to use technology tools appropriately and with confidence. Taking the time to explain how to care for the tools they use not only protects your equipment but also gives children a sense of autonomy as they are trusted with the use of complicated technology tools.

Observing Children's Understanding

Children are often excited to share their technology knowledge and skills with others. Here are a few ways that you may see children demonstrate an understanding of the basic operations and concepts related to technology tools:

- Recognizing when to tap and swipe a tablet screen
- Playing a game on a literacy app by using voice commands
- Taking a picture using the built-in camera in the computer screen

As children become more familiar with technology's basic operations and concepts, ask the following questions:

What does this do?

How can we turn this on? How can we turn it off?

What are the steps for using this?

How do these things work together?

What do you see on the screen that looks familiar?

How do you know that it's ready to use?

Your Teaching Practice

Think about the following questions when determining your own comfort level with the technology tools in your classroom and at home:

- Do you feel that you have a basic understanding of how these tools operate?
- Are you familiar with the terminology associated with their various operations?
- Is there a colleague you can work with to share information about technology tools you are most and least comfortable using?
- Have you thought about the most effective way to use these tools in your classroom?

Tips to Share With Families

- Show your child how to use the technology tools in your home.
- Visit your local library to use and learn about technology tools.
- Include your child in discussions about how your technology tools work and how they help you.
- Encourage your child to independently use various types of technology appropriately.

Tools and Equipment

The subject of tools and equipment is not limited to technology devices. Using tools such as cooking utensils, building tools, and audio players exposes children to the many uses of technology. Look for opportunities to point out the daily use of technology in the classroom:

To chop the strawberries, we can use our paring knife, or we can put the strawberries in the blender.

We can touch each picture on the screen to put the pictures in the correct order.

This butterfly wing will look beautiful if we look at it under the microscope.

What Does Research Say?

"When used intentionally and appropriately, technology and interactive media are effective tools to support learning and development." They can "enhance children's cognitive and social abilities; support inclusive practice; provide tools to support English language learning; enhance early childhood practice when integrated into the environment, curriculum, and daily routines; and help educators make and sustain home-school connections" (NAEYC & Fred Rogers Center, 2012).

One of the benefits of having various technology tools in the classroom is how accessible they are to all children regardless of language, literacy, and physical development. Technology in the classroom "opens up a world of rich expression" and when teachers create "carefully scaffolded opportunities" for children to engage with technological devices, children discover that the tablet that they are engaging with is a "tool that helps them accomplish specific objectives" (Rogow, 2015).

High-quality programs that encourage children's natural curiosity as inquiry-based learners and explorers can be further children's discoveries through all types of materials, "including a variety of strategically selected digital devices that provide a range of opportunities for learning." Technology tools "have the ability to enhance as well as transform many learning activities...serving as "inspiration for further learning" even (Bailey & Blagojevic, 2015).

The Teacher's Role in Promoting Understanding of Tools and Equipment

When children understand that there are different kinds of tools and equipment that can be used in a variety of ways, they gain the ability to explore their surroundings and their creativity in new ways. Using technology tools for the first time or refining their skills with investigative equipment (e.g., magnifying glasses, balance scales, tape measures, etc.), offers children a different perspective on gaining information, creating something from their own ideas, and demonstrating what they know and can do. Here are a few examples:

Remind children that they can record their work throughout the day.
There are so many ways that children can benefit from listening to recordings of themselves and others! Consider asking children to create recordings when retelling a story and then inviting others to listen. Children can also revisit their recordings as inspiration for dramatic play, art, or story writing.

Invite children to explore typing as a means of expression.
In addition to learning how to write their names and other words, preschool children can also begin typing for a variety of projects. They will need to recognize and find the letters they are looking for and use their fine-motor skills to press the keys with the correct amount of force and precision.

Provide exploration tools for children's investigations.
Technology tools such as binoculars, thermometers, and electronic timers invite children to further explore familiar and unfamiliar objects. Paired with scientific inquiry skills, children can use tools to learn about the properties of the objects they investigate.

Observing Children's Understanding

You may find that children are more comfortable and familiar with some tools more than others. It is important to offer a variety of tools so that children can learn the use of new tools and refine their skills with familiar ones. Keep in mind that the use of tools does not need to be limited to the Discovery area, the Technology area, or the outdoors. Here are a few examples of what you might see when observing for children's understanding of tools and equipment:

- Dictating into a recording device for a future dramatic play performance
- Waiting for a tablet to restart before beginning to use it
- Playing a matching game on a tablet by matching photos of flowers
- Using a magnifying glass to follow a line of ants on the playground

As children use the technology tools and equipment in the classroom, ask the following questions:

Which tool should we use for this?

How can this tool help us?

What can we use this for?

What will we see on the screen next?

What can we make with this?

What happens when you…?

What else can this do?

Your Teaching Practice

Think about how children currently use tools in the classroom. Are there other ways you can introduce tools to the interest areas? Which tools do children seem to enjoy using most? Are there tools that perform similar functions that can be introduced (e.g., sharing a telescope or zoom feature of a camera after a child uses binoculars)?

Tips to Share With Families

- Look at the technology tools you have available and think about how else they can be used.
- Ask your child how he uses technology at school. If possible, provide opportunities at home for him to practice those skills.
- Talk with your child's teacher if you have questions about how technology is used in the classroom.

People and Technology

Talking about people and technology not only includes how people safely use and interact with a variety of tools but also how technology is used for different purposes. For example, children might use a drawing app to create a map of the classroom, or figure out a way to replay a video on a smart board. These questions might help you lead regular discussions about how children use technology throughout the day:

- What tools do you use at home? What tools do we use at school?
- How do tools make certain jobs easier?
- What technology tools do we have in our classroom?
- What are some of the ways we can perform tasks with technology?

What Does Research Say?

"Early childhood educators in the 21st century now have a very real responsibility to gain the technology knowledge, competencies, and experiences needed in their work and in their interactions with parents and young children. Digital media literacy is an essential new literacy for those who teach the teachers and those who teach young children" (Donohue & Schomburg, 2015).

As children explore technology tools in the classroom in a learning partnership of active discovery and problem solving and interaction, the Technology area of the classroom with its tablet or computer is becoming another "language-rich" place in the preschool classroom (Sharapan, 2015).

When children have the opportunities to play and engage with technology tools they are becoming digitally literate and developing the "life skills they need to become thinkers and makers in the multimedia environment that is their reality" (Rogow, 2015).

"Digitally literate educators who are grounded in in child development theory and developmentally appropriate practices, and who are technologically and media literate, have the knowledge, skills, and experience to select and use technology and digital media that are appropriate for the ages and developmental levels of the children in their care, and they know whether, how, and when to integrate technology into the program effectively" (Guernsey & Levine, 2015).

The Teacher's Role in Promoting Understanding of People and Technology

In addition to knowing how to use technology tools, it is critical that children learn, from a very young age, how people use technology safely, responsibly, and collaboratively. Technology tools can be wonderful instruments for learning, but only when the users realize the implications of the control (and sometimes lack of control) they have over technology tools. Preschool children are at a wonderful age for learning these principles as they learn how to use the technology itself. As children gain understanding that technology is controlled by people and as they use tools and equipment safely, responsibly, and collaboratively, they are taking the first steps toward becoming successful, lifelong users of technology. Here are a few examples:

Demonstrate the ways that people can control technology.
This can be as simple as showing children how they can create an animated video by tapping a specific icon, or noticing how the letters change when a different font is chosen while typing a letter to a friend.

Encourage children's collaboration.
Not only can children use technology to work together when creating a variety of projects, but they can also rely on each other during the process of learning how to navigate different technology tools. Stand back and observe children as they work together to figure out the best way to use different tools. Ask open-ended questions when needed to prompt children to look at a tool's use in a new way.

Develop clear rules for using technology in the classroom.
Talk with children about the types of rules to have in place regarding use of the technology tools in the classroom. As you talk about the safe and responsible use of these devices, help children decide on the rules to follow and why they are important.

See *Intentional Teaching Card* SE09, "Big Rule, Little Rule" for guidance on leading a discussion about creating rules for the classroom.

Observing Children's Understanding

Observing children's use of technology tools, especially in the very beginning, can be tricky. You want to give them the freedom to use these tools but also keep a close watch on how they are used. Notice when children use equipment appropriately and with an understanding of classroom expectations. Talk with them about how they can use the tools creatively. A few examples you might observe are when a child is:

- Showing another child how to navigate on a tablet to reach a particular screen
- Taking a device to a teacher when it needs to be recharged
- Clicking on icons to determine what each one links to

As you observe children using technology responsibly, ask the following questions:

How can we use this safely?

How can you figure this out together?

What are our rules about using this?

How can you control what you see on the screen?

Your Teaching Practice

As with any classroom experience, children's temperaments play a role in how they choose to participate. Be mindful of how children approach the use of technology tools and how they interact with others during those experiences. For children who fearlessly forge ahead, make sure they understand the rules regarding the use of technology tools. For children who approach new experiences with caution, encourage them to repeat steps of a process (e.g., turning on the computer, adding ideas to a digital class book, etc.) so that they can feel comfortable and confident as they learn.

Tips to Share With Families

- Talk about how to use technology tools safely and carefully.
- Model how to use technology responsibly.
- Ask questions that help your child understand how she is controlling what is happening on the screen or with the tool.
- Read books together about digital citizenship and Internet safety.
- Develop rules at home about using technology.
- Limit your child's use of technology each day.

Studies: Simple Machines

In *The Creative Curriculum®* classroom, teachers use *Teaching Guides* that feature studies on a variety of different topics to help children build content knowledge and develop process skills. Each study is an in-depth investigation of a topic children are interested in learning more about. Children find answers to their questions through firsthand explorations, and they have opportunities to practice and apply science and technology skills in meaningful ways.

Beginning the Study

To illustrate how children use science and technology to learn, consider the study that evolved in Ms. Tory and Mr. Alvarez's 4-year-old class.

The children were excitedly building in the Block area. Ms. Tory had found some scrap wooden boards that were flat and smooth, and she added them to the area. The children were enjoying building new structures using the boards. As they played, they began to make ramps for their cars and trains to zoom down. Since the children were enjoying the boards, Ms. Tory added different types of wood for the children to use in the Block area and outdoors.

Over the next several days, Ms. Tory and Mr. Alvarez observed the children making ramps with the boards and also using them to make seesaws for the classroom dolls and stuffed animals. As they saw the children's curiosity and interest growing, Ms. Tory and Mr. Alvarez began to make comments and ask open-ended questions to discover what about the materials were exciting to the children. Mr. Alvarez asked a group of children building ramps on the playground, "What do you like about making ramps?" and the children responded:

"The cars go down them really fast!"

"We can all build ramps and then race our rocks down them."

"I like making the balls roll far away."

Ms. Tory and Mr. Alvarez reviewed their observations related to how the children were using and talking about the pieces of wood and agreed that the children were showing curiosity and interest in inclined planes and other simple machines. Based on these observations, they chose to use *The Creative Curriculum® for Preschool Teaching Guide, featuring the Simple Machines Study.*

Beginning the Study

During a planning time, Ms. Tory and Mr. Alvarez started creating a web of investigations for the simple machines study. They brainstormed vocabulary and ideas related to the six types of simple machines, people who work with simple machines, and how simple machines are used for work and play. After collecting all of their ideas, they created a web of investigations to group their ideas around each investigation question.

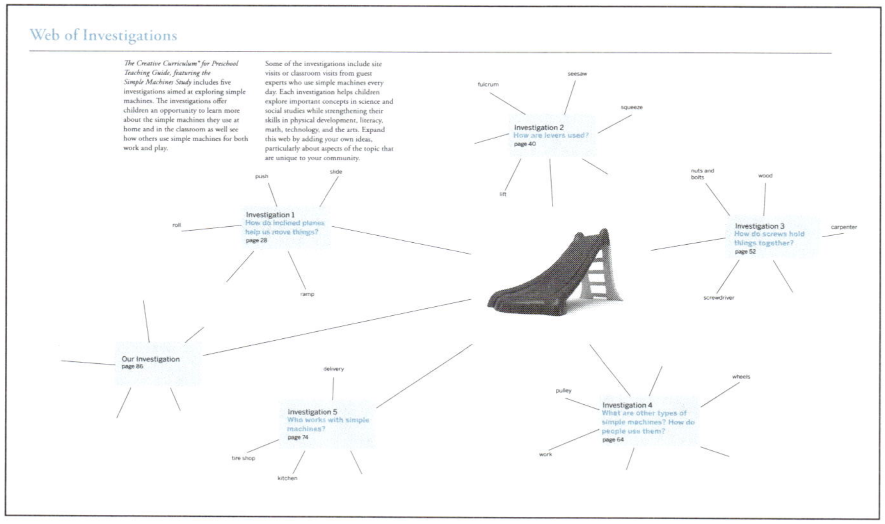

Looking over the web of investigation they created, Ms. Tory and Mr. Alvarez discussed the components of each investigation and planned how they could address literacy, mathematics, science and technology, social studies, and the arts throughout the study in meaningful ways.

To begin the study, Ms. Tory and Mr. Alvarez needed to learn what the children already know about simple machines. Each study begins in this way so that the experiences and investigations can be planned to build on what the children know. To discover what the children already knew about simple machines, Ms. Tory and Mr. Alvarez started gathering a classroom collection of related books, pictures, and materials. They used the "Letter to Families" found in the *Teaching Guide* to inform families about their upcoming study and ask them to donate materials to the collection. They also asked the families if any family members work in a field related to simple machines and invited them to visit the classroom to share their expertise with the children.

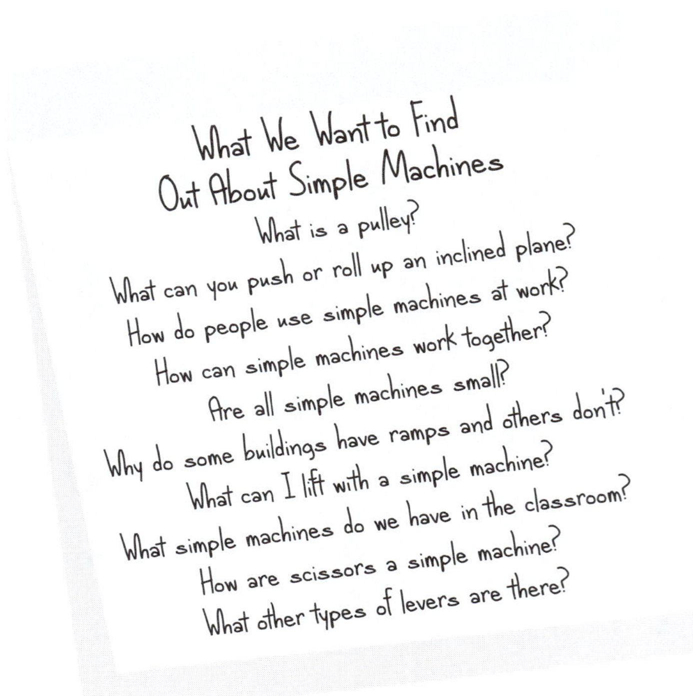

Following the guidance in the *Teaching Guide*, Ms. Tory began the study by exploring the topic. She led discussions about the materials in the classroom collection, and she and Mr. Alvarez carefully documented the children's questions and observations throughout the week. They added the children's questions to a chart titled "What We Want to Find Out About Simple Machines."

Investigating the Topic

The *Teaching Guide, featuring the Simple Machines Study* gives guidance for experiences that help the children discover the answers to their questions and gain a deeper understanding of inclined planes, screws, levers, pulleys, wedges, and wheels and axles. The following shows how these experiences incorporate science and technology skills.

Simple Machines Experiences	Ways to Use Science and Technology Skills
Take a walk to look for simple machines in the neighborhood	Talk about the natural features of your neighborhood. Ask children how people might use the simple machines they find. Take photos and videos of the simple machines the children find. Compare and contrast the simple machines you find. Talk about the materials the simple machines are made from. Take multiple walks during the study and encourage the children to notice how things change.
Site visit to see how simple machines are used in the community	Before the site visit, ask the children to predict how simple machines will be used. Notice how people use simple machines. Take photos and videos of site visits, and review them at the end of the study to compare how different people use simple machines. Talk about how the tools and simple machines are constructed. If possible, give the children time to use and explore the simple machines. Give children time to create observational drawings of what they see.
Class visits from experts and family members who use simple machines	Ask the expert to share and talk about what tools she uses. Take photos and videos of the visit for the children to review. Invite the children to experiment and work with the special visitor. At the end of the study, compare how each visitor used simple machines differently.

Simple Machines Experiences	Ways to Use Science and Technology Skills
Research simple machines	Use the Internet to research simple machines. Copy interesting pages from books or encyclopedias about simple machines. Investigate the properties of simple machines such as what sizes they can be and what they are often made out of. Ask the children to communicate the information they find in various ways such as making a chart.
Compare how different simple machines are used	Invite the children to use and manipulate the simple machines to better understand how they are used. Predict how simple machines will work. Create a chart to share information.
Experiment with using simple machines	Ask children questions and invite them to predict which simple machines would work best in different situations. As children explore, ask them to explain how each simple machine works. Talk about how people use each type of simple machine for work and play. Provide materials for the children to make their own simple machines.

Ms. Tory and Mr. Alvarez studied simple machines with the children over the course of six weeks. During this time, they investigated the following five questions:

How do inclined planes help us move things?

How are levers used?

How do screws hold things together?

What are other types of simple machines? How do people use them?

Who works with simple machines?

Throughout these investigations, Ms. Tory and Mr. Alvarez used planned experiences and gave the children ample time to experiment and explore the materials to discover the answers to their questions. They also used comments and open-ended questions to help the children solve problems, clarify their plans and reasoning, and think about materials in new ways. They connected the investigations to the components of science and technology in meaningful ways that allowed the children to gain a deeper understanding of physical science, life science, Earth and the environment, basic operations of technology, and how people use tools and technology.

Closing the Study

To conclude the study, the children planned a celebration and invited their families and special guests they had met during the study to see what the children learned. They created displays in the classroom interest areas to show the visitors how they investigated simple machines and set up hands-on experiments demonstrating how each simple machine works.

Through this study of simple machines, children used science and technology skills in meaningful and relevant ways. They used scientific inquiry skills to discover how simple machines are used, explored the physical properties of simple machines, and had hands-on experiences with technology.

Including All Children in the Study

Using the *Teaching Guide, featuring Simple Machines*, the teachers can draw on their understanding of each child's behaviors, knowledge, skills, and needs to provide a variety of experiences to include all children. Here are strategies for promoting inclusion of all children during this study.

English- and Dual-Language Learners

- Encourage children to name the simple machines in their home language(s).
- Invite children to work in pairs or small groups to use simple machines. Offer words or phrases for children to take turns or join a group in play.
- Invite families to visit the classroom to demonstrate how they use simple machines at home or in their work.
- Learn a few helpful words in the language(s) spoken by the children related to study (e.g., *wedge, inclined plane,* etc.) to help all children learn key vocabulary words.
- When introducing new ideas, such as the science behind simple machines, determine whether the children are already familiar with the concept. If not, teach children the concept (preferably in their home languages) along with the new words.
- Encourage children to count in their home language(s) and in English as they count the number of simple machines that are in their collection.
- Provide labels for sorting simple machines in English and in the home language(s) of the children.
- Speak clearly when describing simple machines and their uses. Ask closed questions to encourage children to participate in conversations.
- Schedule frequent small-group and individual learning experiences throughout the study to support children in becoming involved and interacting with others.
- Encourage families to join their children in the classroom throughout the study so that children can talk with them to share what they are learning about how people in their community use simple machines.

Children With Disabilities

- Provide adaptive equipment such as large-print books, oversized tools, communication devices, chairs with sides, or allow children more time to process information and respond.
- Use simple language and repeat key words during the experiences.
- Encourage children to participate in the experiences as long as they are interested. Allow children to move on to another experience when they are ready.
- When exploring the collection of simple machines, encourage children to participate however they are comfortable, i.e., observing from a distance.
- Limit the number of items provided for the child to explore. Begin with one or two items for the child to focus on.
- During experiences using simple machines, offer headphones for children with sensory sensitivities who may be averse to loud sounds.
- Connect the experiences to activities that the children are motivated by. For example, if a child loves playing with dolls or stuffed animals, invite children to work together to lift and move the dolls using simple machines.
- Include larger items for children to grasp and manipulate when working with simple machines (e.g., kitchen scissor-style tongs, thick sheets of foam core boards for building ramps, etc.).
- Invite children of different abilities to work together to build and use simple machines.
- Break down exploration activities into manageable steps (e.g., *First we will predict whether our simple machine will work, and then we will give it a try and see what happens.*).

Advanced Learners

- Encourage children to use creativity to improve the performance of a simple machine (e.g., *What can we do to make our wheel turn more smoothly*?). Support children to research related topics such as pulleys, catapults, etc.
- Invite children to lead experiments and activities in which they demonstrate a high level of understanding (e.g., *Zack is an expert at drawing; can you show us how you draw a bicycle?).*
- Provide reading materials in a variety of levels.
- Meet with local librarians, elementary school teachers, and educational specialists to collect resources (e.g., books, equipment, or puzzles) to engage advanced learners.
- Support children to research online videos to learn how simple machines are used in combination to create interesting contraptions (e.g., a complex marble run or a Rube Goldberg machine).
- Encourage children to use materials intentionally or in a new way (e.g., creating a machine to help children put on jackets, or comparing how much weight different simple machines can move or lift). Support children to research answers to their questions as they create.
- Ask questions that encourage children to explore and experiment (e.g., *What would happen if…?* or *How can we make this better*?).

2

Science and Technology Learning in Interest Areas and Outdoors

Science and Technology Learning in Interest Areas and Outdoors 37

The Discovery Area: The Hub of Science and Technology Learning 38

Science and Technology in the Toys and Games Area 42

Science and Technology in the Block Area 46

Science and Technology in the Dramatic Play Area 50

Science and Technology in the Art Area 54

Science and Technology in the Library Area 57

Science and Technology in the Sand and Water Area 61

Science and Technology in the Music and Movement Area 64

Science and Technology in the Cooking Area 67

Science and Technology in the Technology Area 71

Science and Technology Outdoors 74

Science and Technology Learning in Interest Areas and Outdoors

The interest areas in *The Creative Curriculum®* classroom are rich with possibilities for science and technology learning. As we've mentioned before, children's natural curiosity about nature and the world around them gives the teacher a great deal of topics and interests to build on in the classroom. Interest areas allow children to make choices about what they want to explore. Children can look closely at plant life in the Discovery area, or observe and wonder aloud as bread rises as it bakes. Each idea that children show interest in has the potential to become a larger investigation as part of an even larger study. Interest areas are the places where most of that investigation takes place.

In an earlier chapter, you learned how to integrate science and technology throughout the day during your experiences with children. And just as *Volume 3: Literacy* and *Volume 4: Mathematics* of *The Creative Curriculum® for Preschool* explain how to include math and literacy learning in interest areas, this chapter will explain how to incorporate science and technology learning as well. While it may seem that some interest areas are more conducive to science and technology learning than others, this chapter will show you how simple it can be to intentionally plan for and respond to children's learning in all interest areas with regard to science and technology.

Learning about science and technology in a preschool classroom can be spontaneous, and it can be intentionally planned for. Here you will see how to help children make connections between their play, their experiments, and the science and technology concepts found in the world around them.

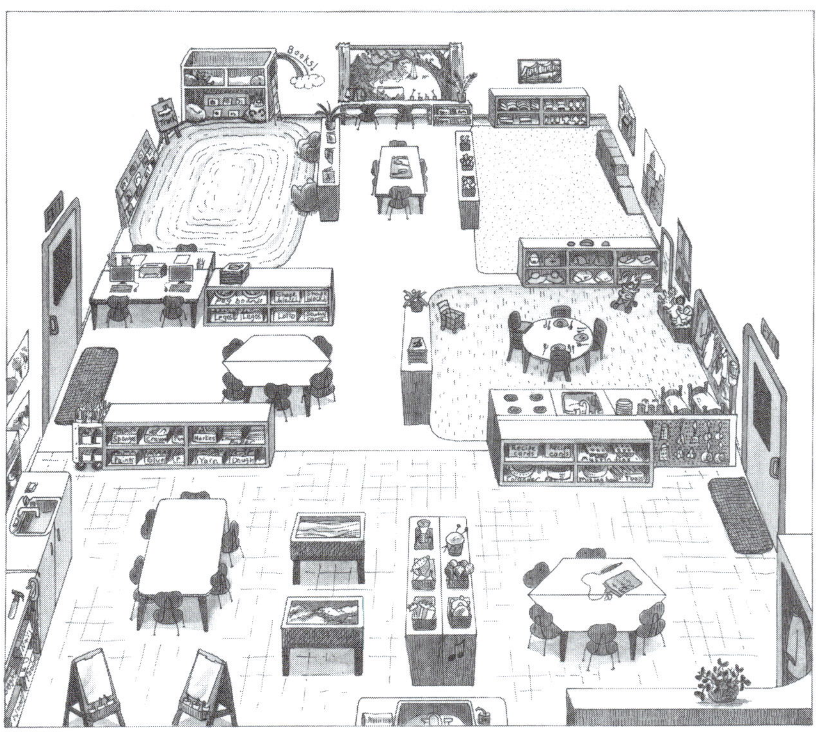

The Discovery Area: The Hub of Science and Technology Learning

The Discovery area is often the interest area dedicated to science and technology learning. You may already have several natural items, artifacts from various studies, books about plants and animals, magnifying glasses, and more in this area. However, it's important to be intentional when planning for and interacting with children in the Discovery area. Think of this interest area as the place where children can have firsthand experiences with some of the objects and materials they read about or see outdoors. Teachers can encourage further exploration by asking open-ended questions and showing interest in children's discoveries. Here are examples of how children's explorations in the Discovery area relate to *The Creative Curriculum® for Preschool* objectives for science and technology.

Examples of What a Child Might Do	Examples of Related Objectives for Development and Learning
Ask, "Why does it only rain when it's cloudy outside?"	24. Uses scientific inquiry skills
Ask questions about the way a beehive is made.	25. Demonstrates knowledge of the characteristics of living things
Look closely at a bicycle chain to see how it connects to a cog.	26. Demonstrates knowledge of the physical properties of objects and materials
Compare samples of different types of dirt from the playground.	27. Demonstrates knowledge of Earth's environment
Use tools to take apart an old telephone to find out what's inside.	28. Uses tools and other technology to perform tasks

Science and Technology Materials for the Discovery Area

Common Discovery area materials, such as magnifying glasses, magnets, prisms, balance scales, eyedroppers, thermometers, tweezers, and clear boxes and cups, are useful for all types of science and technology learning. As you support children to explore their interests, you might reach out to family and community members for additional materials. You can look for new natural items to add to the area on a weekly basis or encourage children to bring in their discoveries from outside.

It's important to keep the area arranged simply so that children have room to use tools and notice details in the materials they explore. Instead of keeping a rock collection, a leaf collection, and a nuts-and-bolts collection out for children to work with, introduce each collection one at a time. You may even want to introduce only one or two objects from the collection so children can really observe and record their findings. Chances are, if you look around the classroom and playground area, you will find items that could be interesting to further explore in the Discovery area. You can also revisit previous objects as children learn more information. Here are additional examples of suggested materials, but remember that this area can include an enormous variety of materials depending on children's interests and investigations.

Materials

collection of natural items (e.g., leaves, sticks, rocks, tree bark, acorns, flowers, dirt, etc.)

sorting trays and bowls

microscopes

writing and drawing materials

informational posters

nature magazines

electronics catalogs

Suggested Books

(Titles preceded by an asterisk are included in the *Teaching Strategies*® *Children's Book Collection.*)

All By Myself (Mercer Mayer)

**Bear on a Bike* (Stella Blackstone)

Birds (Kevin Henkes)

Farm (Elisha Cooper)

First Science Encyclopedia (DK Publishing)

Fossils Tell of Long Ago (Aliki)

From Seed to Plant (Gail Gibbons)

Hello, Rock (Roger Bradfield)

If I Built a Car (Chris Van Dusen)

Lots and Lots of Zebra Stripes: Patterns in Nature (Stephen R. Swinburne)

Meet Einstein (Mariela Kleiner)

Machines at Work (Byron Barton)

The New Way Things Work (David Macaulay)

**Our Tree Named Steve* (Alan Zweibel)

**Peter's Chair* (Ezra Jack Keats)

Pumpkin, Pumpkin (Anne Titherington)

Seasons (Blexbolex)

Seeds! Seeds! Seeds! (Nancy Elizabeth Wallace and Marshal Cavendish)

Sylvester and the Magic Pebble (William Steig)

Ten Flashing Fireflies (Philemon Sturges)

Ten Little Ladybugs (Melanie Gerth)

The Tiny Seed (Eric Carle)

The Weather (Gladys Rosa-Mendoza)

What is the World Made Of? (Kathleen Weidner Zoehfeld)

Using the Discovery Area to Teach Science and Technology

The Discovery area invites children to observe, explore, and investigate natural materials and other objects. Teachers' most effective interactions with children in this area will challenge children to discover more about everyday objects, things they see in nature, and new ideas. Wondering aloud and making predictions prompt children to think beyond their basic understanding of the world around them and explore new investigations. Useful questions and comments to draw children's attention to the details of items found and new ideas discovered during children's explorations include the following:

Physical Science

What do you see inside the tube? What do you think those wires are for?

How can we find out more about how that works?

How would you describe this texture? What does it feel like to you?

I wonder what would happen if we removed the wheels from the bottom.

Can you think of another way to make that work?

Life Science

I see you found a broken egg under the tree. Let's put it in the magnifying box so we can take a closer look.

Can we sort these seeds? We want to know what will grow in this pot once we plant them.

Look at the roots in the bottom of the glass. The potato is growing. It's getting water from its roots.

That was a big sneeze! I wonder why our bodies need to sneeze sometimes.

Let's take a closer look at the ant farm to see what they're up to today.

Earth and the Environment

You chose two different kinds of rocks. Tell me about what you found.

Look at what happens when we add soil to the water.

Where can we find a picture of mountains?

What would happen if we grind up the sand?

Technology

These x-rays are very interesting. I can see the bones in the toes!

This side of the balance scale went down when you put the rock on it. I wonder if you can find another rock that weighs the same.

What do you see in the microscope?

What do you think you'll see inside the clock when you take it apart?

Observing Children's Understanding

As children explore in the Discovery area, notice how they use materials and talk about their discoveries. They may demonstrate understanding of science and technology by:

- Using tools to explore how things work
- Describing the differences between the natural materials they find
- Making a graph of the types of rocks on the playground
- Noticing the details in an abandoned beehive
- Finding ways to fix a broken toy
- Using science and technology vocabulary
- Making predictions about their experiments
- Forming collections of similar natural materials
- Sorting objects by how they work or what their characteristics are
- Explaining why an object works the way it does

Science and Technology in the Toys and Games Area

There are opportunities for children to explore science and technology in all interest areas, and the Toys and Games area is no exception. As children use a variety of toys and manipulatives, they begin to think about how these objects work, how they can be used, and what they're made of. Children may play informative games such as a matching game with animal photos, a game that encourages them to assemble a robot, or a game that requires them to balance objects to keep them from falling over. All of these examples expand children's thinking about science and technology concepts.

Here are more examples of how children's explorations in the Toys and Games area relate to *The Creative Curriculum® for Preschool* objectives for science and technology learning.

Examples of What a Child Might Do	Examples of Related Objectives for Development and Learning
Play a matching game using jar lids and bottle caps and wonder aloud about how lids and caps stay on containers without falling off.	24. Uses scientific inquiry skills
Play a game of "Twister®" and talk about the ways bodies move and balance.	25. Demonstrates knowledge of the characteristics of living things
Sort a collection of beads and buttons and talk about the similarities and differences between them.	26. Demonstrates knowledge of the physical properties of objects and materials
Play a picture card game matching objects to their shadows.	27. Demonstrates knowledge of Earth's environment
Create a marble maze using cardboard tubes and experiment with how to make the marble move quickly or slowly.	28. Uses tools and other technology to perform tasks

Science and Technology Materials for the Toys and Games Area

As you conduct studies and observe children making daily choices in interest areas, reflect on which materials they use most, what you might add to enhance science and technology learning, and what could bring further understanding to the current study topic. The list below is not meant to be comprehensive, and materials should be added and removed from the Toys and Games area as needed to limit clutter and keep children's interest. For guidance about how to introduce new materials to children, see *The Creative Curriculum® for Preschool, Volume 1: The Foundation.*

Materials

- sorting bins of various sizes for sorting small objects, natural materials, and artifacts related to the study topic
- collectibles (e.g., buttons, bottle caps, nuts and bolts, etc.)
- flashlights
- pinwheels
- beads and other small manipulatives
- balls and ramp-making materials
- timers
- wheeled toys
- writing materials
- stacking toys
- movement games
- recording devices to record children's ideas and questions
- magnets and magnetic toys
- gear and pulley toys
- matching games with a variety of subjects (e.g., mammals, cars, butterflies, flowers, toys, etc.)
- board games and quiz games about animals
- wide variety of small building materials (e.g., small plastic building blocks, Lincoln Logs®, table blocks, inch cubes, straws and connectors, etc.)
- locks and keys
- product samples (e.g., paint and fabric swatches, carpet and fabric samples, etc.)
- measuring tools (e.g., measuring tapes, carpenters' rulers, T-squares, etc.)
- puzzles with images (e.g., tools, nature, cars and trucks, trains, etc.)
- sequence cards featuring animal and plant life cycles, weather, or day and night events
- laminated seed packets for matching
- plastic animals and barn

Suggested Books

(Titles preceded by an asterisk are included in the *Teaching Strategies® Children's Book Collection*.)

Alphabet City (Stephen T. Johnson)

Beep Beep, Vroom Vroom! (Stuart J. Murphy)

Big Red Barn (Margaret Wise Brown)

Boats (Byron Barton)

Building a House (Byron Barton)

A Butterfly is Patient (Dianna Hutts Aston)

Cars and Trucks and Things That Go (Richard Scarry)

Curious George Rides a Bike (H.A. Rey)

A Day at the Airport (Richard Scarry)

The Earth and I (Frank Asch)

Freight Train (Donald Crews)

Hello, Robots! (Bob Staake)

The Little Engine That Could (Watty Piper)

Parts (Tedd Arnold)

Ruby's Falling Leaves (Rosemary Wells)

Swimmy (Leo Lionni)

Thump, Quack, Moo (Doreen Cronin)

Who's Hiding? (Agnese Baruzzi)

Using Toys and Games to Teach Science and Technology

Children need time to explore the materials in the Toys and Games area freely. Through their playful manipulation of objects, children discover many scientific relationships on their own. They notice technology concepts in their play. Teachers who carefully observe the ways in which children use materials and listen to them as they talk are able to determine the best way to respond and support their science and technology learning. At times, teachers will ask a question, pose a problem, introduce a new term, or model the steps in solving a problem. At other times, they simply observe.

Talking helps children clarify and organize their thinking. However, young children are not always proficient in expressing their thoughts, particularly if they are English-language learners. Your questions and comments can stimulate children's thinking but be careful not to overwhelm them.

Here are examples of what you might ask and say:

Physical Science

What different types of carpet samples do you have? What is different about them?

Can you stack the boxes so that they don't fall? Which box do you think should go on the bottom?

What happens when you fold the cardboard? Does it stay folded?

How did you make sure the marble stayed in the tube? Can you make the tube longer?

Which key will fit in this lock? How can you find the proper key?

Life Science

Which animal matches the animal on your card? What does that animal look like?

Can you help me put these cards in order? What does the caterpillar do next before becoming a butterfly?

You're stretching your arm up high to catch the balloon! Can you feel your muscles stretching?

This puzzle has so many pretty flowers. Can you find the flower that fits in this space?

You landed on the space that says you need to hop three times. Can you show me how you hop? Now, you can spin the spinner again.

Earth and the Environment

Which of these cards should come first? Yes, the girl puts on her raincoat, and then she goes outside in the rain.

Tell me about your drawing. What colors are you using for the sky?

Your cards have shadows on them. Let's see if we can match the shadows to the pictures on my cards.

You're turning your flashlight on and off. Look, you're making a shadow on the wall just like the sun does!

We have to decide what Jenny should wear in the game. It looks like she's going swimming.

Technology

I see you building a robot with these toys. What will you add next to your robot?

How do these gears fit together? Which gear is the biggest?

Can you lift the basket with this pulley? What else do you need to make it work?

Your boxes are stacked high! How can we measure the height of your tower? What tool should we use?

It looks like the wheel came off of the truck. Can we fix it? What does the wheel attach to?

Observing Children's Understanding

As you observe children playing with toys and games, look for these indications of children learning science and technology concepts:

- Talking about animal characteristics
- Ordering the life cycle of plants and animals
- Using tools to build
- Recognizing differences between natural objects
- Explaining how tools work
- Using physical objects in new ways
- Asking "why" questions
- Building with non-building materials (e.g., nondescript plastic shapes, paper towel rolls, etc.)
- Creating and changing a train track through the Toys and Games area
- Rolling cars down a ramp to see which is the fastest
- Predicting which stuffed animal is heaviest and then weighing them
- Putting together a puzzle of different types of trees and plants
- Using blocks to create a zoo for the plastic zoo animals
- Making animal sounds when playing an animal matching game
- Creating with Tinker Toys® and explaining the function of the creation

Science and Technology in the Block Area

The Block area is a favorite among children and one that presents children with numerous opportunities to explore science and technology concepts such as the characteristics of physical objects, use of tools, and transportation (e.g., driving cars through block tunnels or using a dump truck to haul blocks from one place to another). Children can persist in problem solving when they are fully engaged in their block-building activity. Here are examples of how children's explorations in the Block area relate to *The Creative Curriculum® for Preschool* objectives for science and technology learning.

Examples of What a Child Might Do	Examples of Related Objectives for Development and Learning
Look at a photo of an unusual building and wonder aloud about how the curved walls were made.	24. Uses scientific inquiry skills
Create cages for a toy lion and a toy zebra and say, "They can't live together because the lion might eat the zebra."	25. Demonstrates knowledge of the characteristics of living things

Watch a block tower fall over and say, "The top block was too big and heavy. It should go on the bottom."	26. Demonstrates knowledge of the physical properties of objects and materials
Build a garage for the toy cars because it's a rainy day.	27. Demonstrates knowledge of Earth's environment
Use a measuring tape to measure the height of a block tower.	28. Uses tools and other technology to perform tasks

Science and Technology Materials for the Block Area

Many of the Block area materials suggested in *The Creative Curriculum® for Preschool, Volume 2: Interest Areas* encourage children's thinking across all areas of development and learning. It's possible, though, to focus even more on science and technology when planning for materials and thinking about how to organize this interest area. The materials and books listed in the following chart also support children's science and technology explorations.

Materials

- solid and hollow blocks
- blocks made of different materials (e.g., plastic, wood, cardboard, etc.)
- photographs of buildings and other structures
- drawing and writing materials
- photos of children's block constructions, their neighborhoods, and places the class has visited
- variety of wheeled toys
- small wagon for transporting blocks
- different sizes of boxes for building
- large boxes for building inside
- drawings and floor plans
- magnetic blocks
- lamp or flashlight for making shadows of structures

Suggested Books

(Titles preceded by an asterisk are included in the *Teaching Strategies® Children's Book Collection*.)

Alphabeep (Debora Pearson)

A Boy, a Dog, and a Frog (Mercer Mayer)

**Build It From A to Z* (Trish Holland)

**Building a House* (Byron Barton)

Building With Blocks (Jillian Cutting)

A Busy Year (Leo Lionni)

**Changes, Changes, Changes* (Pat Hutchins)

City Green (Dyanne DiSalvo-Ryan)

Construction Zone (Tana Hoban)

The Curious Garden (Peter Brown)

Little Pink Pup (Johanna Kerby)

Oodles of Animals (Lois Ehlert)

Richard Scarry's Trains (Richard Scarry)

**The Three Little Javelinas* (Susan Lowell)

The Toolbox (Anne Rockwell)

Using Blocks to Teach Science and Technology

Block play involves many skills and concepts as children learn to lift and carry blocks, compare them and determine how to stack them, see them as representations of other objects, and notice their characteristics. As you interact with children in the Block area, you may begin to notice how children experiment with these concepts and apply their learning to their play.

In the Block area, teachers first observe children and listen as children talk about what they are doing. Then, teachers ask thoughtful questions and make responsive comments that prompt children to think further about their experiments. Here are examples of what teachers might say as they interact with children in the Block area:

Physical Science

Which block is bigger? How can you use it in your structure?

Where will the curved piece go? How do you think this curved block was made?

Those blocks make a loud sound when you bang them together! What does it feel like in your hands when the blocks hit each other?

The tower is leaning over. I think it might fall. What can you use to hold it up?

I see that you placed these blocks next to each other. I wonder what would happen if you moved them apart.

Life Science

It looks like you've made a bird house out of blocks. What type of bird will live in it?

You've made a very big zoo for all of these animals! I see that you have a big room for the big animals and small rooms for the small animals.

What do you think would happen if…? Why do you think that?

Your road is big and wide for the trucks to drive on. I see you filled the trucks with fruits and vegetables. Where are they going?

You're right – these blocks are made of wood, just like the trees outside. What else do we have in our classroom that is made of wood?

Earth and the Environment

The light from my desk makes a big shadow of your block tower. Would you like to trace it?

The flower box outside is built up high so the rain water can drain out the bottom. How do you think the flower box is made? Can we make a box like that out of blocks?

I'm glad we brought our large cardboard blocks back inside. What would happen to them if we left them out in the rain today?

I see you built a rocket ship out of blocks. Where will your rocket ship go today?

You have two big mountains of blocks! See the space at the bottom between them? That's called a "valley."

Technology

We can make a recording of you building your tower. That way if it falls, you can watch the recording to see what you want to do differently next time.

You're using the mallet to tap the blocks into place. Is that easier than using your hands?

How can you attach the basket so it hangs off of the top of the structure? What tools can you use?

This tool is called a "level." It will help you see if the blocks are flat.

You would like to research how to build a football stadium? Where can we look to find that information?

Observing Children's Understanding

While children are engaged in block play, look for these indications of children's understanding of science and technology concepts:

- Talking about tools used during construction
- Solving problems related to building with blocks
- Comparing similarities and differences between types of blocks
- Using a variety of materials in block play
- Constructing homes for toy animals and people
- Explaining how to build a tower so that it doesn't fall
- Measuring weight, height, length, and width of blocks using various tools
- Looking at building plans when deciding what to build and how to build it
- Adding to a block structure after watching a video about construction

Science and Technology in the Dramatic Play Area

In the Dramatic Play area, children get a chance to explore firsthand some of the science and technology concepts they observe in the world around them. The props you add to this area can spark new ideas for children and encourage them to think imaginatively. Children also have opportunities to solve problems like determining which animals should be housed together and which should not. Here are examples of how children's explorations in the Dramatic Play area relate to *The Creative Curriculum® for Preschool* objectives for science and technology learning.

Examples of What a Child Might Do	Examples of Related Objectives for Development and Learning
Make a meal in the play kitchen and wonder about the grill marks on a plastic steak.	24. Uses scientific inquiry skills
Plant, water, and harvest a pretend garden of fruits and vegetables.	25. Demonstrates knowledge of the characteristics of living things
Talk about why some of the hats are hard and some are soft.	26. Demonstrates knowledge of the physical properties of objects and materials
Wear old headphones and pretend to be an astronaut.	27. Demonstrates knowledge of Earth's environment
Explain why the broom works better for sweeping up dirt than the rake.	28. Uses tools and other technology to perform tasks

Science and Technology Materials for the Dramatic Play Area

At the beginning of the year, the Dramatic Play area resembles a home so children can take on the familiar roles of their family members. This is a great time to explore some of the science and technology concepts that are prevalent at home. As the school year continues and the Dramatic Play area evolves, children can build on their science and technology learning by applying previously introduced concepts to their new dramatic play roles.

Pay attention to children's interests, their conversations, and their comments and questions during studies to determine how to best outfit your Dramatic Play area for optimal science and technology exploration. The following chart lists science and technology props, accessories, and books for this interest area.

Materials

props for a repair shop

empty food boxes and containers

scales for weighing food in a grocery store or packages in a post office

props to create a woodwork shop or tailor shop

flower shop with artificial flowers

catalogs for various jobs and hobbies (e.g., flower catalogs, sewing supplies, woodworking, shipping materials, etc.)

hats, tools, and gloves for jobs such as gardener, construction worker, veterinarian, etc.

writing materials

lights and props for shadow puppets

props for stores such as sporting goods, work and exercise clothing, appliances, etc.

cooking, baking, and measuring supplies

transportation props such as boxes, chairs, uniforms, etc.

videos of people working in various jobs

cookbooks

doctor's office supplies (e.g., stethoscopes, thermometers, notepads, bandages, etc.)

animal costumes and masks

clothing for a variety of weather conditions

Suggested Books

Bark, George (Jules Feiffer)

Children Make Terrible Pets (Peter Brown)

I Want to Be an Astronaut (Byron Barton)

Let's Say Hi To Friends Who Fly! (Mo Willems)

The Lorax (Dr. Seuss)

My Favorite Time of Year (Susan Pearson)

The Perfect Puppy for Me (Jane O'Connor)

Planting a Rainbow (Lois Ehlert)

The Snowy Day (Ezra Jack Keats)

Stranger in the Woods (Carl R. Sams)

The Story of Ferdinand (Munro Leaf)

The Tale of Peter Rabbit (Beatrix Potter)

The Very Hungry Caterpillar (Eric Carle)

What's the Weather Like Today? (Rozanne Lanczak Williams)

Using Dramatic Play to Teach Science and Technology

Teachers observe children engaged in the Dramatic Play area and then thoughtfully consider ways to promote children's understanding of science and technology concepts. Sometimes a teacher may let a child wrestle with a problem, or she may pose a question, recall aloud previously learned information, or join in the dramatic play. Here are some examples of what teachers might say and do as they interact with children in the Dramatic Play area to promote science and technology learning:

Physical Science

Our stroller has a broken wheel. Will it still work if we take off the broken wheel?

Why do you think this winter coat is so heavy? What makes it heavy?

Your shoe store has so many shoes! Which shoes would work best for climbing? Why do you think those are the shoes I should buy?

This spaghetti box is very long. Why do you think the box needs to be so long?

This fabric is very stretchy. How is it different from this stiff fabric?

Life Science

What will you feed your baby in her bottle? What does she like to drink?

It's time to sell your vegetables at the market. Can you collect them in your basket?

Hi, little puppy! Your tail is wagging and you're barking. You look like a happy puppy.

How can we make room for more bees in our beehive? Where do the bees go to get inside?

It's cold outside today. I wonder what I should put on to keep warm. Will this T-shirt keep me warm? Why not?

Earth and the Environment

We're ready to blast off to the moon. Can you count down for us?

It's snowing today. These boots should help me walk in the snow like Peter in The Snowy Day.

It looks like you're turning out the light. It must be nighttime. What will you do to get ready to go to sleep?

You look ready for your expedition! Where will you go after you visit the jungle?

How is the rain hat different from the snow hat? What will happen when the rain hat gets wet?

Technology

Your baby is getting so big! How much does he weigh? What can you use to measure his weight?

I'm excited that you're making me a cake. How long does the cake need to bake? Can you set the timer?

The video showed us how doctors listen to a patient's heartbeat. Can you use the stethoscope to find your heartbeat?

Which tool would help us stir the soup?

I would like to buy three things from your shop. Here is the money to put in your cash register.

Observing Children's Understanding

As you observe children engaged in dramatic play, look for these indications of science and technology learning:

- Caring for animals in a veterinary office
- Using time measurement words to talk about night and day
- Dressing for all types of weather
- Using a mixer or whisk to cook in the kitchen
- Talking about how to work in the garden
- Explaining why the baby's clothes are small
- Pretending to be an animal in the forest
- Preparing food for a pet
- Planning an expedition into space

Science and Technology in the Art Area

The Art area is ideal for scientific thinking and experimentation. As children create, they are exploring ways to combine materials, mix colors, experiment with textures, etc. When children sculpt with clay or use glue to add a feather to a collage, they are using what they know about the properties of objects and are exploring to find out what art materials can do. Here are examples of how children's explorations in the Art area relate to *The Creative Curriculum® for Preschool* objectives for science and technology learning.

Examples of What a Child Might Do	Examples of Related Objectives for Development and Learning
Predict what will happen when more or less water is added to clay or paint.	24. Uses scientific inquiry skills
Examine closely the design made from painting with a pinecone.	25. Demonstrates knowledge of the characteristics of living things
Set a glued piece of art aside for the glue to dry.	26. Demonstrates knowledge of the physical properties of objects and materials
Make shadow art by leaving objects on dark paper out in the sun.	27. Demonstrates knowledge of Earth's environment
Experiment with different types of sculpting tools.	28. Uses tools and other technology to perform tasks

Science and Technology Materials for the Art Area

All of the items in a well-stocked Art area have possibilities for scientific discoveries. The following materials and books may inspire additional science and technology explorations.

Materials

palettes for mixing paints

variety of painting and sculpting tools

variety of art mediums for drawing, painting, and sculpting

writing materials

collage and construction items of different materials and textures

everyday materials for art exploration

natural items for painting and collage creations

paint, pencils, and crayons in a variety of colors

large paper for body tracing

objects to recycle as collages and constructions

newspapers for papier-mâché

light source for making silhouettes

real flowers for observation when painting and sketching

supplies for flower arrangements

old furniture for painting

photo books of animals and plants

Suggested Books

(Titles preceded by an asterisk are included in the *Teaching Strategies® Children's Book Collection*.)

The Earth Book (Todd Parr)

An Egg is Quiet (Dianna Hutts Aston)

Four Seasons Make a Year (Anne Rockwell)

I Hear, I See, I Touch (Helen Oxenbury)

It Looked Like Spilt Milk (Charles G. Shaw)

The Line (Paula Bossio)

Mouse Paint (Ellen Stoll Walsh)

Ocean (Maurice Pledger)

Our Stars (Anne Rockwell)

**The Pot That Juan Built* (Nancy Andrews-Goebel)

Summer Birds (Margarita Engle)

The Sun in Me (Judith Nicholls)

Too Much Glue (Jason Lefebvre)

Using Art to Teach Science and Technology

Your primary role in the Art area is to facilitate children's art explorations and creations. By observing children and listening to them talk about their work, teachers can decide whether and when to call children's attention to science and technology concepts. Here are examples of what you might say:

Physical Science

Which brush will you use to make a wide line?

What texture does this pinecone make when you rub it over the clay?

What happens when you fold the clay? I see an air bubble in it now!

The paint looks different on this type of paper. I wonder what is different about this paper.

I see that you've made lots of new colors with the paint. Can you tell me about your picture?

Life Science

These autumn leaves are brown, red, and yellow. What color will you make your leaves?

Can you tell me about the clay animal you're making? I see its two ears.

Look at the colors on the butterfly's wing. What colors do you see?

The flower petal is so colorful in your collage. What will you add next?

How do you think the bird keeps the nest together? What materials will you use to build your nest?

Earth and the Environment

Look at the thick fog in your picture! I see the trees behind the fog.

This painting is by an artist named Claude Monet. It's called "Sunset in Venice." I wonder what the sunset will look like today. Would you like to draw it?

I see that you added blue tissue paper to your drawing to make it look like water. What else will you add?

You drew the moon and stars above the house. It must be night. Can you tell me what's happening in your picture?

How would you like to add the rocks you collected to your sculpture?

Technology

The flashlight makes a silhouette on the wall. That means it's the shape of your face. Would you like me to trace it on your paper?

We can print the picture you made on the computer for you to take home. Would you like to make another picture?

I see you're using straws to make the arms and legs of your robot. What can your robot do?

Which tools would you like to use on your clay? How will you divide the clay into smaller pieces?

How long does the glue take to dry? Let's use this stopwatch to time it so we'll know when your collage is ready to go home.

Observing Children's Understanding

As children create and explore in the Art area, look for these indications of children's understanding of science and technology concepts:

- Observing the sky outside and then painting a sky picture
- Using natural materials in their artwork (e.g., sticks, rocks, pinecones, leaves, acorns, etc.)
- Making animals and people out of clay or play dough
- Talking about the characteristics of animals and people as they draw or paint
- Using a variety of tools when modeling with clay
- Describing the changes to the ingredients when making play dough
- Explaining the process of mixing paint to create new colors

Science and Technology in the Library Area

In the Library area, children have the chance to explore books on any subject, write down the information they learn, and retell stories (both fiction and nonfiction) as a way of sharing information with others. When it comes to science and technology, the Library area is a wonderful place to have discussions about fiction and nonfiction stories. For example, comparing *Cloudy With a Chance of Meatballs* with a nonfiction book about weather can be a great way to illustrate the difference between the two genres. With books related to the study topic as well as other interesting topics, the Library area can nurture children's literacy learning while also offering in-depth learning opportunities of science and technology concepts. Here are examples of how children's explorations in the Library area relate to *The Creative Curriculum® for Preschool* objectives for science and technology learning.

Examples of What a Child Might Do	Examples of Related Objectives for Development and Learning
Wonder aloud about volcanoes and then find a nonfiction book of facts about volcanoes.	24. Uses scientific inquiry skills
Use props to retell the story of Goldilocks, and talk about how bears really live.	25. Demonstrates knowledge of the characteristics of living things
Experiment with different types of paper for bookmaking.	26. Demonstrates knowledge of the physical properties of objects and materials
Look at a photo book of the Grand Canyon and ask questions about how it formed.	27. Demonstrates knowledge of Earth's environment
Ask to use the digital camera to take pictures of flowers outside for a class book.	28. Uses tools and other technology to perform tasks

Science and Technology Materials for the Library Area

The Library area in your classroom probably already includes a variety of books on a variety of topics, both fiction and nonfiction. But you can enhance the Library area by periodically rotating books and including books specific to the current study topic. Another idea to consider is to think beyond storybooks and informational books to other genres. For example, you might add a book of poems about the weather or a counting book of insect characteristics. The possibilities are endless!

As with planning for all interest areas, pay attention to children's interests and curiosities and use those conversations to help plan intentionally for the collection in your Library area. The following chart lists materials and a few of the many books that entice children to explore science and technology through literature.

Materials

fiction and nonfiction books about the current study topic

counting and alphabet books in a variety of topics (e.g., insects, trucks, flowers, etc.)

puppets and props of animals for story retelling

magazines and catalogs of cars, machinery, plants, pet supplies

field guides

drawing and writing materials for bookmaking

blank books for writing original stories

poetry books about nature

fiction and nonfiction books about animals, weather, machines, etc.

Suggested Books

(Titles preceded by an asterisk are included in the *Teaching Strategies® Children's Book Collection*.)

A Bad Case of Stripes (David Shannon)

Cinderlily: A Floral Fairytale (Davide Ellwand)

**Dear Mr. Blueberry* (Simon James)

Diary of a Worm (Doreen Cronin)

From Rubber Tree to Tire (Ali Mitgutsch)

The Great Kapok Tree (Lynne Cherry)

**The Grouchy Ladybug* (Eric Carle)

Hedgie's Surprise (Jan Brett)

How to Clean a Hippopotamus: A Look at Unusual Animal Partnerships (Robin Page)

**I Stink!* (Kate and Jim McMullan)

The Legend of the Bluebonnet (Tomie dePaola)

Little Hoot (Amy Krouse Rosenthal)

The Little Kitten (Judy Dunn)

The Lizard and the Sun (Alma Flor Ada)

Make Way for Ducklings (Robert McCloskey)

Movement (John Gaski)

Nothing Sticks Like a Shadow (Ann Tompert)

Our Earth (Anne Rockwell)

**The Paper Bag Princess* (Robert Munsch)

Planes and Rockets and Things That Fly (Richard Scarry)

Recycle That! (Fay Robinson)

Sunflower Sal (Janet S. Anderson)

The Three Little Pigs (Paul Galdone)

**A Tree is For…* (Judith Bauer Stamper)

**We All Went on Safari* (Laurie Krebs)

**When the Monkeys Came Back* (Kristine L. Franklin)

**Who Lives in Trees?* (Trish Holland)

Using the Library Area to Teach Science and Technology

The primary reason for setting up the Library area is to encourage children to enjoy and explore books. Books also offer teachers numerous opportunities for sharing new scientific ideas with children. Here are some examples of questions and comments you might use as you share books with children:

Physical Science

Let's look through this plant book to see if we can find the leaf you brought in. That will help us know what kind of tree it's from.

This book about how pencils are made is very interesting. What did you learn from it?

We can add the word "automobile" to our word wall. That's another way to say "car."

Life Science

Would you like to tell me the story of The Three Little Pigs? *It's fun to pretend that pigs can talk.*

Do you think the ladybugs we see on the window are grouchy?

We can read this book and move our bodies at the same time! I see you're moving like a frog.

Earth and the Environment

The gems in this book are very pretty. I like the picture of the caves they come from.

I like the way they describe the clouds in this poem. The word "wispy" means that it looks feathery and a little bit like cotton candy.

This book about the desert is interesting. I didn't know that these plants and animals live in the desert.

Technology

I see that you're using a magnifying glass to look at the tiny insect legs in that book. Would you like to draw them?

Let's use the computer to make a book about robins. We can read it to our visitors at the end of our study.

This book shows "life-sized" objects. That means the objects are the same size in real life as they are on this page. Look at the tiny bunny! Let's use the ruler to measure how tall it is.

Observing Children's Understanding

As you observe and share books with children in the Library area, look and listen for children's understanding of science and technology concepts:

- Following directions in a "how-to" book about creating an ant farm
- Creating a book about different types of leaves
- Reading a weather book and making comparisons to the weather outside the classroom
- Retelling a story featuring animals
- Describing differences between an animal in a fiction story and a real animal
- Looking through a catalog of tractors and pointing out various features
- Recording when telling a story in order to share a story with a family member
- Looking for more information about bones after seeing someone in a cast
- Reading a poem about seasons and naming characteristics of the current season
- Listening to an audiobook about the life cycle of plants

Science and Technology in the Sand and Water Area

Most children love the sensory experiences at the sand and water table. They can explore using sight, sound, and touch and create endless possibilities for learning. Here are examples of how children's explorations in the Sand and Water area relate to *The Creative Curriculum® for Preschool* objectives for science and technology learning.

Examples of What a Child Might Do	Examples of Related Objectives for Development and Learning
Describe the feel of the sand as it pours out of the cup.	24. Uses scientific inquiry skills
Talk about the pet fish in the classroom while pouring water.	25. Demonstrates knowledge of the characteristics of living things
Demonstrate how sand pours through the funnel slowly.	26. Demonstrates knowledge of the physical properties of objects and materials
Say, "This water is clear. Not like the water in the ocean."	27. Demonstrates knowledge of Earth's environment
Work with a water wheel to move water into a bowl.	28. Uses tools and other technology to perform tasks

Science and Technology Materials for the Sand and Water Area

The addition of props, tools, and containers to the Sand and Water area gives children many opportunities to investigate more intentionally while using sand, water, or other materials. The materials listed in the chart below are not meant to be added all at once. Choose props based on the study topic or children's interests.

Materials

collections for sorting (e.g., shells, rocks, and other natural materials)

forms or containers for molding bricks from damp sand

small construction vehicles

pipes, tubing, connectors, basters, straws

different types of fabric

light sources nearby that can be the "sun"

balance scale

props related to the current study topic

Suggested Books

(Titles preceded by an asterisk are included in the *Teaching Strategies® Children's Book Collection*.)

**The Adventures of Gary & Harry: A Tale of Two Turtles* (Lisa Matsumoto)

Animal Babies in Ponds and Rivers (Editors of Kingfisher)

**Dear Mr. Blueberry* (Simon James)

**Get Set! Swim!* (Jeannine Atkins)

A Hole is to Dig (Ruth Krauss and Maurice Sendak)

I Can Be a Plumber (Katherine Frew)

In My Pond (Sara Gillingham)

Is This a House for Hermit Crab? (Megan McDonald)

Jump Into Science: Sand (Prager)

Mixing and Separating (Chris Oxlade)

**Our Tree Named Steve* (Alan Zweibel)

Sea, Sand, Me! (Patricia Hubbell)

Swing, Slither, or Swim (Patricia M. Stockland)

Tina's Diner (JoAnn Adinolfi)

Using Sand and Water to Teach Science and Technology

Teachers can use the time children spend playing with sand and water to challenge them to think of these materials in new ways. Instead of just scooping and pouring, children can more closely examine whatever might be found in the sensory table that day. Describing the cause and effect of what children are doing draws their attention to the science behind how things move and what things are made of. Begin by observing children before entering their play. Then, thoughtfully determine what questions and comments might further their learning experience.

Physical Science

What happens when the hole in the cup gets bigger?

Where does the water go when you pour it into the pipe?

If you try to pour the sand back into the bowl, will it all fit?

I wonder what would happen if we put a magnet in the sand.

Life Science

You saw a turtle once? Did you know that some turtles lay their eggs in the sand?

What will you do with the plastic fish? How is it going to swim?

Tell me why you think your cat can't swim.

Remember the book we read this morning? What did they make out of sand?

Earth and the Environment

That sand is heavy as you fill the biggest cup!

Where have you seen sand before?

You said that some water is salty. I wonder if the rain is salty.

Technology

Which cup of sand weighs more? Let's use the balance scale to find out.

How can we make the water go faster through the funnel?

What did you find when you used a sifter in the sand?

Observing Children's Understanding

As children explore sand and water, observe for their understanding of science and technology concepts:

- Using tools to move sand or water from one place to another
- Measuring using standard and nonstandard units
- Talking about what comprises sand
- Describing some of water's properties
- Describing the texture of the sand
- Talking about animals who live in sand and water
- Thinking of new ways to use tools in the water
- Making connections between the pipes in the water and the pipes in buildings

Science and Technology in the Music and Movement Area

Music and movement activities provide a chance for children to explore how their bodies balance and move, what makes sound come from an instrument, how animals move, and even how objects in nature move such as rocks, rivers, trees, and flowers. Here are examples of how children's explorations in the Music and Movement area relate to *The Creative Curriculum® for Preschool* objectives for science and technology.

Examples of What a Child Might Do	Examples of Related Objectives for Development and Learning
Wonder aloud about what makes the sound loud when blowing through a horn.	24. Uses scientific inquiry skills
Imitate animal sounds and movements.	25. Demonstrates knowledge of the characteristics of living things
Talk about the way the strings vibrate on the guitar.	26. Demonstrates knowledge of the physical properties of objects and materials
Learn to make sounds using water.	27. Demonstrates knowledge of Earth's environment
Play an electric keyboard.	28. Uses tools and other technology to perform tasks

Science and Technology Materials for the Music and Movement Area

You can support children's science and technology learning by providing materials that encourage children to move in different ways. You can also introduce new and familiar instruments and talk about how they produce sound. Consider the materials in other areas of the classroom. You might find interesting sound makers that invite children to further investigate different types of sound, music, and movement.

Materials

instruments that make different sounds

recordings of different types of instruments

recordings of animal sounds (e.g., birds, insects, whales, etc.)

photos of the inside of various musical instruments

objects from the classroom that can make sound in new ways

animal props for movement

video clips of plants growing over time

natural materials for making music (e.g., small stones to make a shaker, sticks for drumming, etc.)

Suggested Books

(Titles preceded by an asterisk are included in the *Teaching Strategies*® *Children's Book Collection*.)

Birds (Kevin Henkes)

Birdsongs (Betsy Franco)

Bug Music (David Rothenberg)

The Busy Body Book (Lizzy Rockwell)

The Croaky Pokey (Ethan Long)

The Frog Was Singing (Rita Rosa Ruesga)

**From Head to Toe* (Eric Carle)

**Hop, Hop, Jump!* (Lauren Thompson)

Making Sounds (Charlotte Guillain)

Max Found Two Sticks (Brian Pinkney)

Move! (Steve Jenkins and Robin Page)

The Musicians of Bremen (Roser Ros)

Over in the Meadow (Ezra Jack Keats)

A Rock is Lively (Dianna Hutts Aston)

**Whistle for Willie* (Ezra Jack Keats)

Using Music and Movement to Teach Science and Technology

It's fun for children to hear and make music together. They also typically enjoy dancing and moving in silly ways. Teachers can use these moments to reinforce science and technology concepts. Asking "why" and "how" questions might encourage children to think beyond what they already know. For example, a child might play a note on a piano without ever wondering how the sound is made. This would be a chance to apply science concepts to everyday, real-world situations. Here are examples of what you might say and ask as you interact with children in this interest area:

Physical Science

How can we make the guitar sound louder?

What do you hear when I play the drum with my fingers?

What happens when we make the string shorter?

I see the scarf floating in the air while you dance. I wonder how it moves that way.

Your shoes make a tapping sound when you dance. I wonder why my shoes don't make that same sound.

Life Science

We're listening to the sound that whales make in the ocean. It almost sounds like music.

How can we use this shell to make a sound?

I wonder why we breathe faster when we dance.

Why do you think the bird sings that song?

How can we move like a crab?

Earth and the Environment

I wonder if we can make our own shaker using sand.

How does the flower look when we watch a sped-up video of it growing?

Look at the waterfall on this poster. The water moves very fast.

What animal sounds do we hear at night?

I wonder why these rocks make different sounds when I tap them with a stick.

Technology

Listen to the sound of the violin. The sound comes out of these holes on the side.

What tools can we use to make our own instruments?

How can we turn the volume down on our music?

This video shows a bee flying very slowly. Can we move slowly, too?

Observing Children's Understanding

As children explore music and movement, be aware of how they apply their knowledge of science and technology concepts. You may notice children:

- Experimenting with natural materials to make sounds (e.g., shells, sticks, sand, etc.)
- Imitating animal movements and sounds
- Asking questions about how instruments work
- Wondering about how their bodies move
- Describing the motions and making comparisons between animal movements
- Trying to whistle after listening to birds chirping

Science and Technology in the Cooking Area

When children are involved in creating and tasting food, they begin to see the cause and effect of their actions, learn about the drastic difference in tastes and textures across a variety of foods, and discover how food is grown. As teachers prepare food with children, they should take time to explain the process, what ingredients are used, and what tools are needed. Here are examples of how children's explorations in the Cooking area relate to *The Creative Curriculum® for Preschool* objectives for science and technology.

Examples of What a Child Might Do	Examples of Related Objectives for Development and Learning
Ask, "Why do we always wash our hands before we eat?"	24. Uses scientific inquiry skills
Wonder why bananas don't have seeds like other fruits.	25. Demonstrates knowledge of the characteristics of living things
Take a berry basket and say, "This would be good to use in the sandbox."	26. Demonstrates knowledge of the physical properties of objects and materials
Hold a piece of ice and wonder how water freezes.	27. Demonstrates knowledge of Earth's environment
Use a plastic knife to cut a piece of watermelon.	28. Uses tools and other technology to perform tasks

Science and Technology Materials for the Cooking Area

Many standard cooking tools can be used by children as they explore the process of preparing food. Utensils, measuring cups, whisks, and hand mixers are all examples of kitchen tools that might prompt additional comments and questions from children when teachers work with them in the Cooking area. Children can use their five senses to learn about the ingredients and foods they eat. They can learn where their food comes from. And they can learn why a particular cooking tool is used for a particular task.

Materials

standard and unusual cooking tools (e.g., potato masher, garlic press, cherry pitter, etc.)

kitchen timer

balance scale

posters that explain where food comes from

cookbooks

different types of similar foods (e.g., citrus fruits, bread, yogurt, etc.)

food container labels featuring nutrition facts

poster demonstrating how to properly wash hands

Suggested Books

(Titles preceded by an asterisk are included in the *Teaching Strategies® Children's Book Collection.*)

Baby Food (Joost Elffers and Saxton Freyman)

Before We Eat: From Farm to Table (Pat Brisson)

Blueberries for Sal (Robert McCloskey)

Bunny Cakes (Rosemary Wells)

Cloudy With a Chance of Meatballs (Judi and Ronald Barrett)

**Come Cook With Me* (Heather Baker, Kai-leé Berke, and Sherrie Rudick)

Counting at the Market (Amy Rauen)

**Crazy Pizza Day* (by Bonnie Dobkin)

Feathers for Lunch (Lois Ehlert)

Germs Are Not For Sharing (Elizabeth Verdick)

The Giant Jam Sandwich (John Vernon Lord)

Growing Vegetable Soup (Lois Ehlert)

**Guacamole* (Jorge Argueta)

How Many Seeds in a Pumpkin? (Margaret McNamara)

Little Pea (Amy Krouse Rosenthal)

Oliver's Fruit Salad (Vivian French)

Pete's a Pizza (William Steig)

**Rah, Rah, Radishes!* (April Pulley Sayre)

Seaweed Soup (Stuart J. Murphy)

**Stone Soup* (Marcia Brown)

Thunder Cake (Patricia Polacco)

Using Cooking to Teach Science and Technology

As you interact with children in the Cooking area, ask questions and prompt them to think about how they are preparing food and what it tastes like. Invite children to predict how a certain food will taste or what dough will look like when it comes out of the oven. Then, let them test their predictions. Here are examples of what you might say and ask to promote science and technology learning:

Physical Science

Which tool will work best to break up the dough? Yes, that's called a pastry blender.

How can I protect my hand when I touch the hot pan?

What happened to the baking soda when we added it to the batter?

When we close the bag, we'll squeeze the air out first to keep the food fresh.

Life Science

These strawberries we picked are delicious!

We can use these extra carrots to give our pet rabbit a snack.

I wonder what would happen if we cooked the apples without cutting them first.

How can we find out where our milk came from today?

Earth and the Environment

We'll add a little salt to our mashed potatoes. Salt and potatoes both come from the ground.

This recipe is called "Sun Tea." After we put the teabags in the water, we'll set the jar outside so the sun can heat the water.

This bread recipe uses lots of cranberries. Cranberries grow in places with sand and water that are called "bogs."

When we make ice cream, we put rock salt around the bowl to help the ice cream freeze.

Technology

How can we make sure the muffins bake for 20 minutes?

There are different buttons on the blender that change how fast the blade spins.

Which tool will work best for scraping the bowl?

The toaster makes the bread brown and crisp. I like watching the bread pop up!

Observing Children's Understanding

As children participate in cooking experiences or prepare snacks, look for examples of their understanding of science and technology:

- Using measuring tools to measure ingredients
- Talking about where food comes from
- Describing the taste, smell, or texture of food
- Experimenting with different ingredients (e.g., adding or removing dried fruit when making trail mix)
- Explaining what happens when ingredients are cooked or frozen
- Using a thermometer to measure the temperature of food
- Leaving frozen fruit in the bowl for a few minutes so it can thaw
- Using hand tools and appliances when making a recipe
- Asking how long it will take for the bread to cool when it comes out of the oven
- Predicting what will happen when eggs are added to the dry ingredients
- Asking for help using a new kitchen tool

Science and Technology in the Technology Area

By using various technology devices, children can experience learning in new or different ways. They can explore science topics, create books on a study topic, and make an observational drawing. As children learn to use technology, they are also learning how it works and the science behind it at the same time. Children can use the computer to represent their new ideas, predictions, and experiments or use a tablet to investigate a topic that interests them in order to find out more information. Here are examples of how children's explorations in the Technology area relate to *The Creative Curriculum® for Preschool* objectives for science and technology.

Examples of What a Child Might Do	Examples of Related Objectives for Development and Learning
Ask for help researching how cars are made.	24. Uses scientific inquiry skills
Check an online calendar to find out when to feed the classroom pet.	25. Demonstrates knowledge of the characteristics of living things
Follow the steps for turning on the tablet.	26. Demonstrates knowledge of the physical properties of objects and materials
Remember to take the digital camera inside so it doesn't get wet.	27. Demonstrates knowledge of Earth's environment
Know how to navigate a drawing program and use the mouse to draw.	28. Uses tools and other technology to perform tasks

Science and Technology Materials for the Technology Area

The Technology area houses more than just the computer. This can be the place where children go to print a picture, return the digital camera, or get the tablet from where it is being charged. The possibilities are endless when it comes to technology and studies. Children, with adult guidance, can find information on virtually any topic. Choose appropriate computer programs and tablet apps and games, and think about how children might work together when using them.

Limit the number of children using a device at the same time. Provide writing materials nearby so that children can record their online findings. When planning for a study, take time to research available resources so that children can make the most of their time spent on the tablet or computer.

Using Technology to Teach Science and Technology

While children may already have some knowledge of technology tools, your guidance and support will help them use the tablet or the computer as a tool for learning and for diving deeper into a study topic. Remember that technology in the classroom should be used to enhance learning, so your interactions with children are critical in order for children to get the most they can out of the experience.

Physical Science

Do you hear that sound the computer is making? Where do you think it's coming from?

We'll be careful when we use the touch screen so that it stays clean. That will make it easier to use.

Life Science

We can use the tablet to find out more about the zebras you see in your book.

I like to get up and stretch after I sit at the computer.

How can we find out how long it will take for our baby chicks to hatch?

Earth and the Environment

The label on the tablet says it needs to stay around 70 degrees. It can't be too hot or too cold.

Let's make sure we cover up the camera while we're outside so it doesn't get sand in it.

I wonder how we can find out when the sun will set today.

Technology

When I type on the computer, I can fix my mistakes with the Delete key.

The tablet is useful when we need to move the screen around the room. We can't carry the computer that way.

Can you please help me put more paper in the printer? Can you find where I put the paper?

Observing Children's Understanding

As children explore the computer and other technology tools, observe their understanding of science and technology. A few examples are:

- Following the correct sequence to open up a program on the computer
- Finding a familiar icon for a letter game
- Researching to find more information about the study topic
- Handling the equipment gently and explaining why this is important
- Asking questions about how the tablet and other devices work
- Tracking information such as weather predictions or phases of the moon
- Suggesting a technology tool to make a job easier, such as using a calculator to add several large numbers
- Problem solving (e.g., figuring out that the mouse won't work because it's not on the mouse pad)
- Explaining the process for navigating an app on the tablet

Science and Technology Outdoors

The outdoors often provides the ideal setting for science and technology exploration. Children can observe animals, plants, the sky, and other objects in their surroundings. They can make predictions and conduct experiments of plants, weather, animals, etc. They can explore various tools for building, measuring, and other tasks. Outdoors it may be more natural to incorporate new scientific vocabulary. Just as with the indoor interest areas, children's learning outdoors can be both individual and group based. Here are examples of how children's outdoor explorations relate to *The Creative Curriculum® for Preschool* objectives for science and technology.

Examples of What a Child Might Do	Examples of Related Objectives for Development and Learning
Wonder aloud about how the rainspout works.	24. Uses scientific inquiry skills
Notice the caterpillars getting bigger on the milkweed plant.	25. Demonstrates knowledge of the characteristics of living things
Use the fence to hang materials to make a wind chime.	26. Demonstrates knowledge of the physical properties of objects and materials
Observe the sun making the playground warm.	27. Demonstrates knowledge of Earth's environment
Take a photo of a flower instead of picking it.	28. Uses tools and other technology to perform tasks

Science and Technology Materials for the Outdoors

Children can use all kinds of tools to conduct experiments outdoors. Keep the materials simple, and think about the different ways they can be used. See *The Creative Curriculum® for Preschool, Volume 2: Interest Areas* for additional information about setting up your outdoor space. You will find that an organized outdoor space is a welcoming environment for budding scientists and investigators. The chart below suggests books and materials to encourage scientific thinking outdoors.

Materials

pipes and water

wind chimes and materials for making additional chimes

chalk for tracing shadows

gardening tools and supplies

watering cans

building materials

wheelbarrow

magnifying glasses and binoculars

rain gauge

sundial

containers for sorting

writing materials, including clipboards

standard and nonstandard measuring tools

riding toys

Suggested Books

(Titles preceded by an asterisk are included in the *Teaching Strategies® Children's Book Collection.*)

Bugs Are Insects (Anne Rockwell)

**Chrysanthemum* (Kevin Henkes)

**Dinosaur Woods* (George McClements)

**A Grand Old Tree* (Mary Newell DePalma)

**Henny Penny* (Bonnie Dobkin)

In My Backyard (Valarie Giogas and Katherine Zecca)

The Little Leaf That Wouldn't Fall (Phil Scrima)

Our Yard is Full of Birds (Anne Rockwell)

Planes (Richard Scarry)

Sense Suspense: A Guessing Game for the Senses (Bruce McMillan)

Stick! (Andy Pritchett)

Stranger in the Woods (Carl R. Sams)

What Makes Day and Night (Franklyn M. Branley)

Whose Shadow is This? (Claire Berge)

Using the Outdoors to Teach Science and Technology

When outdoors with children, teachers should allow for plenty of time for children to begin their own explorations of their surroundings. As you see children become more engrossed in their investigative play, make simple comments and ask questions that encourage them to use science and technology vocabulary. Regardless of your feelings about the outdoors, remember to show enthusiasm for nature and exploration so that children get the full benefit of your teaching outdoors. Here are examples of what you might say and ask:

Physical Science

You're up high on the ladder! What can you see from up there?

I wonder how the bucket got full of water.

Do you have more red leaves or yellow leaves?

Why do you think the sidewalk has cracks in it?

How can we use this rope to hang the birdfeeder?

Life Science

I wonder what animal ate the grain we left outside yesterday.

Look at all of these ants! They're marching in a line. I wonder where they're going.

It's hot outside today. Let's drink some cold water to cool down our bodies.

How can we help our tree grow taller?

Here is a praying mantis cocoon. We'll put it in the bush so it will be safe.

Earth and the Environment

What is the sundial telling us? Where is the shadow?

There is a ditch here from the rain water. It was rushing like a river.

How can we keep our flowers from getting too much sun?

What animal do you think lives in that nest?

We can use the rain from our rain barrel to water the garden.

Technology

Would you like to take a picture of the butterfly? That way you can draw it later after it's flown away.

This gardening spade will help you make a bigger hole for the seeds.

Look at that birdfeeder. It's made to keep squirrels from eating the bird seed.

Let's see if we can measure how much snow fell this morning. What tools should we use?

I like recording the sounds of the birds outside. We can listen to them later when we're back in the classroom.

Observing Children's Understanding

As children play and explore outdoors, observe the ways that they demonstrate their understanding of science and technology:

- Following a trail of animal tracks
- Checking the temperature on the outdoor thermometer
- Using a tarp to make shade for the sandbox
- Pulling up weeds in the garden
- Harvesting any fruits or vegetables
- Looking for insects on the ground
- Wondering how to ride a tricycle on the bumpy ground
- Comparing the grass by the shed to the grass under the rainspout
- Collecting and organizing natural objects
- Explaining what happens when the sun goes down

3

Planning Your Science and Technology Program

Planning Your Science and Technology Program 79

Objectives for Science and Technology Development and Learning 80

Guiding Children's Science and Technology Learning 81

Creating a Scientifically and Technologically Rich Physical Environment 82

Integrating Science and Technology Throughout the Day 84

Planning Your Science and Technology Program

Chapter 1 explains the components of science and technology. In this chapter, you will see how the curricular objectives for development and learning help you think about the content and process skills of science and technology and understand how science and technology learning takes place in *The Creative Curriculum®* classroom. You will also see how teachers purposefully and intentionally plan for children's science and technology learning and how they use the environment during daily routines and experiences.

In order to plan intentionally and responsively, teachers need to know the objectives for children's development and learning. As you read the at-a-glance chart that is presented in the next section, note the five objectives that are related specifically to science and technology.

Because children's understanding of these concepts is affected by development in other areas, teachers also need to know the objectives for development and learning in those areas. For example, verbal language skills are related to children's understanding of scientific and technological terminology.

This volume of *The Creative Curriculum® for Preschool* focuses on the science and technology objectives for preschool children. Keep these objectives in mind as you plan for each child and the group. Understand that individual children will be functioning at different developmental levels. You will tailor your strategies as you scaffold children's learning and help them expand their knowledge and understanding of science and technology. The assessment information that you collect will guide you in determining how to plan for experiences that support children's development and learning.

Objectives for Science and Technology Development and Learning

The following chart shows the 38 objectives that are included in *The Creative Curriculum® for Preschool, Volume 6, Objectives for Development & Learning: Birth Through Third Grade.* Objectives 24–28 are directly related to science and technology.

Objectives for Development & Learning: Birth Through Third Grade

Social–Emotional

1. Regulates own emotions and behaviors
2. Establishes and sustains positive relationships
3. Participates cooperatively and constructively in group situations

Physical

4. Demonstrates traveling skills
5. Demonstrates balancing skills
6. Demonstrates gross-motor manipulative skills
7. Demonstrates fine-motor strength and coordination

Language

8. Listens to and understands increasingly complex language
9. Uses language to express thoughts and needs
10. Uses appropriate conversational and other communication skills

Cognitive

11. Demonstrates positive approaches to learning
12. Remembers and connects experiences
13. Uses classification skills
14. Uses symbols and images to represent something not present

Literacy

15. Demonstrates phonological awareness, phonics skills, and word recognition
16. Demonstrates knowledge of the alphabet
17. Demonstrates knowledge of print and its uses
18. Comprehends and responds to books and other texts
19. Demonstrates writing skills

Mathematics

20. Uses number concepts and operations
21. Explores and describes spatial relationships and shapes
22. Compares and measures
23. Demonstrates knowledge of patterns

Science and Technology

24. Uses scientific inquiry skills
25. Demonstrates knowledge of the characteristics of living things
26. Demonstrates knowledge of the physical properties of objects and materials
27. Demonstrates knowledge of Earth's environment
28. Uses tools and other technology to perform tasks

Social Studies

29. Demonstrates knowledge about self
30. Shows basic understanding of people and how they live
31. Explores change related to familiar people or places
32. Demonstrates simple geographic knowledge

The Arts

33. Explores the visual arts
34. Explores musical concepts and expression
35. Explores dance and movement concepts
36. Explores drama through actions and language

English Language Acquisition

37. Demonstrates progress in listening to and understanding English
38. Demonstrates progress in speaking English

Guiding Children's Science and Technology Learning

Although opportunities naturally occur every day for science and technology learning, planning is still essential to ensure that learning opportunities are fully explored. A well-planned, project-based approach and carefully considered study topic can address the components of science and technology and make the most of the classroom learning environment and materials. Mindful planning also takes into account children's abilities, interests, and learning styles.

As they plan for children's science and technology learning, teachers must decide what to teach, as well as when and how to teach it. They make these decisions on the basis of:

- what children are interested in and what they already know
- *The Creative Curriculum® for Preschool* objectives for development and learning
- the strengths, needs, and abilities of individual children
- the available resources for hands-on exploration of science and technology concepts

In *The Creative Curriculum®* classroom, the teacher uses a wide range of teaching strategies. Children have unique learning styles, interests, and temperaments, and they progress at different rates. Some children love to scoop and dump sand in the sand and water table, while others gravitate toward the Discovery area and the tools there. An approach that is successful with most 4-year-olds may not work with most 3-year-olds. You might find that some movement activities, experiences with manipulatives, or time spent in the Library area may work best depending on what the children are learning. Because the environment provides the context for young children's learning, consider the ways in which teachers can create and use the environment to promote understanding of science and technology.

Creating a Scientifically and Technologically Rich Physical Environment

Scientific thinking is supported by a thoughtfully arranged, well-organized classroom environment. Focused explorations are more likely to occur in a well-organized environment.

A classroom ready for science and technology learning is full of interesting, novel materials. It fosters the investigation of important concepts such as life science, physical science, Earth and the environment, awareness of technology, basic operations of technology, tools and equipment, and people and technology. The environment should stimulate children's thinking and prompt them to solve problems, reason, communicate, make connections to what they already know, and represent their learning. In an environment such as this, children can make discoveries about the scientific world around them and pose new questions to find the answers to. Here are some basic principles to help you create a rich physical environment that is ideal for children's learning of science and technology.

Strategies for Creating Spaces for Science and Technology Experiences

Strategies	Examples
Organize the classroom environment to invite exploration.	Create interest areas that are inviting and organized with room for children's investigative play.
Highlight scientific ideas and the use of tools and technology in the classroom (asking questions, observing and recording, using technology) in classroom displays.	Create relevant displays, such as: • natural items found outdoors • photos from site visits • instructions for using the computer • class-made charts and graphs of predictions and outcomes • children's artwork (hand-drawn and computer-made) • interest area choice boards • artifacts from the current study • "What Do We Know" and "What Do We Want to Find Out" charts • weekly weather forecasts and measuring tools for temperature and precipitation • instructions for caring for classroom pet or plant
Make time each day for outdoor exploration.	Consider all of the ways to explore the outdoors, such as: • taking measurements of precipitation on a rainy day • bringing in natural objects into the classroom for observational drawing • making predictions and comparisons of outdoor temperatures • looking for wildlife • taking pictures of plant life • observing the sky • using magnifying glasses and/or binoculars • filling bird feeders • measuring growth of plants • creating an outdoor display of natural materials

Strategies	Examples
Look for opportunities to enhance interest areas with science and technology materials.	Include tools and materials for investigation. Incorporate related environmental print appropriate to each area (e.g., computer manuals in the Technology area, seed packets in the Dramatic Play area, etc.). Include appropriate books in each interest area (e.g., field guides in the Discovery area, park and wildlife brochures in the Library area, books about animal habitats in the Block area, etc.).

Integrating Science and Technology Throughout the Day

Most young children enter school having already been exposed to some science concepts, and more and more children come into preschool with a basic understanding of technology tools. Mobile infants use their mouths to explore textures and tastes. They observe animals and feel the wind on their hands when they go outdoors. Toddlers learn about science by picking up objects, stacking, moving, and often using them to make noise. Two- and 3-year-old children help family members feed a pet or put wet laundry into the dryer. Such activities give children a foundation of science and technology knowledge that they take with them to preschool.

Preschool teachers can provide children with meaningful opportunities to investigate, ask questions, predict, research, and observe all day long. Sometimes these occasions happen unexpectedly, like when a child comes to school with a picture he drew of a bluebird or a child brings in a sparkling rock to share. These opportunities are perfect for engaging children in scientific inquiry and technology exploration and expanding what they know. Although these types of examples may occur with some regularity, it is still important to include science and technology experiences when planning for your day. Using *Teaching Guides* is a great way to make sure you are engaging children in thoughtful, in-depth investigative experiences. Additionally, here are a few ways to integrate science and technology.

Arrival

Preparing for the Environment

Ask children about the weather outside and how they dress accordingly.

Post written and illustrated instructions for handwashing.

Post any instructions for classroom jobs involving the care of classroom pets or plants.

Interactions

Have informal conversations about what children do outdoors (e.g., *You're sitting in the shade of the tree. I wonder if it would feel differently if you were sitting in the sunshine.*).

Remind children about how to observe animals respectfully and from a safe distance.

Talk with children about procedures when technology devices.

Interact to facilitate scientific inquiry and technology awareness (e.g., draw attention to how the xylophone works or what happens when paint colors are mixed).

It sounds like you're playing high notes and low notes. Which end do you play for the high notes? How are those keys different from the keys that play low notes?

Which of these icons should I click so that I can write a letter? What do you see on that icon?

Large-Group Time

Preparing the Environment

Refer to the weather chart or daily weather report.

Post a "Question of the Day" that asks children to think about a science topic.

Where should we look to find a bird nest?

Display detailed photos of animals and materials found in nature for observational drawing.

Post a chart with questions and answers related to the current study topic.

Who lives in trees?

Prepare materials (e.g., books, manipulatives, artifacts, photos, etc.) for any science or technology concepts you want to introduce.

Use authentic materials whenever possible. Keep natural materials in clear plastic bags or magnifying boxes (e.g., eggshell, owl pellet, soil sample, etc.).

Interactions

Introduce any new materials for children to see and touch. Talk about how to handle the materials safely, if needed.

Read and review the "Question of the Day." Invite children to predict and later interpret the answers.

Refer to the investigations currently taking place in the classroom. When using a *Teaching Guide*, follow the guidance for incorporating the study topic into your daily experiences. Encourage children to think about what they will choose to investigate or work on during choice time.

Call attention to any science and technology concepts that have been previously discussed and are relevant to daily experiences.

Remember when we visited the quarry and saw how they crush the rocks? How can we do something similar to break up these large chunks of hardened clay from the playground?

Use movement activities that reinforce science concepts such as:

Mighty Minutes 34, "The Wave"

Mighty Minutes 45, "I'm a Sturdy Oak Tree"

Mighty Minutes 67, "Let's Stick Together"

Mighty Minutes 133, "Metamorphosis"

Introduce new science and technology vocabulary.

Invite children to share their discoveries and questions.

Choice Time

Preparing the Environment

Create choice boards for interest areas that indicate some of the materials available for exploration.

Organize materials in ways that encourage children to sort and classify by various characteristics.

Prepare any technology tools so that they are ready for use (e.g., turn on the computer, unlock the screen on the tablet, etc.).

Add writing, drawing, and construction materials so children can represent their discoveries, predictions, and learning.

Interactions

Encourage children to continue the discussion from large-group time.

Talk about how to investigate using the materials in the interest areas.

Discuss ways to find out more information about the study topic and current investigation question.

Interact with children to facilitate their learning. Ask follow-up questions about their discoveries, have informal conversations, pose new challenges, model or demonstrate new materials, etc.

Read science- and technology-related books with individual or small groups of children. Interact with children in ways that intentionally draw their attention to the science and technology concepts presented in the books (e.g., pose a question about how something is built, which tools are used, and help children make connections to what they already know).

Invite an individual child or small groups of children to work with you as you use various technology devices.

Read both fiction and nonfiction books about science and technology topics. Discuss the differences between the two genres.

Encourage children to use a science journal to document or represent their scientific learning.

Give children time to thoroughly investigate materials. Encourage them to work slowly and deliberately with materials to make new discoveries.

Observe children and take notes about children's actions, abilities, and use of materials. Reflect on your observations and think about how you might extend the length of the study to suit children's interests.

Small-Group Time

Preparing the Environment

Think of new ways to incorporate science and technology materials into small-group learning time (e.g., using the computer to write a story, discussing why an ice cube melts faster in the sun, sorting leaves by more than one characteristic, graphing the results of an investigation, etc.).

Interactions

Encourage children to work together to solve problems and test predictions.

Have children create science journals and nonfiction books about the study topic.

Offer sorting and graphing experiences that help children learn more information about their investigations.

Expand children's understanding of science and technology vocabulary through literacy experiences (e.g., writing, researching, retelling information, etc.).

Point out ways that children also use mathematical concepts in their investigations (e.g., using measuring tools, counting and comparing objects, and noticing patterns in nature).

Snack and Mealtime

Preparing the Environment

Post step-by-step instructions for washing hands.

Display photos that depict how food is grown such as farmers harvesting fruits and vegetables.

Display names and pictures of the food being served.

Interactions

As children wash their hands, talk about why it's important. Encourage children to wash their hands for an appropriate length of time and explain the reasons.

Pose open-ended questions to facilitate scientific thinking and learning (e.g., "Why are there small holes in the bread? and, "What happens to the fruit when we turn on the blender?").

Read recipe charts and ask children if they can taste each ingredient in their snack or meal.

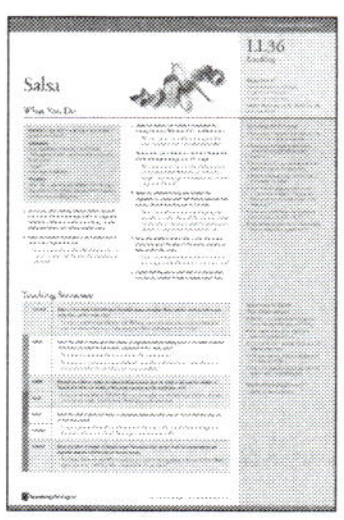

Intentional Teaching Card
LL 36, "Salsa"

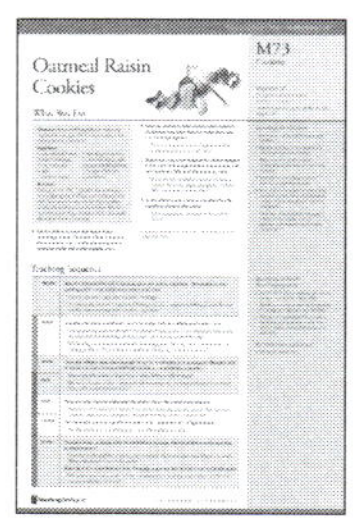

Intentional Teaching Card
M73, "Oatmeal Raisin Cookies"

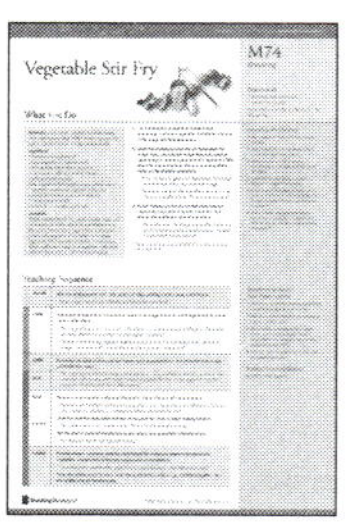

Intentional Teaching Card
M74, "Vegetable Stir Fry"

Interact to help children make connections between science, technology, and everyday experiences.

Your bread is stuck together by a piece of melted cheese. How did the cheese melt?

The bottle says that we should shake the juice before we pour it into our cups. What do you see in the juice? Why do you think we need to shake it?

We have strawberries with our lunch today because they're "in season." That means that this is the time of year when strawberries grow where we live. They grow best when it's not too hot and not too cold outside.

Invite children to taste and make comparisons between foods such as different types of apples. Create graphs that chart the characteristics as well as children's preferences.

Transitions

Preparing the Environment

Plan in advance for any appropriate activities that illustrate science and technology concepts, such as:

Mighty Minutes 31, "What's Inside the Box?"

Mighty Minutes 39, "Let's Pretend"

Mighty Minutes 48, "Feely Box"

Mighty Minutes 179, "Heavy & Light"

Prepare any materials needed for the activity.

> Let's Pretend **39**
>
> Objective 26
> Demonstrates knowledge of the physical properties of objects and materials
>
> Related Objectives: 1, 3, 4, 5, 8, 11, 12, 14, 21, 25, 36
>
> What You Do
>
> 1. Ask the children to make their bodies look flat and small, like a balloon before it's been blown up.
> 2. Tell them that you are going to pretend to inflate them.
> 3. Blow hard, and direct the children to expand their bodies.
> 4. After the children are "inflated," pretend to be a gust of wind that carries them over trees, mountains, and places in the community.
> 5. Afterward, ask a child to gently "pop" each balloon.

Interactions

Physical Science (e.g., *If you have a zipper on your clothes, you may get your coat.*)

Life Science (e.g., *Let's move like frogs when we walk to the sink.*)

Earth and the Environment (e.g., *Find a shadow to stand on before lining up to go inside.*)

Technology (e.g., *We'll pretend to use microphones when we sing our song.*)

Outdoor Time

Preparing the Environment

Provide measurement tools, binoculars, magnifying glasses, and materials for collecting specimens.

Provide safe areas for exploration that are free of trash and debris.

Include writing materials for children to record their findings outdoors.

Interactions

Use science and technology vocabulary when discussing children's outdoor investigations (e.g., *You found a very small insect. It's an insect because it has six legs. What do you see when you look at it with the magnifying glass? When we go inside should we use the computer to research what type of insect it is?*).

Call attention to changes in the environment. Ask open-ended questions that prompt children to notice the changes and think about why they happen (e.g., *I see a big hole in the dirt here under the corner of the roof. What do you think caused that hole? Do you remember the weather we had yesterday?*).

Talk with children about how they might sort and classify any new natural objects they find.

Encourage quiet observation of animals.

Allow children to take some of their findings indoors for further exploration. Designate an area such as the Discovery area for children to temporarily investigate and display the materials they find.

Rest Time

Preparing the Environment

Display a clock.

Prepare an audio device to play soothing music.

Interactions

Point out how you use the clock to determine the beginning and end of rest time.

Talk about the device you're using to play calm, quiet music.

Discuss how rest helps our bodies grow and stay healthy.

Departure

Preparing the Environment

Display any additional information that was added to the chart about the current investigation.

Check the weather outside to help children determine how to dress appropriately.

Interactions

Recall the discoveries children made during the day. Refer to the investigation chart.

Ask children questions about how they'll dress for the weather. Introduce new vocabulary to describe the weather.

Discuss how you will use the technology devices throughout the day. Ask children to help you make sure each device is working and is being used carefully.

Encourage children to make sure the classroom pet or plant has been properly cared for.

What Would Happen If…? 110

Objective 8
Listens to and understands increasingly complex language
a. Comprehends language
Related Objectives: 9a, 10a, 11a, 11e, 12a, 30

What You Do

1. **Explain that you are going to ask some silly questions.**
2. **Ask,** "What would happen if we…[wore socks on our hands]…[brushed our teeth with a hairbrush]…[wore bathing suits in the snow]?"
3. **Give children time to respond.**
4. **Continue asking new, silly questions.**

4 Components of Social Studies

Social Studies 93

Components of Social Studies 95

People and How They Live 95

People and the Environment 99

People and the Past 103

Spaces and Geography 107

Studies: Reduce, Reuse, Recycle 111

Social Studies

When we talk about social studies, we are talking about people and communities. We are talking about how people interact, work, and live. We are talking about changes throughout history and how those changes affect our lives today. As early as infancy, children are aware of certain social studies concepts. They recognize members of their family and understand daily routines. Preschool children pretend and interact as members of the larger community. The Dramatic Play area, in particular, offers many opportunities for introducing and reinforcing social studies concepts such as community jobs, home routines, and the roles of different people.

Children use important process skills when they communicate information about themselves, explore similarities and differences among people and how they live, explore change, and use simple geographic knowledge. For preschool children, social studies learning encourages them to share information about themselves, discuss, and even debate (Bentley & Reppucci, 2013). Preschoolers also begin to learn civics as you teach them to cooperate and to resolve differences in a classroom setting. Young children can understand civics topics having to do with democratic principles of fairness, justice, and equality when teachers provide them with "purposeful and meaningful learning experiences that are challenging, of high quality, and developmentally appropriate" (National Council for the Social Studies, 2009, quoted in Santoli, Vitulli, & Giles, 2015).

Everyday experiences pertinent to children's lives are the foundation for learning social studies. Teachers can build this foundation by beginning social studies learning based on children's interests and questions they ask. This approach engages children, promoting both their critical thinking skills and social–emotional learning, while they gain social studies knowledge and develop social competence (Mindes, 2015). When teachers connect children's social understandings and social studies content learning to their personal development, children gain greater understanding and connection to social studies topics (Mindes, 2015).

As children are introduced and welcomed into a classroom community, they begin to make social–emotional connections with others as well as develop an understanding of what it means to be a part of the group. Children develop "greater and more complex understandings of cultural differences, historic trends, and current events" (Mindes, 2015). When teachers recognize and appreciate the bond between families and their children, are aware of social and cultural contexts, and establish trust with families, they are better able to implement best practices for all learners (Feeney & Freeman, 2012). As teachers connect with families and make them an integral part of the classroom experience, they expand children's knowledge and understanding of social and cultural elements in society.

And just as teachers should make it a priority to educate themselves about their classroom community and keep an open mind about the families they serve, children can also learn from this example being set for them. Teachers are in a wonderful position to model acceptance, inclusion, and tolerance while expanding children's knowledge of the world. An "anti-bias" education strengthens the possibilities for early childhood education programs to foster the development of the whole child. It "supports children in developing a fuller, truer understanding of themselves and the world and strengthens their sense of themselves as being capable and empowered to make 'unfair' things 'fair.'" When incorporating social studies into the daily opportunities of a preschool classroom, teachers can use real-life experiences to expose children to the concepts of civic topics, like fairness (Derman-Sparks & Olsen Edwards, 2010). As teachers incorporate social studies learning into the daily opportunities of a preschool classroom, they are preparing each child for "responsible life in a free society, in the spirit of understanding, peace, tolerance, equality of sexes, and friendship among all peoples, ethnic, national and religious groups and persons of indigenous origin" (United Nations Convention on the Rights of the Child, quoted in Hawkins, 2014).

The four social studies objectives for development and learning in *The Creative Curriculum® for Preschool* are:

Objective 29. Demonstrates knowledge about self

Objective 30. Shows basic understanding of people and how they live

Objective 31. Explores change related to familiar people or places

Objective 32. Demonstrates simple geographic knowledge

The objectives explore how people live in communities, interact with their environment, reflect on their past, and understand their surroundings. This chapter discusses each area in more detail, relating research to the teacher's role and to assessment strategies. With a clear understanding of the components of social studies, teachers will be able to observe children, analyze and evaluate their learning, and plan experiences that engage children as members of their community and the world at large.

Components of Social Studies

As an early childhood teacher, you know the importance of introducing children to the concept of community and helping them feel like valuable members of your class. "From previously being seen as passive vulnerable recipients, children are now acknowledged as competent, resilient and active agents, citizens with the right to be involved and heard in matters that affect them" (Davis, 2013, quoted in Ärlemalm-Hagsér, 2013). By beginning social studies learning in preschool, children are able to apply those areas of knowledge to their lives outside of school. The components of social studies listed here offer a depth and breadth of knowledge that ensures children understand what it means to be a member of classroom community and a global citizen. These components fall into four categories related to individuals and their interactions with others.

Social studies standards focus on history, geography, economics, and civics. These areas can be categorized as follows:

- people and how they live
- people and the environment
- people and the past
- spaces and geography

People and How They Live

"People and how they live" refers to the everyday activities of children, their families, and community members. This also includes similarities and differences between people both physically and culturally. The preschool classroom is a "natural extension" of the world today, a world where "groups of many different ethnicities and extractions have come together to form a culturally diverse, pluralistic, or multicultural society" (Robles de Meléndez & Beck, 2013). Drawing children's attention to these concepts helps them focus on how their daily lives are influenced by social studies. Children should have many opportunities for firsthand social studies experiences; they should "be taken out into the world of people as well as have the world brought to them in the classroom" (Feeney, Moravcik, Nolte, & Christensen, 2010).

Think of the children in your classroom and how they might answer the following questions as you introduce a variety of social studies concepts:

- What are the names of your family members? How many people are in your family?
- What do you like to do with your friends? How do you know if someone is a friend?
- What kinds of jobs do you see people doing at school? At the grocery store? At the post office?
- What do we need to create a pretend shop in our classroom?
- What rules do we follow at school and at home? Why are they important?

What Does Research Say?

In the early childhood classroom, social studies is another "developmentally appropriate link" in the classroom curriculum. Its focus on not only a child's education but concern for and understanding of each child and each child's family and community is a central tenet of social studies learning. This focus on each individual child and her world encourages children's natural enthusiasm for learning about both the cultural world and the environmental world" (Jackman, Beaver, & Skinner Wyatt, 2015).

"Intentional teaching in preschool can expose children to many of the themes developed in the K–12 years, including culture; time, continuity, and change; people, places, and environments; individuals, development, and identity; individuals, groups, and institutions; power, authority, and governance; production, distribution, and consumption; science, technology, and society; global connections; and civic ideals and practice" (NCSS [National Council for the Social Studies] 2010. National Curriculum Standards for Social Studies: A Framework for Teaching, Learning, and Assessment. Silver Spring, MD: NCSS).

When children feel and know that they are part of the school community, when they have a connection to the other children and the teachers in their classroom and know they are an integral part of the class, children understand their personal value as individuals in a community. Children's ownership in being a part of a community lays the groundwork for future success (Howell & Reinhard, 2015).

Through active participation in activities that encourage supporting peers and the classroom community, children's feelings of being helpful "enhance their thinking skills and deepen their sense of pride and belonging in their school and community" (Honig & Mennerich, 2013).

The social–emotional benefits to children's connection to the classroom community include: "increased willingness to learn, better impulse control, and overall increased and improved attention span" (Conscious Discipline, 2014).

The early childhood classroom is often representative of our culturally diverse society, "where different cultures exist, socially interact, and ... remain visible in their own context" (Robles de Meléndez & Beck, 2013).

Research has shown (and teachers and early child care providers and caretakers know) that children's growth and development are strengthened when teachers and schools partner and engage with children's families and their communities in meaningful ways and make strong connections with each other (Couchenour & Chrisman, 2013).

"Social studies learning encourages children to become aware of themselves as valued independent individuals who are also part of various communities: family, classroom, neighborhood, and even the world. This awareness emboldens children as they learn civic values such as respect for all and responsibility and begin to act as independent individuals" (Jackman, Beaver, & Skinner Wyatt, 2015).

The Teacher's Role in Promoting Understanding of People and How They Live

Learning about people and how they live means understanding and accepting similarities and differences in people, understanding how the jobs people do support the community, and knowing what rules are important for creating the best learning environment possible at school.

No matter what study topic your class is investigating or where you are in the school year, you can promote understanding of people in many ways. Here are a few suggestions:

Create rules related to cooperation and fairness.
In the context of real problems that may arise in the classroom, talk with children about the rules that will ensure a friendly and cooperative classroom community (e.g., *It can be frustrating when you feel like people aren't listening while you share a story during our group time. What rule could help us make sure that everyone is politely listening?*).

Make sure that art materials reflect a variety of skin tones.
Give children an opportunity to choose from a variety of materials that reflect the classroom community. Additionally, include art, music, and cooking experiences that represent different cultures.

Encourage families to join in class activities so they can share their own experiences.
By including cultural experiences of the families you serve, you encourage children to learn not just about their peers but also about how their own cultural experiences are alike or different from others.

Look for opportunities to introduce props in Dramatic Play that reinforce children's understanding of community jobs.
There are so many possibilities for enhancing this interest area to invite exploration of jobs in- and outside of your community (e.g., jobs in a child care center, bank, garden center, and pet supply store). Pay attention to the children's interests in the jobs of their families or community members. Invite children to help think of props that would represent a specific job.

Use site visits as a way to give children firsthand experience with a variety of jobs.
Children may be most interested in the jobs of the people they see regularly in the community. Encourage children to ask questions and learn more about the work people do and how this work supports the community.

Observing Children's Understanding

When you begin to observe children in order to determine their understanding of people and how they live, you may begin to notice small moments throughout the day that relate to this concept. A few examples are:

- Pretending to work at a store
- Contributing to a class book about community workers
- Looking at a family portrait and pointing out similar physical traits
- Explaining how to play a game differently to include everyone who wants to play
- Inviting a child who is new to the classroom to play catch with a ball

As children work together as part of the classroom community and learn about the roles that exist at home and in the larger community, ask the following questions:

How did you help your family today?

What jobs do you do at home?

How can we make the new member of our class feel welcome?

What do you notice about…?

What job do you have in grocery store we made?

Can you tell me about your portrait? Who did you draw?

Would you like to invite your family to help us…?

How much money do I need to buy this…?

Your Teaching Practice

Take a few moments to think about your own answers to the questions above. What feelings do you have about the people in your family? What about the jobs of your family, friends, and community members?

How can you ask questions of children to encourage them to share their own experiences with family and friends?

Tips to Share With Families

- Have conversations about what you do at work and what other family members do. Offer information about how your job helps others.
- Encourage friends and other family members to share about their jobs.
- Use positive language to describe your physical features and your child's physical features. Point out similarities and differences between your physical characteristics.
- Teach your child songs that you sang growing up. Talk about where you learned the songs.
- When you are out in the community, describe the jobs you see people doing.
- Include your child in discussions about family rules. Talk about why the rules have been chosen and how they help the family.
- Give your child responsibilities at home that support her to feel like a valuable and contributing member of the family.

People and the Environment

"People and the environment" refers to all of the ways that people take care of their local and global environments. This includes recycling, repairing buildings and roads, building new playground equipment for a city park, and planting a community garden. In preschool, teachers will find eager helpers in the preschool children who want to improve their surroundings and feel like important members of the community.

Here are some questions for children to think about as you help them explore the ways people affect and are affected by their environment:

- What can we do at school that helps the entire Earth?
- What are some good habits we can have that will help the environment? What habits are bad for the environment?

What Does Research Say?

Research has shown that when children gain an awareness of and increased knowledge about the environment and its resources at an early age, they are more likely to support actions and projects for the environment's well-being later in life. Educators now recognize that this environmental and conservation awareness contributes to children's "prosocial behavior" (Honig & Mennerich, 2013).

Children whose social studies education includes learning about the environment and their relationship with the environment recognize the impact of their actions on the environment. This awareness leads children to pay even more attention to the environment and potential actions on the behalf of the environment (Hsiao & Shih, 2015).

Young children who learn about the environment and engage in environmental activities in the classroom and school develop a strong sense of obligation to protecting the environment and its plants and animals. This positive behavior and attitude contributes to children's recognition of the importance of protecting the Earth and the impact recycling has on the Earth (Kahriman-Öztürk, 2010).

Classroom activities that focus on learning about the Earth and protecting the environment, such as celebrating Earth Day, not only give children the knowledge around the concept of sustainability but strengthen children's critical thinking and communication skills. As children acquire new learning knowledge, they gain confidence in themselves as investigators and problem solvers (Sibley & Kurz, 2014).

"By brainstorming together about environmental toxins, recycling or helping conserve resources, peers share their ideas with each other. This sharing may lead to more exciting and creative ideas. ... Children increase their understanding and ability to think of new ways to help the environment when they are encouraged to share ideas, brainstorm with each other and work on projects together" (Honig & Mennerich, 2013).

A crucial component to children's education around the Earth and the environment is for children to be "acknowledged as environmental stakeholders with a right to meaningful participation in environmental issues" (Ärlemalm-Hagsér, 2013).

The Teacher's Role in Promoting Understanding of People and the Environment

Learning about people and the environment means exploring the effects that people have, both positive and negative. Children may also explore how the environment affects people and how people adapt to their surroundings.

There are many ways to draw children's attention to their interactions with their environment. Here are a few simple suggestions:

Keep a collection of various materials for reuse in art projects.
Materials for art creations can come from many places. You may want to invite families to bring in things to add to a junk collection or talk with local business owners about collecting supplies that are no longer needed. Talk with children about how materials can be reused instead of thrown away.

Encourage children to notice improvements to be made to the outdoors.
Taking before and after photos of your outdoor area gives children a chance to see how their changes can improve their environment. If your program has multiple outdoor areas, encourage children to move beyond their own space to improve other areas at school.

Take a neighborhood walk to look for local environmental changes.
Model being an observant community member. Point out changes you see, such as wind damage to a local building or trees that were cut down to make way for a road or parking lot.

Include children in the task of sorting recyclable materials.
Adding this brief extra step to your classroom clean-up routine will help children establish the habit of sorting materials for recycling. You can also talk with children and families about simple ways to recycle materials at home.

Look around your classroom and reflect on the ways that recycled materials may enhance children's learning in interest areas.
Children hardly need encouragement to incorporate boxes and tubes into their play. When new cardboard materials come into the classroom, look for ways to add them to interest areas for as long as they remain sturdy.

Observing Children's Understanding

Children's daily activities may demonstrate many ways that they understand people and the environment. A few examples are:

- Adding a new bin to the classroom to collect scraps of wood
- Saying, "Our rain barrel is full. What will we do with all of that water?"
- Explaining how to reuse empty tissue boxes to build a tower

As you support children's understanding of the environment and their role in caring for it, look for opportunities to ask the following questions:

What do you notice about our building today?

How can we make the sidewalk look clean?

How can we reuse this…?

How do we know if this can be recycled?

What can we do to take care of…?

How can we find out more about that?

What can we do instead of throwing this away?

What happened to the tree outside our window?

Where can we take our empty boxes?

How should we sort these for recycling?

Your Teaching Practice

Think about the ways that you affect your environment. Consider the following questions:

- Do you enjoy looking for ways to help the environment? Do you consider it a nuisance?
- What simple changes can you make in the classroom that give children examples of how to affect their environment in a positive way?
- What experiences can you share with children that demonstrate how you are affected by the environment, both at school and at home?

Tips to Share With Families

- Include your child in tasks such as raking leaves, picking up trash outside, and sweeping the sidewalk. Talk about how these jobs help to keep the neighborhood clean.
- Ask your child to help you sort materials for recycling. Talk about where the items go next.
- Point out ways that you reuse materials at home instead of throwing them away. Talk about the items you do throw away and explain why.
- Encourage your child to think of new ways to use materials at home.
- Talk to your child about donating toys and other items that are no longer needed instead of throwing them away.
- Point out changes you see in the neighborhood such as a new building under construction or a row of newly planted trees.

People and the Past

Preschool children are at a wonderful age to learn more about people and the past. They like to hear about the ways they have grown since infancy, and they are beginning to understand events that either took place in the past or will occur in the future. Think about the ways that you can introduce concepts related to people and the past. The following questions may be helpful:

- What are some of the things that happen when we grow up?
- What do we use to know what time it is?
- Why is it helpful to know the time? When do we talk about time at school?

What Does Research Say?

Social studies learning in the early childhood classroom contributes to children's understanding of not only the various relationships between people, environmental issues, but even the past (National Council for Social Studies, 2009).

Children's introduction to and engagement with social studies concepts and content gives them the "knowledge and understanding of the past" which helps them to engage with the present, even prepare for the future – skills and understanding that lay the foundation for children's role as world citizens (Santoli, Vitulli, & Giles, 2015).

Young children have the capabilities to understand and engage in learning about the past. Preschoolers demonstrate their understanding of sequential events when they talk about events that happened the day before, events that happened today, and events that will happen the next day. Young children can understand the concept of the past when past events are specific and concrete and framed by children's own experiences (Gibson Warash, Day, Workman, Troilo, Law, & Devito, 2013).

Children's understanding of their own personal history and their family's history is extremely important, and social studies content in the classroom should emphasize activities and learning that allow for "the study of the ways human beings view themselves in and over time" to further engage children in this historical understanding (Jackman, Beaver, & Skinner Wyatt, 2015).

One way to present past events to young children is to offer photos of the event for children to explore; this exploration allows children to "observe, discuss, and relate to pictures" and develops not only their understanding of social studies concepts but also their language and literacy skills (Santoli, Vitulli, & Giles, 2015).

Social studies learning should include opportunities for children to learn about themselves and their families. Examples include giving children the opportunity to talk about themselves and their families. When a child has the knowledge of his family history (his families' "attitudes, customs, celebrations, and occupations") his social–emotional skills are strengthened as he creates his own concept of self and has a sense of belonging to the family group (Jackman, Beaver, & Skinner Wyatt, 2015).

Although there are some developmental limits to children's comprehension of the past, children do have some understanding and conception of the past, which is shown in young children's intense interest in the past. Children love to hear about when they were babies and love being told stories from when they were younger. Children's interest in the past is furthered when past events are framed in relationship to the important people in their lives. Children are fascinated by the discovery that their family members were once little like them (Gibson Warash, Day, Workman, Troilo, Law, & Devito, 2013).

The Teacher's Role in Promoting Understanding of People and the Past

Children are regularly exposed to language about the past, present, and future. As they begin to have a better understanding of time, they will notice and use vocabulary about time more and more accurately.

In addition to talking about the daily schedule as well as past and upcoming events, here are some suggestions for new ways to encourage children's interest and learning about people and the past:

Encourage family members to talk with the class about their childhoods.
Although it is difficult for children to think about their older relatives as young children, these experiences help children begin to understand the passing of time over long periods. Children may also enjoy hearing about the similarities and differences between their own childhood experiences and those of their grandparents.

Encourage children to explore artifacts from their earlier years and talk about how they were used.
Baby photos and baby clothes give children tangible objects to explore while thinking about the past. Discuss how the children have changed over time by making comparisons between their baby items and their current selves.

Find opportunities in the day to refer to time.
As you move through your daily routines with children, draw their attention to time by incorporating specific vocabulary and questions (e.g., *What did you do yesterday when you got home?*).

When exploring children's interests, investigate how that topic was relevant in the past.
Many contemporary toys resemble toys from long ago, but some are very different. Share a few old toys with children and make comparisons between the old and new. For example, a toy telephone from 20 or 30 years ago is very different from how toy telephones look today.

Reflect on your own childhood and share your experiences with children.
Children will likely enjoy learning about games from your past. Simple playground games, board games, or word games that are easy to teach give children a chance to experience something from the past that is relevant and interesting to them today.

Observing Children's Understanding

When children learn about the past, they will begin to share more and more details and show interest in the past experiences of others. A few examples of when you might observe this are when a child:

- Looks at tiny baby clothes and says, "This is too small for me now, so my baby sister wears it."
- Says, "I'm going to go to get ice cream yesterday."
- Explains, "I had a blue room at my last house, but I have a yellow room now."

Children are often curious about what they were like as babies and how they've changed. As children reflect on the past, ask the following questions:

How do you think this toy was used?

What did you have for dinner last night?

Can you tell me who is in this picture?

What can you do now that you couldn't do when you were a baby?

Would you like to learn how to play this game?

How is this toy different from that newer one?

Your Teaching Practice

Take a look around the classroom and notice labels and materials that help children understand the past, present, and future. Consider the following questions:

- Are there artifacts from studies earlier in the year that you can draw children's attention to?
- How do you reflect back on children's learning throughout the year?
- What are some of your favorite past experiences to share?

Tips to Share With Families

- Tell your child stories about your childhood. Talk about what has changed from then to now.
- Show your child photos or artifacts from his earliest years. Offer specific memories of what your child could or could not do back then.
- Ask questions about events in your child's past. For example, ask her to recall a favorite game or activity that was recently played.
- Teach your child games you played as a child.
- Include other older family members in discussions about the past. Encourage your child to ask questions of her older relatives.

Spaces and Geography

One of the best ways to help children understand space and geography concepts is to relate them to their everyday experiences at home and at school. They can explore their homes, their favorite neighborhood spots, and their school. They can use and create maps to visualize the places they go. They can create the roads, rivers, and mountains they see represented on maps. Talking about maps is not limited to the outdoors, however. Children can use maps to get all around their school. You can connect children's home and school learning by encouraging families to make and share maps of their homes.

These kinds of questions can help children understand spaces and geography:

- What is your home like? What is near your home?
- How do we get around our community?
- What is close to you? Far from you? Behind you? Beside you?
- Why is it helpful to have a map?

What Does Research Say?

"Geography is a way of thinking, the skill of asking questions through the observation and interpretation of the wider world of people and places. It requires a group of adults and children, both learners and teachers, to share space, seek experiences in the environment, use tools for moving about the world, gather data, develop skills for decision making, and enable children to relate more meaningfully to other people and places" (Ranck, 2012).

Geographic understanding is a crucial social studies concept, for this understanding leads to children's understanding of the various "relationships between people and their environments" (Brillante and Mankiw, 2015).

"Geographic skills enable a person to understand the connections between patterns of rivers and the physical processes that create them, between patterns of cities and the human processes that create them, and between what happens in the places in which we live and what happens in places throughout the world, near and far" (Heffron & Downs, 2012).

"Young children are capable, competent and intelligent thinkers and learners in many areas, including geography." Geographic learning, with its study of maps, also encourages the development of children's literacy skills (Fantozzi, Cottino, & Gennarelli, 2013).

The foundation for social studies learning and understanding the concepts of geography is young children's own experiences (Jackman, Beaver, & Skinner Wyatt, 2015).

Children's explorations of the classroom, the home, and the neighborhood are "geographical exercises" that demonstrate their natural ability to be investigators and observers (Ranck, 2012).

Research has shown that mapmaking is a common activity for young children and also occurs across various cultures. Three-year-old children "use maps to solve problems," and 4-year-olds are able to interpret aerial photos. "Young children are capable of making meaning of maps and, perhaps more important, have the natural inclination and curiosity to want to explore the world through many different media" (Fantozzi, Cottino, & Gennarelli, 2013).

The Teacher's Role in Promoting Understanding of Spaces and Geography

As children develop and gain a stronger sense of self, they become more aware of the physical world around them and how they move through the world. The classroom is a safe and comfortable place for children to explore and experiment with movement in the space around them. Below are examples of ways to guide children's understanding of spaces and geography:

Introduce mapping concepts.
Providing games like "Chutes and Ladders®" introduces mapping concepts related to position and direction. Use words related to the placement and movement of the game pieces as you play.

Use everyday materials to make an obstacle course with children.
An obstacle course, either in- or outdoors, provides children with a movement experience that places them in and around a variety of spaces. As children move around and through obstacles, include directional and positional vocabulary as part of the experience.

Show children how to make a simple map.
Children can work with you to make a simple map of a familiar area. Adding the sandbox and storage closet on a simple map of the playground is a great way to reinforce this new skill.

Invite children to talk about what they can see from the classroom.
Point out objects both near and far, such as the gate to the playground and the hills in the distance, and encourage children to notice where objects are in relation to others.

Observing Children's Understanding

Children's daily movements around the classroom will give you insight into their understanding of spaces and geography. Here are a few examples:

- Navigating a board game to get to the finish line
- Using sticks to make roads outdoors
- Explaining that the ground is hot lava and finding new ways to move around the playground
- Working with another child to plan a hike around the park

As children become aware of and interact with their environment, ask the following questions:

Where can we find it on the map?

How can we move through this obstacle course?

What can you see from our sidewalk? What can you see from the top of the rock wall?

What does this map tell us?

What is near the picnic table?

Is the gate near or far from where you are standing?

What does your neighborhood look like?

How did you get to school today? Did you go over any hills or bridges?

How can we make a map of our classroom?

How can we see what's behind our building?

Your Teaching Practice

Both teachers and children can become so accustomed to their classroom surroundings that they no longer notice them. Are there big changes you can make to room arrangement or the placement of materials that would challenge children to focus on the space and their place in it? What about small changes that are more temporary?

Tips to Share With Families

- When going to or from home, talk about familiar features in the neighborhood.
- Explain how to get to your destination when leaving your house.
- Go outdoors with your child and talk about what you can see from your front door.
- Help your child create a map of the place where you live.
- Use distance words (e.g., near, far, close, etc.) to describe objects in your home and community.
- Use pillows or other objects around the house to create a simple obstacle course.

Studies: Reduce, Reuse, Recycle

In *The Creative Curriculum*® classroom, teachers use *Teaching Guides* that feature studies on a variety of different topics to help children build content knowledge and develop process skills. Each study is an in-depth investigation of a topic children are interested in learning more about. Children find answers to their questions through firsthand explorations, and they have opportunities to practice and apply social studies skills in meaningful ways.

Selecting a Topic

To illustrate how children use social studies to learn, consider the study that evolved in Ms. Tory and Mr. Alvarez's 4-year-old class.

As the children were cleaning up in the Art area Ms. Tory reminded the children to decide which scraps of paper they could use again and which should be recycled. She pointed out the scrap bin for the paper to reuse and the recycle bin for the paper they could not use again. She thought about what she was asking the children to do and said, "The paper we put in the recycling bin gets recycled, which means it is used again to make something else. What do you think happens to the paper that we recycle?" The children thought for a moment and then shared all of the interesting ways they thought their paper might be used.

Over the next several days, Ms. Tory pointed out other ways the children reuse and recycle materials. She noticed the children's curiosity and interest in the recycling and observed the children talking about how they can recycle and reuse materials throughout the day. On a walk around the neighborhood, the children noticed some paper and bottles on the ground and asked, "Why didn't they recycle that?" At lunchtime Mr. Alvarez pointed out the recycling symbol on the children's milk cartons, and after lunch, the children pulled out the food boxes and containers from the Dramatic Play area to look for the recycling symbols on them as well. During large-group time, the conversation continued and Ms. Tory asked the children what else they would like to find out about recycling and reusing materials. The children shared their questions and Ms. Tory documented them on a chart.

Ms. Tory and Mr. Alvarez reviewed their observations and agreed that the children were showing curiosity and interest in recycling. Based on these observations, they chose to use *The Creative Curriculum® for Preschool Teaching Guide, featuring the Reduce, Reuse, Recycle Study.*

Beginning the Study

Ms. Tory and Mr. Alvarez started planning for their study by creating a web of investigations that they will explore throughout the study. They brainstormed words related to reusing and recycling materials and grouped them around each investigation question. The webbing process helped them identify important vocabulary and plan how they will address literacy, mathematics, science and technology, social studies, and the arts throughout the study.

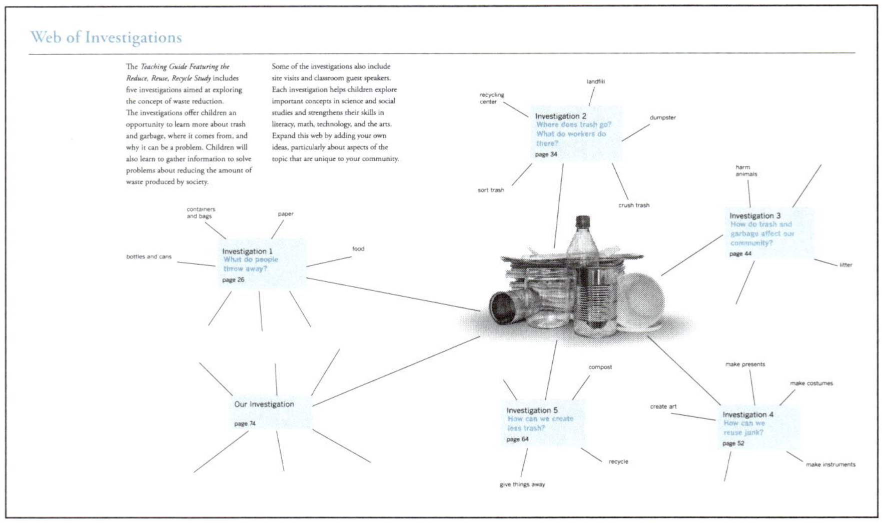

A good study begins with what children already know and then builds upon their knowledge through exploration and investigation of children's questions. To discover what the children already knew about reducing, reusing, and recycling, Ms. Tory and Mr. Alvarez started gathering a classroom collection of related books, pictures, and materials. They used the "Letter to Families" found in the *Teaching Guide* to inform families about their upcoming study and ask them to donate materials to the collection. They also asked the families if any family members work in a field related to reducing, reusing, or recycling and invited them into the classroom to share their expertise with the children.

Following the guidance in the *Teaching Guide*, Ms. Tory began the study by exploring the topic. She led discussions about the materials in the classroom collection, and she and Mr. Alvarez carefully documented the children's questions and observations throughout the week. They added the children's questions to a chart titled "What We Want to Find Out About Reducing, Reusing, and Recycling."

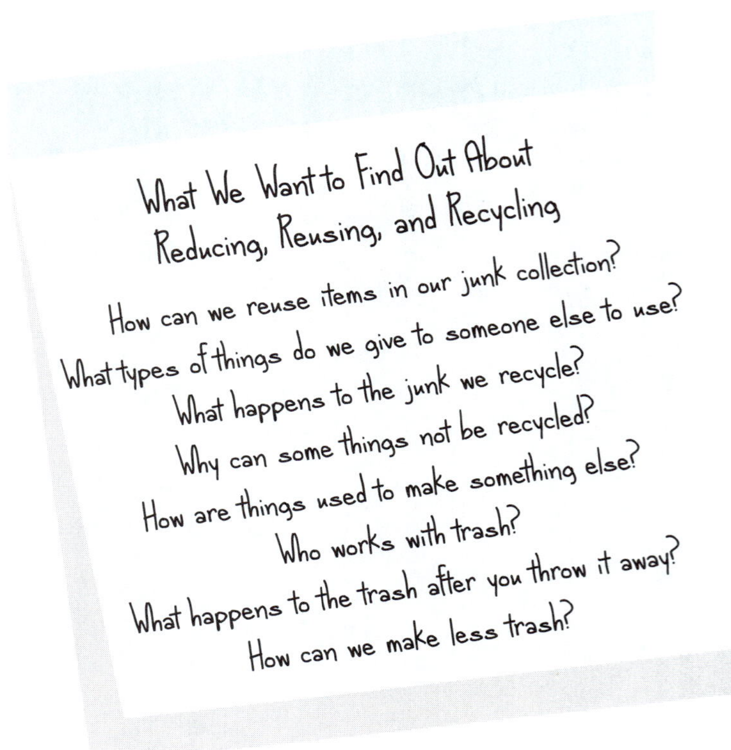

Investigating the Topic

The *Teaching Guide, featuring the Reduce, Reuse, Recycle Study* gives guidance for experiences that help the children discover the answers to their questions and gain deeper understandings about the reducing, reusing, and recycling process. The following shows how these experiences incorporate social studies skills.

Reducing, Reusing, and Recycling Experiences	Ways to Use Social Studies Skills
Walk in the community to look for litter	Talk with the children about how litter has an impact on their neighborhood environment. Take several walks throughout the course of the study and ask children to notice how the environment changes. Create a neighborhood map and add features related to reducing, reusing, and recycling such as where trashcans and recycling bins are located. Observe what kinds of things people throw away or leave on the ground.
Classroom visits from experts	Prepare for the visit by asking children to think of questions they would like to ask the visitor. Invite a special guest in who reduces, reuses, or recycles in various ways. Ask her to share what she does. Ask children to compare how they reduce, reuse, and recycle with how the visitor reduces, reuses, and recycles. Ask the visitor to talk about how his job was done long ago.
Explore the classroom junk collection	Look at the items in the junk collection and talk about how they were originally used. Talk about products and packing people used long ago. Invite the children to think of ways the junk in the collection can be used to benefit others or make something new.
Interview the school custodian	Talk about how the custodian's job benefits the classroom and school. Create a map of the path the custodian takes and where he works. Ask the children, "What would happen if we did not have a school custodian?"
Use the Internet to research on reducing, reusing, and recycling	Create a list of the people who work with recycling and trash. Research ways that other countries handle trash and recycling. Look for pictures, videos, and photos of how trash has an impact on the environment. Research what people did with trash long ago.

Ms. Tory and Mr. Alvarez studied reducing, reusing, and recycling with the children over the course of five weeks. During this time, they investigated the following five questions:

What do people throw away?

Where does trash go? What do workers do there?

How do trash and garbage affect our community?

How can we reuse junk?

How can we create less trash?

As the teachers guided the children through the investigations and activities to answer the questions, they used comments and questions to help the children solve problems, clarify their plans and reasoning, and think about materials in new ways. They connected the investigations to the components of social studies in meaningful ways that supported the children in gaining a deeper understanding of how reducing, reusing, and recycling all have an impact on people and the environment; learning about people whose jobs relate to reducing, reusing, and recycling; and discovering how they can reduce the amount of trash they make and how to reuse materials.

Closing the Study

To conclude the study, the children planned a celebration and invited their families and special guests they met during the study to share what they have learned. They created displays in the classroom interest areas to show the visitors how they investigated reducing, reusing, and recycling and set up a "beautiful junk" art show where they displayed everything they made using found objects.

As you can see, the study of reducing, reusing, and recycling enabled children to use social studies skills in meaningful and relevant ways. It helped children understand and apply skills related to people and how they live, the environment, the past, and geography and supported children to use social studies process skills to gain a deeper understanding of the topic.

Including All Children in the Study

Using the *Teaching Guide, featuring the Reduce, Reuse, Recycle Study,* the teachers can draw on their understanding of each child's behaviors, knowledge, skills, and needs to provide a variety of experiences to include all children.

Below are some general strategies for promoting inclusion of all children during this study.

English- and Dual-Language Learners

- Include items with print in the children's home language(s) in the junk collection.
- Make sorting category signs for the junk collection in the languages spoken by the children in your class.
- Learn a few helpful words in the language(s) spoken by the children related to the study (e.g., *garbage, recycle,* etc.) to help all children learn key vocabulary words.
- Encourage children to count in their home language(s) and in English as they explore the junk collection.
- Schedule frequent small-group and individual learning experiences throughout the study to encourage children to become involved and interact with others.
- Encourage families to join their children in the classroom throughout the study so that children can talk with them to discuss what they are learning about how people in their community reduce, reuse, and recycle trash.

Children With Disabilities

- Provide adaptive equipment such as large-print books, communication devices, chairs with sides, or allow children more time to process information and respond.
- Use simple language and repeat key words during the experiences.
- Encourage the children to participate in the experiences as long as they are interested. Allow children to move on to another experience when they are ready.
- When exploring the junk collection, encourage children to participate however they are comfortable, i.e., observing from a distance.
- Limit the number of items provided for the child to explore. Begin with one or two items for the child to focus on.
- Provide plastic gloves or tongs for children with sensory sensitivities who may be averse to handling items in the junk collection.
- Connect the experiences to activities that the children are motivated by and interested in. For example, if a child loves trains, include activities about how people reduce, reuse, and recycle on trains.
- Include larger items of junk in the collection for children to grasp and manipulate (e.g., cereal boxes, milk cartons, etc.).
- Add sand to empty containers to weigh them down and make holding and examining them easier.
- Break down exploration activities into manageable steps (e.g., *First, we will gather the cans near the trash bin, and then we will count how many uncrushed cans fit inside the bin.*).

Advanced Learners

- Encourage children to use creativity to solve a problem in the community (e.g., *What can we do with the food scraps we throw away in the kitchen?).* Support children to research related topics such as composting, zero waste, etc.
- Invite children to lead experiments and activities in which they demonstrate a high level of understanding (e.g., *Karina is an expert in building sculptures; can you show us how you made a tower with the materials from our junk collection?).*
- Provide reading materials in a variety of levels.
- Meet with local librarians, elementary school teachers, and educational specialists to collect resources (e.g., books, equipment, or puzzles to engage advanced learners).
- Encourage children to use materials intentionally or in a new way (e.g., using a magnifying glass to examine small print on empty food containers, or using a magnet to see which metal objects are steel and which are aluminum). Support children to research answers to their questions.
- Ask questions that encourage children to explore and experiment (e.g., *What would happen if...? or How can we make this better?*).

5

Social Studies Learning in Interest Areas and Outdoors

Social Studies Learning in Interest Areas and Outdoors 119

The Library Area: The Hub of Social Studies Learning 119

Social Studies in the Toys and Games Area 122

Social Studies in the Block Area 125

Social Studies in the Dramatic Play Area 128

Social Studies in the Discovery Area 131

Social Studies in the Art Area 134

Social Studies in the Sand and Water Area 137

Social Studies in the Cooking Area 140

Social Studies in the Technology Area 143

Social Studies in the Music and Movement Area 145

Social Studies and the Outdoors 148

Social Studies Learning in Interest Areas and Outdoors

In *The Creative Curriculum*® classroom, children spend a significant part of each day in interest areas designed thoughtfully by teachers. When a teacher prepares interest areas in a way that promotes social studies learning, they can seamlessly incorporate concepts and build on what children already know. This chapter describes how to make each interest area a valuable place for in-depth social studies learning and gives suggestions for how to best interact with children in those areas to further their understanding.

The Library Area: The Hub of Social Studies Learning

There are a few interest areas that may be most effective for social studies learning. The Library area is one of them. Here children can research their study topics, read about different cultures, write stories about their families, and more. As your study topics change, look for ways to include new reading and writing materials in this area to reflect the topic. Here are more examples of how children's explorations in the Library area relate to *The Creative Curriculum*® *for Preschool* objectives for social studies learning.

Examples of What a Child Might Do	Examples of Related Objectives for Development and Learning
Use family photos to make a book.	29. Demonstrates knowledge of self
Read a book about the work police officers do.	30. Shows basic understanding of people and how they live
Write in an old day planner.	31. Explores change related to familiar people or places
Create a map of the classroom.	32. Demonstrates simple geographic knowledge

Social Studies Materials for the Library Area

Some materials will always be in the Library area such as writing materials, dictionaries, etc. Others will be added and removed over time depending on the current study topic. Below is a list of general suggestions for materials to support social studies learning.

Materials

- phone books
- address books
- daily, weekly, or monthly planners
- books in a variety of genres related to the study topic
- books about the past (e.g., children's books that depict people living in the past)
- recycling guides from the community
- mirror
- book of maps
- envelopes and stamps for writing letters
- sequencing cards

Suggested Books

(Titles preceded by an asterisk are included in the *Teaching Strategies® Children's Book Collection.*)

- *The Bus Ride* (William Miller)
- **A Chair for My Mother* (Vera B. Williams)
- **Charlie Anderson* (Barbara Abercrombie)
- *Duck For President* (Doreen Cronin)
- *The Family Book* (Todd Parr)
- *The Garden Wall* (Phyllis Limbacher Tildes)
- **The Girl Who Wore Too Much* (Margaret Read MacDonald)
- *Knuffle Bunny: A Cautionary Tale* (Mo Willems)
- *Leo the Late Bloomer* (Robert Kraus)
- *Librarians at Work* (Karen Latchana Kenney)
- *Richard Wright and the Library Card* (William Miller)
- **Sam Helps Recycle* (Judith Bauer Stamper)
- **A World of Families* (Trish Holland)
- *Yours Truly, Goldilocks* (Alma Flor Ada)

Using the Library Area to Teach Social Studies

In the Library area, children are exposed to books and materials about a wide variety of topics. While reading books with children, teachers can think about how a text relates to children's own experiences. Children can also learn information that they can apply in other interest areas as they continue to investigate their social studies study topic. Here are examples of what teachers might say as they interact with children and support their social studies learning in this interest area:

People and How They Live

Where can we find the address we need to mail this letter?

This book should tell us more about entomologists. That's a long word for someone who studies insects.

I see you're reading the book you made about your sisters and you.

What do you notice that's different about the people in this picture?

People and the Environment

What should we add to our chart so everyone will know what can be recycled?

Since we're finished with this magazine, what else could we use it for?

How can we find out where trash goes when it leaves our school?

Which book should we read about…?

People and the Past

What do you see in this picture? I wonder if people still drive cars that look like that.

Can you help me put these cards in order? Which picture shows what happened before?

I see that picture of you when you were a baby! You're holding your special puppy.

This story takes place in the past because it was written a long time ago. Let's look at the copyright date to find out when it was written.

Spaces and Geography

This book has beautiful photos of mountains all over the world. Which do you like best?

When you're finished writing your letter, I'll help you take it out to the mailbox. It will be a few days before your cousin gets the letter.

This map shows us what time it is in different places. See, when it's 4 p.m. in this place, it means it's 6 p.m. in that place.

Where does this story take place? How do you know?

Observing Children's Understanding

As you interact with children in the Library area, look for examples such as these that demonstrate children's understanding of social studies:

- Talking about a past family celebration when looking at a book that includes a celebration
- Using an address book to find a person's address
- Writing a letter to someone who lives far away
- Explaining the details of a story about a job in the community
- Putting scrap paper in the recycling bin after illustrating a story
- Choosing a book about a child with the same name
- Asking about the similarities and differences between how people used to live and now

Social Studies in the Toys and Games Area

In the Toys and Games area, children have daily opportunities to practice the skills they will need later in life that will help them participate as members of a community. This interest area encourages cooperation, fairness, and an understanding of rules and why they're important. Here are a few examples of how children's explorations and interactions in the Toys and Games area relate to *The Creative Curriculum® for Preschool* objectives for social studies.

Examples of What a Child Might Do	Examples of Related Objectives for Development and Learning
Express a preference between two games when asked to choose.	29. Demonstrates knowledge of self
Play a matching game that pairs a job with its corresponding tools.	30. Shows basic understanding of people and how they live
Say, "I have to make a new bead bracelet for my baby sister. It needs to be bigger because she growed."	31. Explores change related to familiar people or places
Follow the correct path around a board game.	32. Demonstrates simple geographic knowledge

Social Studies Materials for the Toys and Games Area

As you think about how to best equip this interest area to support social studies learning, refer to your *Teaching Guides* and current study to find suggestions for what to include. Remember to rotate materials in the Toys and Games area so that children have plenty of room to play in a clutter-free environment.

Materials

fabric scraps for weaving

games that encourage cooperation (e.g., indoor bowling, bean bag toss, etc.)

puzzles and games representing a variety of jobs and cultures

building materials (e.g., bristle blocks, small plastic building blocks or Lincoln Logs)

doll house and toy people representing different ages and cultures

miniature job stations (e.g., fire station, gas station police station, airport, etc.)

examples of toys from other countries

toys from the past

plastic animals and barn

toy clocks

props representing a variety of celebrations

collection of clean, recyclable items

globe

collection of junk for building

Suggested Books

(Titles preceded by an asterisk are included in the *Teaching Strategies® Children's Book Collection*.)

**Abuela's Weave* (Omar S. Castañeda)

Alphabet City (Stephen T. Johnson)

**A Birthday Basket for Tía* (Pat Mora)

Cássio's Day (Maria de Fatima Campos)

The Clock Struck One (Trudy Harris)

**Estela's Swap* (Alexis O'Neill)

**The Happiest Tree: A Yoga Story* (Uma Krishnaswami)

I Live in Tokyo (Mari Takabayashi)

If You Lived Here: Houses of the World (Giles Laroche)

Illustrated Children's Map of the World (National Geographic)

In Lucia's Neighborhood (Pat Shewchuk)

**Quinito, Day and Night* (Ina Cumpiano)

Trash and Recycling (Stephanie Turnball)

Unicorn of the West (Alma Flor Ada)

The Rainbow Fish (Marcus Pfister)

A Rainbow of Friends (P. K. Hallinan)

Why Should I Share? (Claire Llewellyn)

Using Toys and Games to Teach Social Studies

When observing children investigating a topic or playing a game together, support them to notice and understand how working together helps them accomplish a task. While young children will likely still play and work individually, they are learning how to play near others and will begin to see themselves as part of the classroom community. By including toys and games that represent different jobs, cultures, homes, and people, you're introducing children to the world around them. Here are examples of what you might ask and say:

People and How They Live

How many people are in this family? How many people are in your family? Let's count them together.

I landed on the green circle. That means I need to use my play money to buy something at the store.

Which job card do you see that uses this tool?

I see you two working together to complete the puzzle.

People and the Environment

What can the doll family do to help the environment?

How can we sort these materials so that we can recycle them in the right place?

We have left over cups from our picnic. What else can we do with them?

Let's make sure we find all of the puzzle pieces before we put it away. We don't want it to go in the trash.

People and the Past

Remember when we played this game on Monday? Can you please explain the rules again?

Look at this toy phone. This is what telephones used to look like.

When I was little, I liked to play this game.

Your house looks like a log cabin. I wonder if we can find a picture of a real log cabin.

Spaces and Geography

Where do you think this game came from?

Can we make a road for the toy people to follow?

Which way should your piece move?

You want to find that country on the globe? Let's see where it is.

You made a mountain with those blocks! That looks like the mountain we can see from our classroom window.

Observing Children's Understanding

As you observe children playing with toys and games, look for these indications of understanding social studies concepts:

- Teaching another child how to play a game
- Using the doll house or toy station to imitate real life
- Sorting materials for recycling
- Cooperating with another child while building
- Making a path with building materials
- Talking about the difference between toys for babies and older children
- Talking about different jobs while putting together a jobs puzzle
- Moving game pieces in the right direction while playing a board game
- Rearranging the objects in the doll house to make it look more like home

Social Studies in the Block Area

As children participate in block play, they are often modeling their constructions on roads, buildings, and geographic elements that they have seen and are familiar with. You can expand on their knowledge by providing additional resources, asking open-ended questions, and describing what you see. Here are examples of what you might see in the Block area that relates to *The Creative Curriculum® for Preschool* objectives for social studies.

Examples of What a Child Might Do	Examples of Related Objectives for Development and Learning
Build a structure and say, "This is almost as tall as me!"	29. Demonstrates knowledge of self
Say, "I'm also going to build a store so they can buy their food."	30. Shows basic understanding of people and how they live
Say, "This looks the new building across the street."	31. Explores change related to familiar people or places
Say, "Look! I made a playground for the little kids. They can climb up here and slide down."	32. Demonstrates simple geographic knowledge

Social Studies Materials for the Block Area

The Block area is the obvious place for children to create, investigate, examine, and explore buildings, roads, and other familiar structures. Enhancing the interest area with materials related to the current study topic can help to support children's learning and go deeper than simply building a tower. Remember that materials in the Block area do not need to be limited to blocks and people. Introducing materials from other areas, such as Dramatic Play or Discovery, may help children make connections between their block play and social studies.

Materials

photos of buildings around the world

depictions of vehicles used around the world

props related to the current study topic

props that encourage other types of building (e.g., plastic fruit for a grocery store, plastic animals for a zoo, flowers for a flower shop, etc.)

tools used in a variety of jobs

depictions of jobs and workers

maps

cardboard tubes and boxes

photos of neighborhood buildings and signs

Suggested Books

(Titles preceded by an asterisk are included in the *Teaching Strategies® Children's Book Collection*.)

**Alexander, Who's Not (Do you hear me? I mean it!) Going to Move* (Judith Viorst)

The Big Orange Splot (Daniel Manus Pinkwater)

**Changes, Changes* (Pat Hutchins)

Community Helpers From A to Z (Bobbie Kalman)

Cross A Bridge (Ryan Ann Hunter)

**House, Sweet House* (Judith Bauer Stamper)

In Our House (Anne Rockwell)

The Little House (Virginia Lee Burton)

Make Way for Ducklings (Robert McCloskey)

**My Steps* (Sally Derby)

Tar Beach (Faith Ringgold)

Using Blocks to Teach Social Studies

Block play gives children a great opportunity to represent their ideas by creating models. This helps them make comparisons between real-life structures and their own constructions. Using blocks also offers opportunities for more in-depth thinking of social studies topics. For example, when building a tower to look like a skyscraper, a child might ask how the materials are carried up to the top of the building. This type of question is a start to further investigation about how buildings are constructed, who constructs them, and the different types of buildings found around the world.

Here are examples of what teachers might say as they interact with children in the Block area:

People and How They Live

I see that you're building a hospital. What block will you use next?

Thank you for reminding us about the rule. You're helping to keep us safe.

I wonder what it would look like if you both built the tower.

People and the Environment

Your recycling center has so many places to put things! That will make it easier for people to recycle.

I see you're building a wall around the garden to protect the flowers so they don't get stepped on.

How can you reuse the cardboard tubes as you build?

I wonder what we can do with this box.

People and the Past

Look at this picture of the Great Pyramids. I wonder if we can build a pyramid.

How are these blocks different from the blocks you had in your classroom last year?

Spaces and Geography

I see you using the dump truck to move blocks. What else could you use to move them?

You made two roads that meet in the middle. That's called an intersection.

You're building a fire station like the one we saw on our site visit. What will you build next to it?

Observing Children's Understanding

While children are engaged in block play, look for indications of their understanding of the components of social studies, such as:

- Talking about where they've seen structures like the ones they're building
- Looking at photos of buildings from long ago
- Using the blocks to create roads
- Talking about the jobs of the people who construct
- Making connections between the rules for the Block area and the reasons why the rules are important
- Asking a teacher for more blocks so that there are more to play with
- Talking about past building experiences

Social Studies in the Dramatic Play Area

In the same way that the Block area allows children to make connections between real-life and pretend buildings, the Dramatic Play area gives children endless opportunities to explore all types of jobs and real-world scenarios. This interest area also works well for group play, giving children a chance to practice their social skills and cooperation. Here are examples of how children's explorations in the Dramatic Play area relate to *The Creative Curriculum® for Preschool* objectives for social studies learning.

Examples of What a Child Might Do	Examples of Related Objectives for Development and Learning
Describe hair color while looking in a mirror.	29. Demonstrates knowledge of self
Say, "I made cupcakes. You can buy one for one dollar."	30. Shows basic understanding of people and how they live
Dress a baby doll and talk about how to take care of it.	31. Explores change related to familiar people or places
Get dressed for an expedition to the jungle.	32. Demonstrates simple geographic knowledge

Social Studies Materials for the Dramatic Play Area

When the Dramatic Play area is set up as a home at the beginning of the year, you can take this opportunity to discuss social studies topics and encourage children to think critically about the things they do with their families at home every day. Then, as the school year progresses and the children begin to investigate study topics, the Dramatic Play area can transform into a place related to the topic that children can explore firsthand. Practicing the skills and behaviors that would be seen and expected in those real-life situations gives children a chance to stretch their knowledge and understanding of the world around them.

Materials

variety of dress-up clothes (e.g., for jobs, celebrations, adults and children, etc.)

props for current study topic

props that represent different jobs (e.g., cash register, building tools, medical equipment, etc.)

world maps and maps of the community

dress-up clothes and props that represent the past

store flyers and catalogs

kitchen and restaurant supplies

photos of people of all ages

shoes of various sizes and types

board books (for children to read to their baby dolls)

mirrors

Suggested Books

(Titles preceded by an asterisk are included in the *Teaching Strategies® Children's Book Collection*.)

Abuela (Arthur Dorros)

At the Supermarket (Anne Rockwell)

Busiest Firefighters Ever (Richard Scarry)

**Caps for Sale* (Esphyr Slobodkina)

Career Day (Anne Rockwell)

Counting at the Market (Amy Rauen)

Diary of a Pilot (Angela Royston)

Jobs People Do (DK Publishing)

Look Where We Live!: A First Book of Community Building (Scot Ritchie)

**Mama & Papa Have a Store* (Amelia Lau Carling)

Martin's Hats (Joan W. Blos)

Max's Dragon Shirt (Rosemary Wells)

**Neighborhood Song* (Trish Holland)

Tortoise Brings the Mail (Dee Lillegard)

What Do People Do All Day? (Richard Scarry)

**Who Wears What?* (Judith Bauer Stamper)

William's Doll (Charlotte Zolotow)

Using Dramatic Play to Teach Social Studies

When children dress up, pretend to work in a restaurant, or take care of a baby doll, they are exploring social studies concepts. But their learning doesn't need to end there. By interacting with children during these times, you can make comments and ask questions that will extend their learning. For example, when a child pretends to work in a doctor's office, encourage her to think of all of the different types of doctors she knows of and then discuss more. Here are some examples of what teachers might say and do as they interact with children in the Dramatic Play area to promote social studies learning:

People and How They Live

This cake looks delicious! Let's wait for everyone to be seated before eating.

I see you're wearing a construction vest. What does a construction worker do?

You would like to be a teacher? What will you teach to the children in your class?

Remember when we saw the bus driver this morning? Where do you think she was going? What will happen if she doesn't get there in time?

Your baby has brown hair like yours. Does anyone in your family have brown hair, too?

People and the Environment

I see that you're gathering apples from your apple tree. Where will you take the apples so other people can buy them?

I'm so thankful that the custodian helps us keep our room and playground clean. What will you clean while you're wearing your custodian uniform?

You would like to wear a hard hat like the workers outside who are cutting down that tree. Why do they wear a hard hat? What else should you wear to be safe?

People and the Past

You're cooking the soup over the fire just like people did long ago.

Let's see if we can find a picture of the hat that would go with the outfit you're wearing. People used to wear those clothes every day.

Which shoes will you put on? Why can't you wear these small shoes?

What did you make to see in your store? Have you seen that in a store before?

Spaces and Geography

People wear those type of shoes in places where there is a lot of snow on the ground.

I wonder if children in that city wear the same clothes that you do. How can we find out?

I see that you're packing the map to take with you on the airplane. It will help you find where you're going.

This store flyer shows us where to find the store. Can you make a map to help people find your store?

Observing Children's Understanding

As you observe children engaged in dramatic play, look for these indications that they are understanding these social studies concepts:

- Working with others to create a store
- Deciding what to wear to go to work
- Taking on the role of a family member
- Recalling details from a recent site visit and modifying the Dramatic Play area
- Explaining how the bowls can be used for cooking and for washing the babies
- Talking about why it's important to pick up the flowers gently in the flower shop
- Looking at the dress-up clothes and offering suggestions of what jobs they could be used for
- Dressing up like a family member
- Making a sign that says when the store will be open

Social Studies in the Discovery Area

The Discovery area is a great interest area for supporting children's learning of a study topic. Investigations in this area help children uncover answers to questions they have about everyday life. Children can also make connections between their firsthand explorations and how things may have been different in the past. Here are examples of how children's hands-on investigations in the Discovery area relate to *The Creative Curriculum® for Preschool* objectives for social studies.

Examples of What a Child Might Do	Examples of Related Objectives for Development and Learning
Use a mirror to closely examine physical features.	29. Demonstrates knowledge of self
Create rules for using the microscope.	30. Shows basic understanding of people and how they live
Compare photos from before and after a storm.	31. Explores change related to familiar people or places
Use natural materials to make a collage of the community.	32. Demonstrates simple geographic knowledge

Social Studies Materials for the Discovery Area

When children bring in natural materials from outside to create collections or you take photos of the neighborhood for observational drawing, these artifacts can help establish the Discovery area as a place to learn more about the community and the world. Children can also experiment with tools and other items that they see community workers using each day. Look to the current study topic for additional ways to support children's investigations in the Discovery area.

Materials

clothing samples made of different materials

mirrors

drawing materials

large paper for body tracing

old and current small gadgets and appliances (e.g., old telephone to compare with cell phone)

samples or photos of tools used in the past

old and current maps that show changes

photos of various geographical features (e.g., mountains, rivers, creeks, deserts, etc.)

photos that show changes of the school over time

props related to the current study topic

Suggested Books

(Titles preceded by an asterisk are included in the *Teaching Strategies® Children's Book Collection*.)

Castles, Caves, and Honeycombs (Linda Ashman)

A Cool Drink of Water (Barbra Kerley)

**The Girl Who Wore Too Much* (Margaret Read MacDonald)

Harbor (Donald Crews)

Hide and Sneak (Michael Arvaarluk Kusugak)

I Read Signs (Tana Hoban)

Machines at Work (Byron Barton)

Our World: A Child's First Picture Atlas (National Geographic Society)

Recycle! A Handbook for Kids (Gail Gibbons)

Recycle Everyday! (Nancy Elizabeth Wallace)

Smoke Jumpers One to Ten (Chris L. Demarest)

**Wash and Dry* (Trish Holland)

Using the Discovery Area to Teach Social Studies

When interacting with children in the Discovery area, make sure to observe first before entering their play. Giving children a chance to make predictions, test their predictions, and record their results helps them gain a deeper understanding of their investigation topic. Before offering your own ideas, encourage children to share theirs and explain why they think what they do. Here are some examples of what teachers might say and do as they interact with children in the Discovery area to promote social studies learning:

People and How They Live

You see freckles on your face. Do you see them anywhere else? I wonder where freckles come from.

Look at this coin under the microscope. What do you see?

That book shows homes that are built into the side of a mountain. What do you think people use to build them?

I remember when we saw the man using the leaf blower. What other tools does he use to do his job?

What do you notice about the different scraps of fabric? Which do you think would keep you warm?

People and the Environment

What can we do with this banana peel instead of throwing it in the trash?

Why do you think this empty soup can goes in the recycle bin but the plastic bag doesn't?

This is a piece of bark from the tree that fell across the road. What do you notice about it?

People and the Past

What buttons do you see on that old camera? What do you notice when you compare it to our digital camera?

What do you think would happen if we...?

How can we fix the chair so that we can use it again?

Spaces and Geography

Here is a piece of concrete and a piece of metal. Which do you think would be better for building?

I wonder what would happen if we didn't have cars any more.

This map shows us where mountains and rivers are. These are the lines that show us.

Observing Children's Understanding

As you observe children in the Discovery area, look for indications such as these that demonstrate their understanding of the components of social studies:

- Comparing old and new devices
- Explaining how mountains are formed
- Examining physical features up close
- Filling in a body tracing of himself
- Wondering how tools were used throughout history
- Asking questions about how to compost
- Pointing out geographical features on a map
- Describing how different tools are used in different jobs

Social Studies in the Art Area

One thing that makes social studies concepts interesting and relevant for children is children's ability to have firsthand experiences with a variety of ideas, materials, and experiments. In the Art area, children can express their ideas about the world in myriad ways. When planning, consider the natural connections between the arts, the current study topic, and children's everyday activities. What this allows teachers to do is observe children's understanding from a new angle and respond with consideration and intention. Here are examples of how children's art experiences relate to *The Creative Curriculum® for Preschool* objectives for art.

Examples of What a Child Might Do	Examples of Related Objectives for Development and Learning
Create a self-portrait.	29. Demonstrates knowledge of self
Cut paper to make play money.	30. Shows basic understanding of people and how they live
Look at a book of art throughout history.	31. Explores change related to familiar people or places
Paint from a photo of a landscape.	32. Demonstrates simple geographic knowledge

Social Studies Materials for the Art Area

Children can use all kinds of materials in the art area that relate to social studies. Include materials that are relevant to the current study topic, places, and people in the community, as well as previously used materials that can be repurposed. Invite children's suggestions for art materials as they learn more about and explore the world around them.

Materials

photos of art from around the world

images of foreign buildings, roads, and signs

paint, crayons, markers, and construction paper in various skin tones

photo book of children and school faculty

digital camera

collection of junk

cardboard tubes and boxes

maps

recordings of world music

fabric scraps

materials for creating fabric dye

variety of sculpting materials

props related to the current study topic

mirrors

Suggested Books

(Titles preceded by an asterisk are included in the *Teaching Strategies® Children's Book Collection*.)

**Abuela's Weave* (Omar S. Castaneda)

The Art Book for Children (The Editors of Phaidon Press)

Children's Introduction to Art: The World's Greatest Paintings and Sculptures (Heather Alexander)

The Colors of Us (Karen Katz)

Follow That Map! (Scot Ritchie)

Hairs/Pelitos (Sandra Cisneros)

**Hooray, A Pinata!* (Elisa Kleven)

I Wish I Had Glasses Like Rosa (Kathryn Heling)

Ish (Peter Reynolds)

**The Pot That Juan Built* (Nancy Andrews-Goebel)

**Something From Nothing* (Phoebe Gilman)

There's a Map on My Lap! (Tish Rabe)

When Big Artists Were Little Kids (Greg Constantine)

Whoever You Are (Mem Fox)

Using the Art Area to Teach Social Studies

When you introduce new materials to the Art area, observe children before interacting with them and see where the experience takes them. Think about questions you can ask and comments you can make that will prompt children to think of connections between their art and social studies concepts. Here are examples of what you might say and ask:

People and How They Live

What will you add next to your self-portrait?

What story is your drawing telling about your family?

Your drawing shows you giving someone a tattoo. Would you like me to write "tattoo artist" at the bottom of your paper?

I see that you're painting a picture of our street. This looks like the shop next door.

People and the Environment

Which of these materials will you add to your sculpture?

I see that you're making a sign to help people remember to recycle.

Look at this sculpture! It's made out of traffic cones.

People and the Past

What do you notice about this old painting?

This painting shows a girl close to your age. What is she doing?

Would you like to make a piñata like the one you saw at your friend's party?

Spaces and Geography

You painted a landscape with lots of trees. Let's look in this book to find a photo of a place like that.

What would you like to add to the mural to make our building look beautiful?

Listen to this music. What does it sound like to you? Can you draw something that you think of when you hear this music?

Observing Children's Understanding

Although children should be able to freely explore art materials, there are still opportunities for intentional social studies learning and observation of children participating in social studies experiences. Notice when children are applying their knowledge of social studies to their work and play in the Art area. You may observe children:

- Drawing or painting family and friends
- Using art to tell a story about the past
- Looking at world art books for inspiration
- Creating a sculpture out of everyday materials
- Taking photos outdoors and then drawing from the photos
- Talking about the details in various works of art from the past
- Thinking of ways to improve the appearance of the school
- Using cloth to weave after reading about weavers in another country
- Asking questions about the people in an antique photograph

Social Studies in the Sand and Water Area

As children learn about the local landscape as well as different geographic features found in the world, they can use their sand and water experiences to learn about how some of these features are formed and how they have changed over time. Children can talk about people who live near the water and the kinds of jobs they have. They can replicate what they've seen people do in their environment or in books about the past. Here are examples of how children's explorations in the Sand and Water area relate to *The Creative Curriculum® for Preschool* objectives for social studies learning.

Examples of What a Child Might Do	Examples of Related Objectives for Development and Learning
State a rule about using materials in the interest area.	29. Demonstrates knowledge of self
Use a toy truck to move sand to the "construction site."	30. Shows basic understanding of people and how they live
Recall a trip to the beach.	31. Explores change related to familiar people or places
Make a pile of sand and say, "Look, I made a mountain."	32. Demonstrates simple geographic knowledge

Social Studies Materials for the Sand and Water Area

Materials

recyclables for washing

small bags for holding sand

small plastic pipes

vehicles and small traffic signs

variety of toy boats

images of cities and towns on the water

photos of people working with sand or water

plastic blocks or bricks

Suggested Books

(Titles preceded by an asterisk are included in the *Teaching Strategies® Children's Book Collection*.)

**The Adventures of Gary & Harry: A Tale of Two Turtles* (Lisa Matsumoto)

Anna Carries Water (Olive Senior)

At the Beach (Huy Voun Lee)

Earthscapes (Jerry Wermund)

Fireboat: The Heroic Adventures of the John J. Harvey (Maira Kalman)

A Good Trade (Alma Fullterton)

Little Tug (Stephen Savage)

My Visit to the Aquarium (Aliki)

No More Water in The Tub! (Tedd Arnold)

Sand Sister (Amanda White)

Water Stories: From Around the World (Radhika Menon)

Water Up, Down, and All Around (Natalie Rosinsky)

Why Should I Save Water? (Jen Green)

Using Sand and Water to Teach Social Studies

As you interact with children in the Sand and Water area, think about how water (and sand, depending on your community) affect their daily lives. Children may hear of sandbags used during storms or dams changing the course of a river. They might wonder where the water comes from in your community or how it gets to the desert for people who live there. All of these ideas can be explored firsthand as sensory experiences for children. Here are examples of what you might say and ask to promote social studies learning:

People and How They Live

We saw fish for sale at the supermarket. I wonder how the fish got there.

How can we make sure everyone has a chance to use the big scoop?

Have you been to the beach before? What did you see there?

Sometimes we have to call a plumber to come fix the pipes so they don't leak.

People and the Environment

Why do we turn the water off while we brush our teeth?

I wonder how we can use sandbags to keep this area from getting wet.

Let's wash these plastic bottles so they can go in the recycle bin. Is there a way that we can reuse them instead?

People and the Past

Do you remember last week when the faucet wouldn't turn on? What did we do to get it fixed?

I wonder how we can use the water in the water table when we're finished playing.

Look at this picture of the Hoover Dam. What do you think it's used for?

Spaces and Geography

Where do you think people work with sandbags like the ones we're making?

I wonder what would happen if you poured all the water into the little stream you made.

What happens to the sand when the water washes over it?

Observing Children's Understanding

As children explore with sand and water and investigate social studies concepts, look for examples of their understanding, such as:

- Creating geographical features out of sand and water
- Explaining how sandbags work to hold back water
- Recalling a visit to a body of water
- Demonstrating how sand is moved by dump trucks and excavators
- Asking about how people get water to drink in different places
- Describing the recycling process while washing recyclables
- Exploring the various functions of different types of boats
- Talking about who works on boats and in the water
- Using water pipes to investigate how water travels through buildings
- Brainstorming materials in the community that come from the ocean
- Thinking of ways to repurpose water, such as using it to water plants after playing in it

Social Studies in the Cooking Area

Preschool cooking experiences give teachers a natural way to involve children as they plan for snack and mealtime and prepare food daily. Cooking activities are also a great way to involve families in the program. When investigating social studies study topics, teachers can look for opportunities to share ideas about individuals, communities, and cultures, as well as how food has been grown, prepared, and shared throughout history. Here are examples of how children's explorations in the Cooking area relate to *The Creative Curriculum® for Preschool* objectives for social studies.

Examples of What a Child Might Do	Examples of Related Objectives for Development and Learning
Say, "I like these sweet potatoes. And they're good for me."	29. Demonstrates knowledge of self
Examine a food container and talk about where it came from.	30. Shows basic understanding of people and how they live
Use a timer to know how long to bake muffins.	31. Explores change related to familiar people or places
Talk about the vegetables growing in the class garden outside.	32. Demonstrates simple geographic knowledge

Social Studies Materials for the Cooking Area

As you plan cooking experiences, think of how the current study topic might offer ideas for more in-depth investigations. Include a variety of cooking tools, foods, and environmental print related to food so that children have opportunities to talk about how these things are used and relied on every day. Include materials that are familiar to children but also new materials that children can explore for the first time.

Materials

- variety of cookbooks from around the world
- recipe cards featuring interesting ingredients
- maps
- manual and electric cooking tools
- food containers from a variety of foods
- environmental print related to food (e.g., coupons, store flyers, menus, etc.)
- images of people doing jobs related to food and cooking (e.g., chef, fisherman, waiter, grocery store clerk, etc.)

Suggested Books

(Titles preceded by an asterisk are included in the *Teaching Strategies® Children's Book Collection.*)

Bread and Jam for Frances (Russell Hoban)

Chopsticks (Amy Krouse Rosenthal)

Cleversticks (Bernard Ashley)

Daddy Makes the Best Spaghetti (Anna Grossnickle Hines)

Everybody Bakes Bread (Norah Dooley)

Follow the Drinking Gourd (Jeanette Winter)

**The Gigantic Turnip* (Aleksei Tolstoy and Niamh Sharkey)

**Guacamole* (Jorge Argueta)

Harry's Box (Angela McAllister)

The Little Mouse, the Red Ripe Strawberry, and the Big Hungry Bear (Don Wood)

Mama Panya's Pancakes (Mary Chamberlin and Rich Chamberlin)

**Peeny Butter Fudge* (Toni Morrison and Slade Morrison)

**Rice Is Nice* (Nancy Noel Williams)

Round is a Mooncake: A Book of Shapes (Roseanne Thong)

The Sandwich Swap (Queen Rania of Jordan Al Abdullah)

Sit-In: How Four Friends Stood Up by Sitting Down (Andrea Davis Pinkney)

Spoon (Amy Krouse Rosenthal)

**Stone Soup* (Marcia Brown)

**Too Many Tamales* (Gary Soto)

Why Should I Help? (Claire Llewellyn)

Using Cooking to Teach Social Studies

Children can learn a great deal about how people live when interacting during a cooking experience. They practice cooperation, taste unusual ingredients, and begin to understand how food is different in different places. Here are some examples of what teachers might say and do as they interact with children in the Cooking area to further promote social studies learning.

People and How They Live

Let's read the recipe to find out how many bananas we need to cut. Then, each of you can cut a banana.

For tomorrow's recipe we'll need black beans. I wonder where I can buy those.

You said you make a different kind of bread at home. Tell me about your bread.

It was helpful to have your grandpa here to make sushi. He taught us how to roll it out with a bamboo mat.

People and the Environment

What can we do with our left-over snack so that it doesn't go right in the trash?

How can we reuse the can that the black beans came in?

I wonder what will happen to this egg shell when we put it in the compost.

This small box with berries in it has the word "compostable" on the bottom. What do you think that means?

People and the Past

This is the recipe I used to make with my teacher when I was a young girl. I like to make it at home, too.

What do you think your uncle can tell us about the food he's preparing?

How did we mash the fruit the last time we made this? What tool did we use?

You said your baby sister can't eat this because she's too little. What kind of food does she eat? Did you eat that food when you were a baby?

Spaces and Geography

Let's look on the map and find Ecuador. That's where this cookbook came from.

We can line up the bowls like this. Then we can move around the table and take some from each bowl.

Our book said that this type of fruit grows in the mountains because it needs a colder climate to grow.

Observing Children's Understanding

As you observe and interact with children in the Cooking area, look for these indications of social studies understanding:

- Talking about foods eaten at home
- Remembering a celebration and the special food that was served
- Using a variety of kitchen tools
- Asking questions about where food comes from
- Looking at environmental print and relating it to a personal experience
- Explaining why it's important to compost
- Making comparisons between the foods they used to eat and the foods they eat now
- Choosing a reusable container to store food instead of a plastic bag
- Recalling a site visit to a restaurant or grocery store
- Talking about jobs related to food

Social Studies in the Technology Area

In preschool classrooms today, children have access to unlimited information about communities and cultures around the world. They can learn how to research, make comparisons, and investigate questions they have about how or why something happens in their own community or elsewhere. Children also practice working together to find out more information about their current study topic as well as create artifacts from the study to be shared with families at the end-of-study celebration. Here are examples of how children's explorations in the Technology area relate to *The Creative Curriculum® for Preschool* objectives for social studies learning.

Examples of What a Child Might Do	Examples of Related Objectives for Development and Learning
Create a digital "me" book.	29. Demonstrates knowledge of self
Help generate a list of rules for using the smart board.	30. Shows basic understanding of people and how they live
Research games children played in the past.	31. Explores change related to familiar people or places
Use a video calling system to talk to a person in another place.	32. Demonstrates simple geographic knowledge

Social Studies Materials for the Technology Area

In addition to using the tablet or the computer to research and investigate ideas related to the current study topic and other social studies concepts, the Technology interest area offers opportunities for children to learn about themselves and their place in the world. The computer, digital camera, tablet, or digital device for audio/video recordings can all be used as tools to express children's ideas and document their findings. Be sure to provide writing materials in this area, and limit the number of children using a mobile digital device at the same time.

Using Technology to Teach Social Studies

From the moment children sit down to use the tablet, they are applying social studies concepts. They cooperate with others to coordinate computer use. They refer to and follow the rules of the classroom related to use of technology devices. They think about the information they're looking for, and they recognize that the computer offers a way to find information about almost any topic. They also learn digital citizenship and begin to understand the responsibility, both personally and communally, that comes with using technology devices. Here are examples of what you might say and ask to promote social studies learning in this interest area:

People and How They Live

What rule can we add to our list to make sure there isn't any food near the tablet?

I wonder how you can swipe the screen to draw the hair on your portrait.

We saw the bank teller using a computer when we visited. What do you think she uses the computer for?

How can you two work together to solve the mystery?

People and the Environment

How does sending an e-mail instead of mailing a letter help the environment?

This paper printed without enough ink. Can we reuse this paper for something else now?

Where can we find information about how cardboard is recycled?

We save electricity each day when we power down the tablet when we are not using it.

I wonder where computers go when they don't work anymore.

People and the Past

Do you remember what we learned last week when we read about our community?

We can save pictures on the computer to look at later. It's like the photo album we have on our bookshelf.

How do you use your tablet at home?

What game do we have in our Toys and Games area that is similar to this computer game?

Spaces and Geography

You want to find more information about how people hike in the mountains? Where can we look for that?

Here's a picture of a beautiful valley. When we have a video call with our friend later, we can ask her if she has ever seen a valley where she lives.

Observing Children's Understanding

As children use technology devices to investigate a variety of concepts, look for their understanding of social studies, such as:

- Using the computer to find out more about a different country
- Asking questions about how to send an e-mail to a friend
- Working with a partner to research the history of a celebration
- Explaining how to tap an icon on the tablet screen to play a game
- Taking pictures and using them to make a book of the classroom community
- Downloading facts about recycling to share with families
- Demonstrating how to play a computer game for a child who is new to the program
- Describing and documenting research found from an online search

Social Studies in the Music and Movement Area

Listening to music, playing instruments, dancing and moving are all a part of the classroom and world communities. Even among the families in your program you may find a broad range of preferences and talents when it comes to music and movement. Starting with the classroom and community, children can investigate questions that arise from sharing their knowledge of music with others. From there, they can explore the wealth of resources pertaining to this interest area. Here are examples of how children's explorations in the Music and Movement area relate to *The Creative Curriculum® for Preschool* objectives for social studies.

Examples of What a Child Might Do	Examples of Related Objectives for Development and Learning
Sing a song taught by a family member.	29. Demonstrates knowledge of self
Listen to music played on an unfamiliar instrument.	30. Shows basic understanding of people and how they live
Look in a book that shows how musical instruments have changed over time.	31. Explores change related to familiar people or places
Sing in a particular area outdoors because of the way the sound projects.	32. Demonstrates simple geographic knowledge

Social Studies Materials for the Music and Movement Area

A well-equipped music and movement is already prepped for social studies learning. Each instrument, song, and dance has a history and relationship to a culture that can be shared with children. Children can share their own knowledge and adapt their play in this interest area to incorporate what they know and can do. Use the current study topic for ideas on expanding the offerings in the Music and Movement area. Introduce new sounds, movements, and materials that will help children understand how people outside of their community live.

Materials

writing materials for creating songs and dances

variety of nonstereotypical costumes

audio and video recordings of musicians and dancers around the world

junk collection for making musical instruments

examples or photos of musical instruments from the past

photos and/or video recordings of costumes and dances from the past

books about world music

maps

mirrors

examples of instruments made from natural materials

Suggested Books

(Titles preceded by an asterisk are included in the *Teaching Strategies® Children's Book Collection.*)

**Abiyoyo* (Pete Seeger)

Anna Hibiscus' Song (Atinuke)

Baby Dance (Ann Taylor)

Dragon Dance (Joan Holub)

**The Happiest Tree: A Yoga Story* (Uma Krishnaswami)

**Hush! A Thai Lullaby* (Minfong Ho)

Making Sounds (Charlotte Guillain)

My Family Plays Music (Judy Cox)

**My Name is Celia: The Life of Celia Cruz* (Monica Brown)

Our Global Community: Music (Lisa Easterling)

**Radio Man* (Arthur Dorros)

Skit-Skat Raggedy Cat: Ella Fitzgerald (Roxanne Orgill)

Tap Dance Fever (Pat Brisson)

Under the Mambo Moon (Julia Durango)

What a Wonderful World (George David Weiss and Bob Thiele)

Using Music and Movement to Teach Social Studies

Feel free to share music and traditions from your own culture and invite families to come to the class to share theirs as well. Encourage children to investigate further when they find a new song, dance, or instrument that interests them. Refer to your current study topic to help narrow the focus of exploration. Ask children questions that prompt them to wonder about the relationships between their own music and movement experiences and the experiences of those living in other places. Here are examples of what you might say and ask to promote social studies learning:

People and How They Live

What instrument does your papa play? We will ask him to come play for us.

What questions do you have about the music you hear?

I wonder if this instrument is used in other countries. How can we find out?

Who wrote this song? What do you think she meant by these words?

People and the Environment

This song is about taking care of the earth. We can make up our own dance to go with it.

I'm going to use this cardboard tube as an instrument instead of throwing it away.

What is this instrument made of? Where do you think the wood came from to make it?

People and the Past

This is a song that someone wrote a long time ago. We can hear many different ways it is played.

What kind of music did you hear at your family's celebration? How did you dance to it?

The person in this video is a professional cellist. That means his job is to play the cello. I wonder how much he has to practice.

This is music that is sometimes played for little babies to help them fall asleep. Why do you think babies might like it? Do you think you liked it when you were a baby?

Spaces and Geography

This music is only played in the mountains. The people there make their own instruments and write their own songs.

What do you think of when you hear this music? How do you like to move when you hear it?

Observing Children's Understanding

As children participate in music and movement activities, look for examples of their understanding of social studies concepts, such as:

- Creating a new dance
- Showing a preference between two types of music
- Looking at a map to find where a particular type of music is played
- Explaining how the musicians work together to play a song
- Watching a dance from a different culture and practicing it
- Learning how to make music from repurposed materials
- Asking questions about why music changes over time
- Researching the ways to play an instrument
- Reading a book about a famous musician
- Singing a song and adding new verses
- Asking the school music teacher about his job

Social Studies and the Outdoors

On the playground, children have an opportunity to observe and recreate the different types of transportation they see each day. This can be a special time when children's investigations help them connect social studies concepts, such as where their food comes from and how it gets to school, or how materials from inside the classroom can be repurposed outside. They become more familiar with teamwork as they play group games. Here are examples of how children's outdoor explorations relate to *The Creative Curriculum® for Preschool* objectives for social studies.

Examples of What a Child Might Do	Examples of Related Objectives for Development and Learning
Say, "I'm really good at basketball, but I don't know how to play soccer."	29. Demonstrates knowledge of self
Use trucks in the sandbox to move materials.	30. Shows basic understanding of people and how they live
Say, "I used to only be this tall, but now I'm *this* tall and I can touch the top of the ladder!"	31. Explores change related to familiar people or places
Say, "Look! I poured water into the hole to make a pond."	32. Demonstrates simple geographic knowledge

Social Studies Materials for the Outdoors

When children play on the climbing structure or invent games on the blacktop, they are using their knowledge of social studies to interact. Working together, imitating certain jobs such as a crossing guard or police officer, and tending the garden are all ways that children expand their understanding of social studies concepts. Using your current study topic as your guide, think about how you can introduce open-ended materials outdoors that encourage children's movement as well as exploration and investigation of new ideas.

Materials

- mirrors
- measuring tools
- chalk
- murals of various people and cultures
- props for jobs related to the outdoors (e.g., construction worker, police officer, athlete, park ranger, etc.)
- recycle bins
- compost and garden areas
- images of different types of buildings
- maps of the school and other places
- examples or images of outdoor games from the past
- images of various geographical features

Suggested Books

(Titles preceded by an asterisk are included in the *Teaching Strategies*® *Children's Book Collection*.)

- **The Adventures of Gary & Harry: A Tale of Two Turtles* (Lisa Matsumoto)
- *And the Good Brown Earth* (Kathy Henderson)
- *Bear About Town* (Stella Blackstone)
- *Beautiful Blackbird* (Ashley Bryan)
- *Busy, Busy Town* (Richard Scarry)
- *The City Kid & The Suburb Kid* (Deb Pilutti)
- *Diary of a Firefighter* (Angela Royston)
- *Good Sports* (Jack Prelutsky)
- **Just Like Josh Gibson* (Angela Johnson)
- *Soccer Counts!* (Barbara Barbieri McGrathy and Peter Alderman)
- *We Are Extremely Very Good Recyclers* (Lauren Child)
- *What Does It Mean To Be Green?* (Rana DiOrio)
- *Whose Vehicle Is This?* (Sharon Katz Cooper)
- **Xochitl and the Flowers* (Jorge Argueta)

Using the Outdoors to Teach Social Studies

Sometimes teachers use outdoor time only for observation and not for interaction. By observing and then entering children's play, you show them that their ideas are important. You also then have a chance to extend their play beyond what they already know and encourage them to consider ideas beyond their current understanding of the world. Here are examples of what you might say and ask:

People and How They Live

I see you lined yourselves up by height. Where should I stand in the line?

This wagon has a broken wheel. May I visit your repair shop so that you can fix it?

What can we do to make sure people can cross safely where you're riding?

People and the Environment

Let's see how our compost looks. We can put food in there instead of throwing it away. Then we will use it to help our garden grow.

I wonder how we can make sure that people put trash in the trash can outside instead of on the ground.

You've built an enormous structure with those cardboard boxes!

People and the Past

This is a game that has been played by children for a long time.

What game did we play yesterday outside? Do we want to play it again?

I remember when the bike was too big for you to ride. Now it's just the right size for you!

Spaces and Geography

I see you're wearing your construction vest. What repair work do you need to do on the hill?

How can we reuse these materials to make an obstacle course?

What do you think was here before our school was built?

Observing Children's Understanding

As you observe and interact with children outdoors, notice when they demonstrate an understanding of social studies concepts. A few examples are:

- Creating a road and intersection for bikes and wagons
- Imitating outdoor jobs
- Talking about how to keep the school and playground clean
- Remembering games they liked to play when they were younger
- Explaining how to play an outdoor game
- Creating an obstacle course using playground equipment
- Inviting others to play in a group game
- Asking about the community features that can be seen from the playground
- Talking about how people get from one place to another

6 Planning Your Social Studies Program

Guiding Children's Social Studies Learning 153

Creating an Environment for Social Studies Learning 153

Integrating Social Studies Throughout the Day 155

Guiding Children's Social Studies Learning

Young children are curious and eager to learn about themselves, their peers, and their environment. As they play and interact with others, they express and represent what they know and what they want to learn more about. When they engage in classroom play, they are observing similarities and differences among people, learning the rules of a community, and navigating their way through the classroom space.

Teachers can create opportunities for children to expand their knowledge of social studies by being intentional when adding or changing materials in the interest areas and the outdoors. The classroom is an ideal place for children to work and play together, use pretend play and props to represent another time or place, and experiment with different roles in the community. Adaptations to interest areas should reflect children's interests and further support their learning of social studies concepts.

Keep the following questions in mind when planning for children's learning of social studies concepts:

- What interests have children shown related to social studies?
- What events are taking place in our community that could give children a firsthand experience with social studies concepts?
- What available resources do I have to make social studies learning part of children's everyday experiences?

Creating an Environment for Social Studies Learning

Social studies can easily be incorporated into your daily plans and everyday experiences. It is important to plan intentionally and responsively for these experiences but also remember that new opportunities may arise each day depending on children's interactions and experiences with you and with others. While teaching social studies concepts can be as simple as drawing children's attention to their surroundings, their community, and their peers, there are also ways to ensure quality social studies learning experiences through thoughtful planning. Here are some basic principles to help you create a classroom environment conducive to exploration of social studies concepts and study topics.

Strategies for Creating Spaces for Social Studies Experiences

To create an environment for social studies learning, consider the basic principles that are presented in the following chart.

Strategies	Examples
Organize space and materials to encourage individual and group activities.	Create spaces for large-group discussions as well as spaces for small-group or one-on-one conversations. Include print and pictures in all interest areas that show a variety of people and cultures depicted in non-stereotypical ways.
Display references to class schedules, rules, and members as well as the school and neighborhood communities.	Create meaningful displays such as • photos of children and their families (both recent and from years ago) • photos of school workers with labels for their jobs • examples of environmental print found in the community such as images of signs, community newsletters, newspapers, and community event calendars • images depicting a variety of jobs • display of classroom rules • poster explaining which classroom materials can be recycled and how to sort them • maps of local areas such as the school, city, state, etc.
Include social studies learning materials in all interest areas.	Provide books on and learning materials related to the current study topic that are also about social studies (e.g., phone books in the Dramatic Play area, maps in the Discovery area, video recordings of local performances in the Technology area, photos of local buildings in the Block area, etc.).

Your Teaching Practice

Think back to your experiences learning social studies when you were younger. Which types of experiences did you find most interesting? Cooking? Site visits? Dressing up? Keep these experiences in mind as you plan. You may also want to collaborate with other teachers to hear their ideas and plan larger school events such as festivals and performances.

Materials and displays alone do not make the environment rich for social studies investigations. These concepts must be incorporated thoughtfully into events throughout the day. Children need to see ways in which social studies is part of their everyday experiences. For example, learning to put scraps of paper in the recycling bin instead of the trash can helps introduce children to one simple way to care for the environment.

Integrating Social Studies Throughout the Day

Some children enter preschool with prior experience in a classroom community. For others, this is the first time they are part of a group other than their immediate families. In order to engage children at all levels in social studies learning, it is most appropriate to not only focus on social studies topics for investigation but also to keep social studies concepts in mind during your daily routines and interactions with children. In addition to using *Teaching Guides* for in-depth studies, consider the following ideas for incorporating social studies into daily experiences and reinforcing children's knowledge of social studies.

Arrival

Preparing the Environment

Create an attendance chart with a photo name card for each child.

Post arrival instructions for the daily routine (e.g., place lunch in cubby, hang up jacket, wash hands, etc.).

Create job and helper charts. Post any directions children might need for completing a job (e.g., how to care for the class pet).

Create a message board for children and families to send and receive notes.

Post a daily and weekly schedule. Include any community events that families may be interested in.

Interactions

Have informal conversations about the previous evening's events.

Ask children questions about something from home (e.g., sibling, pet, favorite game, etc.).

Talk with children about how they got to school, which roads they took, familiar landmarks, etc.

Ask children about any changes to the environment they observed on their way to school.

Large-Group Time

Preparing the Environment

Display a schedule or calendar of the day's, week's, and/or month's events.

Display a chart with words to a song or a story you'll share.

Display classroom rules.

Prepare any materials to be introduced related to the current social studies study topic.

Interactions

Introduce any new materials related to the current study topic. Ask questions about the materials that encourage children to apply their knowledge of the topic.

Ask questions that prompt children to think about past events (e.g., *Do you remember what we saw the desk clerk doing yesterday on our site visit?).*

Encourage children to think about what they might investigate during choice time.

Refer to the schedule throughout the day. Talk about what the children did in the past and prompt them to think about how it might relate to the study.

Call attention to upcoming or past events on the calendar. Discuss things that happened yesterday.

Introduce a new song and use the song chart to share the lyrics.

Choice Time

Preparing the Environment

Set out materials in some interest areas that encourage multiple children to work or play together.

Include a mirror in one or more interest areas.

Display intriguing pictures of people and social events.

Include a variety of books in each interest area.

Add materials to interest areas that are related to the study topic.

Invite family members to come and share other languages, songs, games, recipes, etc.

Interactions

Interact with children to draw their attention to new information learned.

Notice aloud when you observe children working together to accomplish a task.

Encourage children to write in their journals to record their thoughts for the day. Talk about how a journal can be read later to recall past events and ideas.

Call attention to the jobs children are doing. Talk about the ways in which those jobs are done by adults outside of the classroom.

Invite children to explore the current study topic by asking and researching questions.

Prompt children to think critically about the roles they play in the classroom.

Small-Group Time

Preparing the Environment

Gather materials that are relevant to the topic.

Prepare print or other visual materials.

Keep blank chart paper and markers ready for recording children's questions and ideas.

Interactions

Make simple books about the study topic.

Encourage children to retell stories from the past.

Play games that support children's understanding of rules.

Ask questions that invite children to share information about themselves, their families, and their homes.

Snack and Mealtime

Preparing the Environment

Display recipes of foods from around the world.

Have informal conversations about the foods children prepare and eat with their families.

Interactions

Point out how ingredients are packaged and whether or not materials can be reused or recycled.

Explain to children why you store food in a bowl with a lid instead of a plastic bag.

Ask questions that prompt children to consider why snacks and meals are always eaten in the same place in the classroom.

Transitions

Preparing the Environment

Choose *Mighty Minutes®* and *Mega Minutos®* to introduce children to new songs.

Plan in advance for any appropriate activities that illustrate social studies concepts, such as

Mighty Minutes 01, "The People in Your Neighborhood"

Mighty Minutes 11, "What Is My Job?"

Mighty Minutes 63, "Going on a Journey"

Mighty Minutes 71, "Recycle Song"

Mighty Minutes 165, "I've Got a Friend"

Mighty Minutes 173, "Tiny Teamwork"

Interactions

People and How They Live (e.g., *If I use a mail box and a bag to hold letters, what is my job?*)

People and the Environment (e.g., *Each person can carry a plastic cup to the recycling bin.*)

People and the Past (e.g., *What song did we sing yesterday before snack? Let's sing it again.)*

Spaces and Geography (e.g., *You may line up by walking next to the bookshelf and then standing at the door.)*

Outdoor Time

Preparing the Environment

Create a map of the outdoor space.

Place bins on the playground for children to easily clean up materials and throw away trash before going inside.

Provide materials that will encourage children to explore their surroundings such as binoculars.

Include map-making materials.

Interactions

Talk about the differences between any paved and green spaces outside.

Ask children to think about ways to preserve the outdoor space.

Help children complete any assigned classroom jobs outside.

Encourage children to create a map of the outdoor space.

Rest Time

Preparing the Environment

Prepare the rest space in the same way every day for each child.

Offer books on a variety of social studies topics.

Play soft music from various cultures.

Interactions

Read a story related to the study topic.

Talk about how children like to prepare for rest at home with their families.

Departure

Preparing the Environment

Display a map of the community.

Display a clock.

Display a list of questions for children to ask their families that are related to the study topic.

Interactions

Talk about the events of the day. Encourage children to recall past events.

Ask children about where they will go after school. Talk about the ways they will travel and what they will see in the community.

Draw children's attention to the clock in the classroom to determine the time.

Tell the children where you will go after school by pointing to the map.

7

Components of the Arts

The Arts	161
Components of the Arts	163
Visual Arts	163
Music	166
Dance	169
Drama	173
Studies: Music Making	177

The Arts

The arts have an extremely powerful impact on the development of young children's comprehension of the world in which they play a significant part as individuals. Along with nurturing children's development of a sense of self, children's imagination and creativity are encouraged and "evoked, stimulated, and developed" through young children's active engagement in various artistic endeavors (Klerfelt, 2011). Research around the arts confirms the connections that arts learning has to all areas of learning and its impact on children's development as independent, engaged, active learners and discoverers. For as Bentley states, "when we come to know the child as an everyday artist, we frame the child as an inquirer, an investigator who navigates the world through inquiry, perceiving experiences through possibility rather than probability. This perspective of inquiry powerfully shapes children's processes of learning and their understanding of themselves as thinkers, learners, and contributors to their educational process" (2013).

Other research such as the United States of the National Education Longitudinal Survey (NELS) data found "significant improvement in achievement, attitudes, and behaviors for children who were highly involved in music or drama activities regardless of their socioeconomic status" (Catterall, Capleau, & Iwanaga, 1999). Children's arts education then becomes a "great leveler" for all children (Roy, Baker, & Hamilton, 2015).

Art involves imagining, investigating creative materials, and experimenting. Children use eye droppers to mix paint, add various materials to clay; design and build structures; sing and dance; and act out stories. These artistic activities "actively engage children's imagination" and engage "children across all domains – cognitive, language, social, emotional, and physical," and when these activities are deliberatively open-ended, when children are able to freely engage in various art activities, children's creative thinking and development of learning processes are encouraged and strengthened (Mills, 2014).

"The arts as a learning and symbolic tool is particularly valuable not only because it embraces the talents often overlooked in education but also because it crosses and links all of the intelligences" along with the development domains (Koster, 2012). For example, children sorting beads might talk about the colors and relate them in their artwork. When children sing a song and pretend to be a bear they are also using and strengthening their gross-motor skills.

In fact, a child who is encouraged to think creatively when very young will likely have a stronger foundation for learning at the beginning of school. Young children's exposure to and engagement with the arts fosters their imagination and their creativity, their "tendency toward exploration, discovery, and imagination" (Suskind, 2015). Teachers can continue to foster this development by providing high-quality classroom experiences and activities to young children that nurtures their artistic thinking and the refinement of their creativity and imagination (Kom-Bursztyn, 2012).

The "everyday artmaking" of young children includes children's singing, dancing, and peer interaction reflecting the complex nature of young children's artistry (Bentley, 2013). This complexity is also seen in creative arts involvement in each and every classroom activity and in the classroom environment itself. As Koster notes, the creative arts in the classroom include "the clapped rhythms used to capture (children's) attention, in building blocks children play with, the books used in read-alouds and other literacy activities, along with the classroom decorations, floor patterns, and the general sound environment" (2012). Young children's early exposure to the arts and to arts learning in an early childhood classroom encourages the development of various learning skills: language, cognitive, and social–emotional. "When children experience arts learning, they are empowered and introduced to a great source of joy and pleasure" (Roy, Baker, & Hamilton, 2015).

The arts in preschool do not need to be limited to drawing, painting, or dancing with scarves. Art can serve as both a creative outlet and a means of exploration as children spend time on and think critically about their work. "Young children's creative acts give expression to their growing capacity to act in the world" (Kom-Bursztyn, 2012). From around age 3 and beyond, children begin to talk about their artwork. This gives adults a chance to ask questions and make comments that encourage children to explain their processes and the meaning behind their work (Charlesworth, 2011). When children can describe their creations in their own words, when the focus of the back-and-forth conversation is on the creative act itself, children "develop the ability to analyze, communicate ideas" and gain "independence of thought and self-confidence" (Suskind, 2015).

It is important to keep in mind that adults should respond to children's comments and describe what they see in a child's work instead of asking too many questions about the subject of the art. Instead, teachers can ask questions that promote creative thinking, such as "What if?" and "How would you?" questions (Charlesworth, 2011). These types of questions not only encourage children to think about their creative work in new ways but also promote language development as children learn to express their ideas. Teachers can best support children's creativity through the arts by offering open-ended art experiences instead of theme-based crafts that result in each child producing the same thing. Instead, teachers should offer a variety of materials and then observe how children decide to use them.

The guidance found in the *Daily Resources* of *The Creative Curriculum® for Preschool* offers teachers ideas for supporting children's learning of the arts in alignment with the related objectives for development and learning.

The four arts objectives found in the *Objectives for Development & Learning* are:

Objective 33. Explores the visual arts

Objective 34. Explores musical concepts and expression

Objective 35. Explores dance and movement concepts

Objective 36. Explores drama through actions and language

Components of the Arts

For beginning artists, the creative process includes figuring out what can be done with different materials and is less about representation (Charlesworth, 2011). Children's participation in various classroom art activities strengthens their inquiry-based learning skills, for "art is a way of solving problems, conceptualizing the world, and creating new possibilities" (Bentley, 2013). Preschool presents an atmosphere that is ideal for creative work, because social interactions, both with adults and peers, are the foundation for many of the ideas that children develop artistically (Charlesworth, 2011). One of the greatest things that occurs in the brain when children express themselves through the creative arts is independence of thought, for the arts are not dependent on rules. When children are given the freedom to create, arts learning helps a child "make sense of the world to establish a sense of self in it." This development of independent thought in very young children may in fact "lead years and years later, to positive innovative improvements" in the world (Suskind, 2015).

Visual Arts

Children's engagement with the visual arts encourages their exploration of the world around them. As they mold with clay, draw with markers, paint with water colors, and become the designers and inventors of puppets, collages, and sculptures, children can share their knowledge of what they have learned and are learning in the classroom. As investigative learners, children often create to further and refine their understanding, and this evolution of understanding in turn inspires even more artistic creation.

When children have the opportunity to experiment and play with all types of art materials, their exploration and engagement with the arts is reaffirmed along with the development of their understanding of themselves as artists. Children's artistic expression as they share their feelings and their experiences and their discoveries through what they are making, creating, designing, and inventing is enhanced as well. As teachers talk with children about children's ideas for all the possibilities of using materials, children begin to recognize themselves as artists and that there are so many things that they can create.

These questions about children's understanding of and experience with visual arts will help you design ways to further include learning experiences in your classroom:

- What does visual art tell us?
- What are the different types of visual art?
- How do people use visual art to express their feelings and ideas?

What Does Research Say?

One way for young children to express their thoughts and feelings is through visual arts such as painting and drawing. The visual arts also support children's gross-motor and fine-motor development. Studies have shown that an additional benefit to children's engagement in visual arts is an improvement in reading and self-regulation (Suskind, 2015).

"The visual arts allow people to express feelings and thoughts that are difficult to put into words, such as grief, fear, and anxiety. Overall, creating visual art was found to be a positive activity that provided release from anxiety-producing situations" (Koster, 2012).

Children's participation in sustained, high-quality visual arts experiences help build children's self-efficacy and original thinking (Catterall & Peppler, 2007).

Children's experiences painting, drawing, and sculpting enhance their thinking and encourage them in their interactions with the world. "Artistic practice is deeply integrated into the life of the child and shapes the ways children interact with the world" (Bentley, 2013).

The Teacher's Role in Promoting Understanding of Visual Arts

Learning about visual arts in a preschool classroom is more than just learning how to use various art materials. It should also be an exploration of how different types of media are and can be used to communicate. Visual arts experiences in preschool should also expose children to a broad range of art forms in order to help children begin to appreciate the many ways that art can help them express their thoughts, feelings, and ideas. Below are examples of ways that you can guide children's exploration of visual arts:

Provide a variety of materials for children to use to express their thoughts and discoveries.
Art materials can be as diverse as your creativity and funds allow. Be sure to provide the basics, including materials children can paint on and with, draw on and with, put things together with, cut with, mold, construct, and clean up with. When children draw people, encourage them to look at each other and also set up mirrors so each child can study her own face.

Honor children's artistic endeavors by highlighting their work through classroom displays.
Children's drawings and paintings, prominently displayed, enhance the charm and warmth of any classroom. They also provide concrete documentation of what children have learned. When hanging children's artwork, treat it as if it were on display in a museum. A simple construction paper backing can be used as a frame to give children's art a professional look. Make sure it is also at children's eye level so they can appreciate and admire their own work and that of their classmates.

Draw children's attention to book illustrations during read-alouds and model noticing different things about an illustrator's work and details in the illustrations. Point out and explain techniques such as torn-paper pictures, watercolors, and pastels. Introduce children to some of the many wonderful children's books and other texts on art that call attention to artists and their styles of painting, such as *Camille and the Sunflowers,* about impressionist Vincent Van Gogh or *Picasso and the Girl with a Ponytail* about painter and sculptor Pablo Picasso.

Observing Children's Understanding

When using the Art area to promote children's learning, through observation you will get clues to how they are developing and the skills that they have mastered. Here are a few examples:

- Saying, *I made a grasshopper* after making a sculpture of clay, twigs, yarn, and disposable foam peanuts
- Using markers and gluing objects on a small paper bag to make an animal puppet
- Pounding and rolling clay to form snakes
- Describing a drawing by saying, *It stopped raining. Here's the sun making everyone happy because they can go out to play.*

As children work on their own artistic creations and explore materials in new ways, ask the following questions:

What do you think we can make with these?

Can you tell me about your painting?

How can we make new colors from this paint?

What do you think this painting tells us?

How did the artist make this shape?

What will you add to your drawing?

What happens when you paint with a different brush?

Your Teaching Practice

In addition to encouraging children to create with art materials, teachers can help children learn to appreciate art. Take a few moments to think about your own creative process. What inspires you to be creative? Are there changes you can make in the classroom to make it a place where children feel comfortable expressing themselves artistically? What can you do to help children reflect on their work and appreciate what they've created? How do you talk about your own art abilities with children?

Tips to Share With Families

- Offer your child everyday household items to use for art experiences (e.g., bottle caps, buttons, scraps of paper, etc.).
- Point out art that you see in your community (e.g., murals, artwork hanging in offices and stores).
- Ask your child questions about his or her artwork.
- Practice drawing and painting with your child.
- Offer your child blank paper and drawing materials instead of coloring books.
- Describe the art you see your child creating.
- Check out art books from the library to look at with your child.

Music

Music, when an instrument (or instruments) is played with or without vocals, gives children another opportunity to engage in the creative process and is another way for children to explore how they are feeling and what they want to express and share with the world. Children's interest in and exploration of music and using music to express their thoughts is encouraged the more children listen to all types of music and sounds and participate as music makers themselves. As children sing songs, hum tunes, and play various instruments, they develop their own artistic sensibilities and recognition of various types of music.

These kinds of questions can help children understand music and musical expression:

- What songs do you like to sing with your family?
- What music do you like to dance to?
- Does anyone in your family play a musical instrument?
- Do you have a favorite musician that you like to listen to?

What Does Research Say?

Music learning and music knowledge demand an independent set of understandings and skills. Music is a "critical domain of learning" in the preK classroom, just like "mathematics, science, and literacy" (McDonel, 2015).

Music has numerous benefits to children's brain development: teaching language skills, encouraging gross-motor development, and strengthening children's social–emotional development as children gain self-confidence, self-esteem, empathy, the ability for imaginative thinking and the ability to express emotions creatively. Music also "strengthens neural pathways to the brain that are responsible for abstract thinking, empathy, and mathematics" (Suskind, 2015).

Children's emotional, cognitive, and physical needs are met through music in the classroom, for music can soothe, and energize children. It can be a way for children with special needs to express themselves. Other benefits include music as a "pathway to literacy," a classroom tool for engaging children and encouraging them to "question the world around them" (Bond, 2015).

Areas of learning for music include: "discerning different aspects of music (e.g., the sound of specific instruments, pitch, tempo), developing different ways of representing music (visually, bodily, and verbally), and learning to listen in a musical way" (Samuelsson, Carlsson, Olsson, Pramling, & Wallerstedt, 2009).

The Teacher's Role in Promoting Understanding of Music

Music naturally delights and interests children. Encouraging exploration of music helps children to develop an awareness of different kinds of music and helps them to become comfortable with different forms of music expression.

There are many ways to explore music with children. Here are a few simple suggestions:

Provide an area that has instruments for children to play and create their own music, and also encourages children to listen as others play.
You can hang musical instruments on a pegboard, and make labels by cutting out silhouettes of the instruments on construction paper or solid adhesive paper and taping them on the pegboard. Place instruments such as a keyboard, xylophones, and melody bells where children can reach them easily.

Use correct musical terminology in the classroom.
Introducing children to concepts such as *tune, melody, rhythm, beat, quickly, slowly, loudly, softly* can help to enhance their understanding and enjoyment of music and can help build vocabulary that's connected to the musical experience.

Teach new songs to add to children's knowledge of music.
When children sing familiar songs at home, family members recognize them and can join in. Songs like "Baa, Baa, Black Sheep," "B-I-N-G-O," and "She'll Be Comin' Round the Mountain" are likely songs that family members learned growing up.

Look for opportunities to create new songs or clap a beat.
By the age of 3 or 4, children can typically keep time to a regular beat. They begin to adjust their body movements with changes in the music, adapting to contrasts such as slow and fast, or light and heavy.

Observing Children's Understanding

Children's daily activities may demonstrate many ways that they are engaged in exploration of music and musical concepts. A few examples are:

- Enjoying listening to music and moving to the beat
- Experimenting with different instruments
- Making up new words to songs
- Interacting with others in music and movement activities

Your Teaching Practice

Think about the ways that music impacts your life and your work. Consider the following questions:

- Do you enjoy listening to music or creating music? Do you have a particular musical talent or skill that you feel comfortable sharing with children?
- What experiences can you share with children that demonstrate your feelings about music and the role it plays in your life, both in the classroom and at home?
- What memories do you have about musical experiences? How have they impacted you?

Tips to Share With Families

- Share your favorite music with your child and talk about what you like about it.
- Spend time singing songs with your child.
- Listen to different types of music with your child and talk about what you like/dislike about it.
- When singing with your child, make up new words to familiar songs.
- Ask your child to share his or her music experiences at school with you.
- Look for ways for your child to see live music played.
- Add your child's name to songs that you sing together.
- Make up songs to sing while doing chores around the house.

Dance

As children listen to music, they often begin to move their bodies in response. As children dance, teachers can encourage them to move with the music and to try different movements and motions to different instruments or verses in the song. Child explore and make discoveries through dance, learning how dancing helps them explore how they feel and that there are so many ways they can move their bodies.

Here are questions for children to consider as they dance:

- How do you want to move to this music?
- What are all of the ways we can move our bodies?
- What does it feel like to move slowly? Quickly?

What Does Research Say?

Dance "helps children understand the structure of movement and promotes their bodily skills and coordination. They learn to modify movements to elements of space, various tempos and speeds, various levels, different quantities of individuals, differences of force and intensity, and various shapes of small and large objects" (Fumoto, Robson, Greenfield, & Hargreaves, 2012, quoted in Saracho, 2012).

As both a physical activity and as a way for children to express themselves, dance has a strong influence on children's lives both inside and outside of the classroom. Dance allows children to explore and create through "lively movement" (Dow, 2010).

"Children involved in creative movement activities discover ways to physically control and coordinate the rhythmic movement of their bodies in a specific environment, alone and in cooperation with others" (Koster, 2012).

Some researchers believe that movement should be considered the primary intelligence as it "precedes both vocal and verbal language development and is informed by and informs visual-spatial, auditory, and other sensory development." In fact, researchers such as Bradley and Szegda consider the learning process of children as a type of dance, i.e., an "increasingly conscious choosing to explore and interact with data that is based in rhythmic and spatial sequences of movement" (Bradley & Szegda, 2012).

The Teacher's Role in Promoting Understanding of Dance

An early childhood program that includes time for music and movement provides an outlet for children's high spirits and creative energy. Music and movement experiences help develop both sides of the brain—an important finding in brain research—and contribute to children's social-emotional, physical, language, and cognitive development and learning.

No matter what study topic your class is investigating or where you are in the school year, you can create an environment for music and movement in many ways. Here are a few suggestions:

Set up an environment that makes floor space available for movement activities.
In this space, children can be free to make or listen to music and dance to the music if they wish. Group music and movement activities may occur wherever space permits. When the weather is good, take music and movement materials outdoors for a very different kind of experience.

Offer props that encourage children to move to the music.
Offering a variety of props and colorful objects to use as they dance can help children to learn about using rhythm and space in different ways and encourages creative movement.

Invite families to participate in the classroom and share songs and dances from their cultures.
Your best resource is the children's families. Invite them to teach a song or a dance to the class if they feel comfortable doing so. Continue the tradition of passing their cultures from one generation to the next by having them share the stories behind their songs and dances. This encourages children to learn about their peers, and also see how their own cultural songs and dances are alike or different from others.

Join children in their music and movement activities.
Enrich a child's experience with moving to music by simply joining in while the child is dancing. Children love to have adults follow their lead, and you can add a variation to the dance later to spark a child's desire to explore new possibilities.

Describe what you see or hear children doing to expand their music and movement activity.
When exploring movement and dance with children, you can introduce words such as *sway, prance, glide,* or *bounce.* You can help children make connections between music and movement (e.g., *The way you're moving is called "gliding." Do you think the music sounds like gliding?*).

Observing Children's Understanding

When you begin to observe children in order to determine the ways they respond to music, you can encourage their development in this area by talking with them about what they are doing, reacting to and encouraging their explorations, and asking open-ended questions. A few examples are:

- Asking questions that call for movement (e.g., *How many different ways can you think of to get from this side of the mat to the other?*)
- Introducing dance by having children move in different ways to music (e.g., flying like a butterfly, walking like an elephant, picking apples off a tree)
- Pointing out sounds and rhythms in the environment (e.g., a dripping faucet or a ticking clock)
- Offering questions and comments after a child finishes dancing (e.g., *You were dancing a special way to that music. I wonder whether this next tape will make you want to dance the same way or differently?*)
- Inviting a child to teach you a dance that she made up

As you support children's understanding of dance concepts, look for opportunities to ask the following questions:

How can we move our bodies to this music?

What do you think this dance could be called?

What does this dance make you think of?

How would you dance if the music was faster?

Is it possible to dance with just your arms? Legs?

Your Teaching Practice

Take a few moments to think about your own feelings about movement and dance. What memories do you have of exploring movement and dance? What makes you want to move and dance? How do you express yourself through movement?

What questions can you ask children that will encourage them to share their experiences with movement and dance with their family and friends?

Tips to Share With Families

- Look for opportunities to dance and move with your child.
- Show your child dances from your family, culture, and community.
- Talk with your child about how dancing makes you feel.
- Point out any examples you see of professional dancers and talk about how they work.
- Together with your child, make up a new family dance.
- Use dancing as a way to make chores more interesting (e.g., dancing while you sweep, swaying while cooking, etc.).
- Talk about the ways you held and danced with your child as a baby.
- Notice your child's interest in dance and look for ways to include dancing in your daily experiences.

Drama

"Drama is based on the presentation of ideas and actions through pantomime, improvisation, play acting, literature, and storytelling to create a visual and auditory performance. Dramatic activities engage children in verbal and physical communication through imitative role behavior, make believe, and social interaction with real and imaginary others" (Koster, 2012). Drama is portraying characters and telling stories through action, dialogue, or both and is an important part of development and learning for young children (Dodge, Colker, & Heroman, 2002). It positively affects children's language development and literacy, self-awareness, social–emotional reasoning, and problem-solving (Brown, 1990; Pinciotti, 1993; Wright, et al., 2008). As children participate with others in drama-related play, they develop basic skills and knowledge in the use of props, movement, pantomime, sound, speech, character, and story making (Pinciotti, 1993).

Children learn to tell stories through repeated exchanges with people who are important to them. Experiences and cultural traditions influence what stories children tell and how they tell stories (Curenton & Ryan, 2006; Wright et al., 2008). Adult guidance is important in helping children develop the skills they need to act out scenarios and stories. When teachers read stories for later dramatization or provide children with puppets to act out a story, clothing they can use for dress up, and props that can transform blocks into an imaginary city, they are teaching children drama.

As children play with materials such as these, they express their feelings and process their experiences. "A preschooler's pretend-play starts to be interactive, including role-play and dress-up. Being part of it is another aspect of building brains, relationships, and creative skills, with the added bonus of being fun. … For example, an older child wearing a superhero cape while acting the part is demonstrating creative thinking" (Suskind, 2015).

What Does Research Say?

Dramatic play or pretending occurs when young children "tap into [their] imagination" as they explore their world and "add [their] own stamp to it." Its impact on a child's development is immense as children learn to express their thoughts and feelings and learn social skills (social–emotional development) and communicate with each other (language development). Pretending also facilitates the development of young children's preliteracy skills and sets the stage for children's "higher, more profound, ways of thinking" (Suskind, 2015).

Children's dramatic play is "the depiction of imaginary worlds while dialoguing with the materials." Drama as a component of arts in the classroom involves this pretend and imaginary play (Klerfelt, 2011).

"Dramatic interpretation of literature supports children's understanding of the text and provides children who struggle with reading comprehension with a way to interact with the story for an extended amount of time and develop the more complex themes and issues. This type of interaction with text is shown to grow children's love of reading" (Sayers Adomat, 2012).

Dramatic interpretation or reenactment supports not only literacy development but also children's science learning. It "can be used in science education to give children a physical way to interact as and use their entire bodies to simulate particles and molecules" (Varelas, Pappas, Tucker-Raymond, Kane, Hankes, Ortix, & Keblawe-Shamah, 2010).

The Teacher's Role in Promoting Exploration of Drama

Dramatic play is central to children's healthy development and learning during the preschool years. Children explore their experiences by pretending to be someone or something different from themselves. They make up situations and actions that go along with the roles they choose. When children engage in dramatic play, they deepen their understanding of the world and develop skills that will serve them throughout their lives.

To support children in communicating a message or story through action and dialogue, there are a few simple things you can do:

Join in as children create dramatic play scenarios.
The more that adults participate with children and talk with them about their experiences, the richer their dramatic play is likely to be. You can stimulate dramatic play by observing what is happening and commenting or asking questions about what you see. By talking about what children are doing, you make them more aware that they are pretending. You can also make suggestions that will extend their play.

Add props to interest areas that invite dramatic story retelling.
Stories like *Caps for Sale* or *The Three Billy Goats Gruff* offer children the opportunity to explore drama and pretend. Encourage this by teaching them the skills they need to pretend while acting out the stories. Provide puppets and encourage children to put on a puppet show.

Ask children to explore a variety of facial expressions.
Encourage children to show you what people's facial expressions look like when they are happy, sad, angry, tired, excited, or afraid.

Provide dramatic play props.
In selecting materials and props for the Dramatic Play area, consider the developmental abilities of the children in your classroom and what will be most familiar to them. Organize them in a logical way to encourage children's creativity, enable them to work independently, and help them make choices. You can also use the children's suggestions for what props to add to the Dramatic Play area—this will make them more likely to use the materials you provide and direct their own learning, which builds their confidence as learners.

Observing Children's Understanding

When children engage in dramatic play, they will begin to expand upon the range of skills and experiences they use to pretend. A few examples of when you might observe this are:

- Placing a dress on the ironing board, running the wooden iron over it, and saying, *I'm getting ready for a party*
- Saying, *Here are some beans for dinner* after going to the collage box and bringing back disposable foam peanuts
- Lining up dolls and putting a puppet show on for them, using several puppets and different voices for different characters

As you support children's understanding of drama concepts, look for opportunities to ask the following questions:

How can we retell the story and act it out?

Why do you like to pretend to be that character?

What can you do to show me what the character is feeling?

What else do you think the character would do?

What props do you need to be...?

Your Teaching Practice

Take a look around the classroom and notice the range of props and materials that help children to explore dramatic play. Consider the following questions:

- Are there props and materials that reflect the cultural and ethnic backgrounds of the children in the group?
- How do you take an active role in teaching children the skills to make believe?
- How do you feel about participating in dramatic play?

Tips to Share With Families

- Talk about the actors your child sees on TV and in the movies.
- Look for ways to pretend play with your child by taking on different roles.
- Describe the facial expressions and actions of your child when he or she is pretending.
- Ask questions that help your child continue to play a role.
- Encourage your child's pretend play, even if he or she pretends to be an animal, someone of the opposite gender, or a villain.
- Help your child think of new ways to pretend to be a character.
- Act out familiar stories with your child. You may also want to change the story as you play.

Studies: Music Making

In *The Creative Curriculum*® classroom, teachers use *Teaching Guides* that feature studies on a variety of different topics to help children build content knowledge and develop process skills. Each study is an in-depth investigation of a topic children are interested in learning more about. Children find answers to their questions through firsthand explorations, and they have opportunities to practice and apply skills related to the arts in meaningful ways.

Selecting the Topic

To illustrate how children use the arts to learn, consider the study that evolved in Ms. Tory and Mr. Alvarez's 4-year-old class.

A small group of children in the Music and Movement area planned how they could play music together in a band. They chose instruments and excitedly started playing music together and marching around. The band continued to play for the rest of choice time with children leaving and joining the group. As the children used the instruments, Ms. Tory listened to what they said:

"I want to play the tambourine because I like shaking it."

"Can we play a fast song?"

"I saw a man play a recorder like this at the library once."

"My dad plays a real guitar and sings too!"

She noticed that the children were excited about playing instruments and experimented with different types of music and tempos as they played together. Over the next few days, the children continued to play the instruments together during choice time. Mr. Alvarez talked with the children about the music they were making during a large-group time. He asked what they enjoyed about playing the instruments together, and the children excitedly talked about making music and their favorite instruments.

Ms. Tory and Mr. Alvarez reviewed their observations related to how the children were using and talking about the instruments and agreed that the children were showing curiosity and interest in music making. Based on these observations, they chose to use *The Creative Curriculum*® *for Preschool Teaching Guide, featuring the Music Making Study.*

Beginning the Study

To start planning for the music making study, Ms. Tory and Mr. Alvarez brainstormed vocabulary and ideas related to music making. They thought about who makes music and uses instruments, how they could make their own music, how instruments are played, what types of music there are, and how music impacts people emotionally. After collecting all of their ideas, they created a web of investigations to group their ideas around each investigation question.

Through the webbing process, they gained a clear idea of the components they could include in each investigation. They also planned how they could address literacy, mathematics, science and technology, social studies, and the arts throughout the study in meaningful ways.

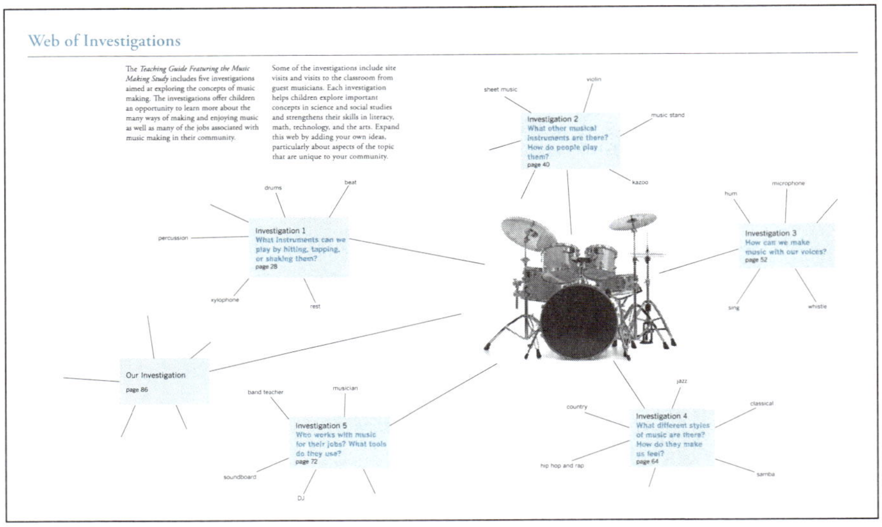

Each study begins with exploring the topic to discover what the children already know. Then, based on the children's curiosity and questions, a series of investigations are planned to build on what the children know. To discover what the children already know about music making, Ms. Tory and Mr. Alvarez started gathering a classroom collection of related books, pictures, and materials. They used the "Letter to Families" found in the *Teaching Guide* to inform families about their upcoming study and ask them to donate materials to the collection. They also asked the families if any family member works in a field related to music and invited them to visit the classroom to share their expertise with the children.

Following the guidance in the *Teaching Guide*, Ms. Tory began the study by exploring the topic. She led discussions about the materials in the classroom collection and she and Mr. Alvarez carefully documented the children's questions and observations throughout the week. They added the children's questions to a chart titled "What We Want to Find Out About Music Making."

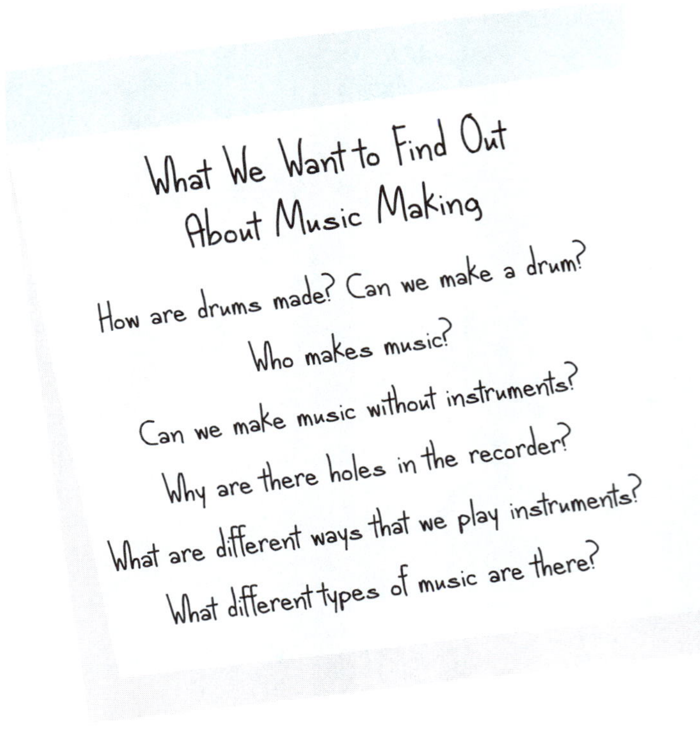

Investigating the Topic

The *Teaching Guide* gives guidance for experiences that help the children discover the answers to their questions and gain a deeper understanding of music making. The following shows how these experiences incorporate skills related to the arts.

Music Making Experiences	Ways to Use Skills Related to the Arts
Classroom visits and site visits to meet musicians and singers	Talk about the type of music the musician plays and ask the children how it makes them feel. Ask the visitor to play music and invite the children to dance to it. Add instruments, like the ones the children see on the site visit, to the Dramatic Play area so the children can reenact what they observed. Record and discuss music you hear from the classroom visitors and on the site visits. Invite the children to play music or sing with the musicians.
Listen to different types of music	Dance and move to the different tempos. Ask the children to listen to the music and discuss what instruments they hear. Talk about the different styles of music and learn their names. Listen to music as an inspiration for creating other types of visual art.
Make different kinds of instruments	Experiment with using different materials to make instruments and compare their sounds. Compare the components of real instruments with those the children make. Talk about the different types of sounds the children's instruments can make. Experiment with pitch, tone, and tempo using handmade instruments.
Play music together	Ask the children to listen to the music other children play. Record the music the children make and listen to it at a later time. Talk about the tempo and rhythms that they hear. Invite the children to play different styles of music together. Encourage the children to make up their own songs. Make music together using instruments and voices.

Use the Internet to research music, singing, and instruments	Listen to and discuss different styles of music. Add props and materials that the children find on their Internet search to the Dramatic Play area. Research different styles of dance and practice different moves and steps together. Choose a performer the children discovered during their research and reenact their performance. Research paintings, sculptures, and other works of art that feature instruments or musicians.
Make a concert hall in the Dramatic Play area	Invite the children to act out their own musical performances. Include roles such as conductor, musicians, and the audience. Encourage the children to put on shows that feature different styles of music. Provide props to dance and play music with. Provide both conventional and handmade instruments for the children to play. Create scenery and backdrops for their performance.

Ms. Tory and Mr. Alvarez studied music making with the children over the course of six weeks. During this time, they investigated the following five questions:

What instruments can we play by hitting, tapping, or shaking them?

What other musical instruments are there? How do people play them?

How can we make music with our voices?

What different styles of music are there? How do they make us feel?

Who works with music for their jobs? What tools do they use?

Throughout these investigations, Ms. Tory and Mr. Alvarez used planned experiences and gave the children ample time to experiment and explore the materials to discover the answers to their questions. They also used comments and open-ended questions to help the children solve problems, to clarify their plans and reasoning, and to think about materials in new ways. They connected the investigations of the components of music making in meaningful ways that allowed the children to gain a deeper understanding of dance, music, performing arts, and visual arts.

Closing the Study

To conclude the study, the children planned a celebration and invited their families and special guests they had met during the study to see what they have learned. They created displays in the classroom interest areas to show the visitors how they investigated music making. The children planned performances using their handmade instruments, dance, and other performing arts skills.

Including All Children in the Study

Using the *Teaching Guide, featuring the Music Making Study*, the teachers can draw on their understanding of each child's behaviors, knowledge, skills, and needs to provide a variety of experiences to include all children. Below are some general strategies for promoting inclusion of all children during this study.

English- and Dual-Language Learners

- Include music with lyrics in the children's home language(s) and instruments used in the cultures of the children in the classroom.
- As you play and sing songs in English, emphasize sounds that may be new or unfamiliar.
- Encourage children to work in pairs or small groups to play or move along with music. Offer words or phrases for children to describe the music.
- Invite families to visit the classroom to share music or instruments that are used in their home culture(s).
- Encourage children who are reluctant to join conversations to participate in musical experiences by dancing or moving along to the rhythm.
- Learn a few helpful words in the language(s) spoken by the children related to study, e.g., *tempo, concert,* etc., to help all children learn key vocabulary words.
- Encourage children to count in their home language(s) and in English as they count the number of instruments in their collection.
- Schedule frequent small-group and individual learning experiences throughout the study to encourage children to become involved and interact with others.
- Encourage families to join their children in the classroom throughout the study so that children can talk with them about what they are learning about how people in their community make music.

Children With Disabilities

- Provide adaptive equipment such as large-print books, oversized instruments, communication devices, chairs with sides, or allowing children more time to process information and respond.
- Use simple language and repeat key words during the experiences.
- Encourage the children to participate in the experiences as long as they are interested. Allow children to move on to another experience when they are ready.
- When exploring the instrument collection, encourage children to participate however they are comfortable, i.e., observing from a distance.
- Limit the number of items provided for the child to explore. Begin with one or two items for the child to focus on.
- Provide headphones for children with sensory sensitivities who may be averse to loud sounds.
- Connect the experiences to activities that the children are motivated by. For example, if a child loves horses, invite children to listen for the *clippity cloppity* sound of horse hooves in the song "Sleigh Ride." Encourage children to find ways to recreate a similar sound using recycled materials.
- Include larger items for children to grasp and manipulate when making instruments, e.g. milk cartons, car tires for drum, etc.
- Invite children to work together to play an instrument.
- Break down exploration activities into manageable steps (e.g., *First we each take an instrument, and then we will start to play when I lower my hand.*).

Advanced Learners

- Encourage children to use their creativity to improve the sound of an instrument (e.g., *What can we do with the strings on the guitar to make them tighter like on the guitar that Sergio's dad brought?).* Support children to research related topics such as composing, beats per measure, etc.
- Invite children to lead experiments and activities in which they demonstrate a high level of understanding (e.g., *Noni plays the recorder at home; can you show us how you cover the holes to make different sounds?*).
- Provide reading materials in a variety of levels.
- Meet with local librarians, elementary school teachers, and educational specialists to collect resources, e.g., books, equipment, or puzzles to engage advanced learners.
- Support children to research online videos to watch how professional musicians play instruments, e.g., a traditional snare drum grip.
- Encourage children to use materials intentionally or in a new way, e.g., using other items such as paintbrushes, as drumsticks, or comparing a variety of hollow containers to create a xylophone. Support children to research answers to the questions they come up with as they create.
- Ask questions that encourage children to explore and experiment (e.g., *What would happen if…?* or *How can we make this better?).*

8

Learning the Arts in Interest Areas and the Outdoors

Learning the Arts in Interest Areas and the Outdoors 185

The Arts in the Library Area 186

The Arts in the Art Area 189

The Arts in the Discovery Area 192

The Arts in the Toys and Games Area 195

The Arts in the Cooking Area 198

The Arts in the Block Area 201

The Arts in the Technology Area 203

The Arts in the Dramatic Play Area 205

The Arts in the Sand and Water Area 208

The Arts in the Music and Movement Area 210

The Arts and the Outdoors 213

Learning the Arts in Interest Areas and the Outdoors

The Creative Curriculum® preschool classroom is designed to encourage exploration and creativity. No matter where children are working or playing, there are opportunities for them to express themselves creatively. Planning thoughtfully for art experiences in the interest areas takes little time but results in spaces that welcome children's artistic explorations. Drawing, painting, singing, dancing, acting – all of these experiences can be found taking place throughout the classroom, giving children the chance to develop their skills, learn more about their abilities, and explore their interests.

The Arts in the Library Area

The Library area is a great place for children to learn more about the arts as they explore books that cover a broad range of art topics. You may be able to find beautiful art books that bring paintings and sculpture to life or stories about famous dancers and musicians. Using these resources can serve as a first step toward helping children figure out how art speaks to them and how they can create their own works of art. Here are a few examples of how children's explorations and interactions in the Library area relate to *The Creative Curriculum® for Preschool* objectives for the arts.

Examples of What a Child Might Do	Examples of Related Objectives for Development and Learning
Look at a book of abstract paintings.	33. Explores the visual arts
Write a poem and create a tune to go with it.	34. Explores musical concepts and expression
Read a book about a music festival and create a list of materials needed for a classroom celebration.	35. Explores dance and movement concepts
Retell a folktale using props and costumes.	36. Explores drama through actions and language

Materials for the Arts in the Library Area

Materials for art experiences in the Library area can be simple. Their purpose is to expose children to new art experiences, and encourage children to explore their creative ideas that come from the books they read, the writing they do, and the stories they hear. Rotate the materials regularly, and be sure to include materials relevant to the current study topic as well.

Materials

photos of artwork and artists

biographical books about artists, musicians, dancers, actors, etc.

props for retelling stories

drawing and writing materials

books about art from around the world

pamphlets from community art experiences (festivals, parades, concerts, etc.)

posters of artwork found on book covers

Suggested Books

(Titles preceded by an asterisk are included in the *Teaching Strategies® Children's Book Collection*.)

An ABC of What Art Can Be (Meher McArthur)

The Art Book for Children (Editors of Phaidon Press)

Art Treasury (Rosie Dickins)

The Book With No Pictures (B.J. Novak)

Dance! (Elisha Cooper)

Diego (Jonah Winter)

**The Dot* (Peter H. Reynolds)

Elmer (David McKee)

Frida (Jonah Winter)

Get Into Art Telling Stories (Susie Brooks)

Henri's Scissors (Jeanette Winter)

Here's Looking at Me (Bob Raczka)

Katie Meets the Impressionists (James Mayhew)

My Pen (Christopher Myers)

Oliver Button is a Sissy (Tomi dePaola)

Olivia (Ian Falconer)

Papa Chagall, Tell Us a Story (Laurence Anholt)

The Pencil (Allan Ahlberg)

Philadephia Chickens (Sandra Boynton)

The Rainbow Fish (Marcus Pfister)

The Stories of the Mona Lisa (Piotr Barsony)

The Story of the Orchestra (Robert Levine)

Through Georgia's Eyes (Rachel Rodriguez)

Where Are My Books? (Debbie Ridpath Ohi)

Zin! Zin! Zin! A Violin (Lloyd Moss)

Using the Library Area to Teach the Arts

In the Library area, children have a chance to explore the arts beyond what they can create on their own. In this interest area, children have an opportunity to read books and hear the ways that art of all kinds is described. They can relate the stories and experiences they have in the Library area to their own creations when writing, drawing, dancing, etc. Teachers can read with children and focus on the arts by pointing out illustrations, defining rich language, and asking children to think critically about what they see in the books they read. Here are some examples of what teachers might say as they interact with children and support their learning of the arts in this interest area:

Dance

How are people moving their bodies in this picture? They look like they're having fun.

Can you move like the animals in this story?

I like the rhythm of this poem. It makes me want to dance, too.

This character describes his dance as jerky, and this dancer is smooth. Can you show me how you can move like that?

Music

This poem sounds like a song. Can you sing it with me?

I like how this book has illustrations that look like musical notes.

Would you like to write your own music?

I wonder what the violin in this picture sounds like.

Drama

Let's use these masks to retell the story. Which character would you like to be?

This book is written as a play. That means that actors would say the words in front of an audience.

How can you make your voice sound like the daddy bear and the baby bear?

Visual Arts

This art book has so many beautiful paintings.

What do you notice about the sculpture in this book?

I wonder where this giant sculpture is. How can we find out?

Look at the name of this painting. It's called "Night and Day." Do you think it looks like night and day?

Observing Children's Understanding

As you interact with children in the Library area, look for examples such as these that demonstrate children's understanding of the arts:

- Describing illustrations found in books
- Drawing to illustrate a story
- Retelling a story using props
- Looking at a songbook and singing along
- Asking questions about pictures
- Choosing books featuring different examples of art
- Adding a tune to a poem

The Arts in the Art Area

The Art area can serve as a hub of learning where children can apply their knowledge, explore their ideas, and investigate a variety of questions. Here are a few examples of how children's explorations and experiences in the Art area relate to *The Creative Curriculum® for Preschool* objectives for the arts.

Examples of What a Child Might Do	Examples of Related Objectives for Development and Learning
Use paintbrushes with different textures and talk about the differences between them.	33. Explores the visual arts
Listen to music as inspiration when drawing.	34. Explores musical concepts and expression
Sculpt with play dough to make a ballerina after looking at a Degas sculpture.	35. Explores dance and movement concepts
Create masks for retelling the story of Goldilocks.	36. Explores drama through actions and language

Materials for the Arts in the Art Area

There are endless possibilities for materials to enhance children's learning of the arts in the Art area. Materials do not need to be expensive, or cost anything at all, if you plan to introduce items already available in the classroom or the outdoors. You may also consider rotating materials by sharing with another teacher in your program so that children learn all the ways that materials can be used for art experiences. It is important to offer children open-ended experiences. This ensures that they will be able to fully explore their creativity without being restricted to a specific desired outcome. It's okay if everyone's art looks different hanging on the wall!

Materials

fabric scraps for weaving

a variety of music samples

images of famous works of art from around the world

natural items for painting (e.g., pinecones, sticks, rocks, leaves, etc.)

cardboard boxes and tubes for creating musical instruments

hats and clothing to decorate for dramatic play

materials for creating masks

variety of types of paper

mirrors

books on famous works of art

Suggested Books

(Titles preceded by an asterisk are included in the *Teaching Strategies® Children's Book Collection*.)

Abuela's Weave (Omar S. Castañeda)

Art Is… (Bob Raczka)

The Art Lesson (Tomi dePaola)

The Art of Miss Chew (Patricia Polacco)

Artist to Artist (Eric Carle Museum of Picture Book Art)

Bartholomew and the Oobleck (Dr. Seuss)

Beautiful Oops! (Barney Saltzberg)

The Big Book of Art (Hervé Tullet)

Color Dance (Ann Jonas)

The Day the Crayons Quit (Drew Daywalt)

A Day Without Crayons (Elizabeth Rusch)

I Ain't Gonna Paint No More (Karen Beaumont)

I Spy: An Alphabet in Art (Lucy Micklethwait)

Ish (Peter H. Reynolds)

Louise Loves Art (Kelly Light)

Madeleine's Light (Natalie Ziarnik)

The Maestro Plays (Bill Martin Jr.)

Museum Trip (Barbara Lehman)

Prancing Dancing Lily (Marsha Diane Arnold)

**Something from Nothing* (Phoebe Gilman)

The Usborne Book of Famous Paintings (Rosie Dickens and Philip Hopman)

What is Contemporary Art? A Guide for Kids (Jacky Klein and Suzy Klein)

Using Art to Teach the Arts

When observing children in the Art area, support their learning by first watching them create and explore and then asking questions about their creations. You may be surprised to see how children use the materials in new and unexpected ways. Avoid offering advice or directing children's artwork in order to attain a specific outcome. Help children make connections between what they are doing in the Art area and how it applies to their overall understanding of the arts. Here are examples of what you might ask and say:

Dance

I see that you're making big movements with your arms while you paint.

You said you wanted to draw the dancing cats you saw in the book. What will you do first?

This pictures shows the dance steps to follow. I wonder if we can make our own dance steps and draw the directions like this.

Music

What do you think of when you hear this music? Can you paint it?

It looks like you're making your own musical instrument with those straws. What kind of music will you play?

I see you painted short strokes when the fast music played and long strokes when the slow music played.

Let's sing our song while we pound, pound, pound the clay.

Drama

You're using so many colors to make your mask! What character will you be when you're wearing it?

You're weaving fabric to make a blanket for your teddy bear. I wonder how big it will be when you're finished.

We saw a play about three girls at the zoo. What do you want to draw about the play?

Visual Arts

How will you use these feathers for your mask?

I wonder how you created that color.

Which brush did you use to make that texture on your paper?

How can we make our own flower out of clay that is like the flower in this painting?

Observing Children's Understanding

As you observe children playing and creating in the Art area, look for these indications that children are demonstrating artistic concepts:

- Showing another child how to mix colors
- Creating props for dramatic play
- Experimenting with different amounts of water in a watercolor painting
- Asking for help to tie fabric together to make a hat
- Talking about the different drawings displayed in the classroom
- Comparing two works of art by the same artist
- Describing the process for creating a play dough sculpture
- Explaining the meaning of a painting
- Making a collage using different types of paper

The Arts in the Discovery Area

As children explore in the Discovery area, they may naturally be inclined to include their experiences in their art creations. For example, a child who looks closely at a butterfly's wing under a microscope might be inspired to make an observational drawing of what she sees. You can encourage children's art experiences in the Discovery area by talking about the beautiful patterns, colors, and designs found in nature. Here are examples of what you might see in the Discovery area that relate to *The Creative Curriculum® for Preschool* objectives for the arts.

Examples of What a Child Might Do	Examples of Related Objectives for Development and Learning
Look at a collection of John Audubon drawings.	33. Explores the visual arts
Listen to recordings of different animal sounds and songs.	34. Explores musical concepts and expression
Look out the window at leaves blowing and then create a dance to look like the blowing leaves.	35. Explores dance and movement concepts
Pretend to be an insect and fly around the classroom.	36. Explores drama through actions and language

Materials for the Arts in the Discovery Area

Sharing art experiences with children in the Discovery area is a great way for them to recognize how the arts can play a role in their experiences in the classroom, at home, outside, or at the park. Children can connect music, drama, dance, and visual art to all types of learning in the Discovery area. Adding materials to help children make those connections will enhance both their learning of the arts and their learning of the world around them.

Materials

images of animals

props for pretend play

mirrors

musical instruments made from natural objects

digital camera

writing and drawing materials

junk collection

examples of works of art made from natural materials (e.g., sand mandalas, mosaics, etc.)

close-up images of animals

recordings of animal songs and sounds

displays of patterns, colors, and designs in nature

displays of children's artwork made from natural materials

Suggested Books

(Titles preceded by an asterisk are included in the *Teaching Strategies® Children's Book Collection*.)

Buffalo Music (Tracey E. Fern)

Can You Find It? (Judith Cressy)

The Cat and the Bird (Géraldine Elschner)

Chandra's Magic Light (Theresa Heine)

Color Zoo (Lois Ehlert)

The Dance of the Caterpillars (Adele Marie Crouch)

Dinothesaurus: Prehistoric Poems and Paintings (Douglas Florian)

Elmer in the Snow (Davide McKee)

Extra Yarn (Mac Barnett)

Georgia's Bones (Jen Bryant)

Hugo and Miles in I've Painted Everything! (Scott Magoon)

I Face the Wind (Vicki Cobb)

**Joseph Had a Little Overcoat* (Simms Taback)

Leonardo the Flying Boy (Laurence Anholt)

Little Wolf's Song (Britta Teckentrup)

Making Amazing Art (Sandi Henry)

The Most Magnificent Thing (Ashley Spires)

My Best Friend is as Sharp as a Pencil (Hanoch Piven)

Tuesday (David Wiesner)

Uncle Andy's (James Warhola)

When Pigasso Met Mootisse (Nina Laden)

Using the Discovery Area to Teach the Arts

Children can often see the creative promise in materials that adults would readily discard. For example, a collection of small nuts and bolts can be made into a musical shaker and a broken seashell can inspire a painting that incorporates a newly discovered pattern. When observing and interacting with children in the Discovery area, ask open-ended questions that encourage them to describe the artistic elements they notice in the materials they use for work and play. Here are examples of what teachers might say as they talk with children in the Discovery area:

Dance

I see that you used our junk collection to make clackers for your shoes. Now when you dance and move your feet, you can make music, too!

I wonder what will happen to the pinwheel when you twirl around with it.

Do you remember what types of animals we saw at the aquarium? Can you move like they do?

I see you looking closely at the colors on that eggshell. What are you going to add to your drawing of the egg?

Music

What does the whale sound like in this recording? Can you make a sound like the whale?

I wonder how we can make an instrument out of these things we found.

That music makes me think of the way a bumblebee moves very quickly.

Why do you think these two instruments sound different? How can we find out what they're made of?

Drama

What animal would you like to be today?

How can we make puppets out of these materials? What can we use for the eyes?

This story is about a big wolf and a little wolf climbing a tree to reach the last leaf. Can you help me retell the story? We can use these real leaves to help us.

Visual Arts

The spider web in that photo has a beautiful pattern. I see you're making a pattern on your paper, too.

I wonder how we can add these materials to our mural.

What do you think it would look like if we used these pinecones instead of paintbrushes?

You have blue, green, and pink in your painting. We saw those same colors when we looked at the butterfly's wing under the magnifying glass.

Observing Children's Understanding

While children are engaged and active in the Discovery area, look for indications of their understanding of the arts, such as:

- Incorporating natural materials into their artwork
- Pretending to be different animals
- Looking closely at designs in nature
- Asking questions about how patterns are made in nature
- Looking at drawings of animals and plants
- Singing songs about animals and their movements
- Creating animal masks for dramatic play
- Mimicking movements seen in nature, such as leaves blowing, rain falling, etc.

The Arts in the Toys and Games Area

Because the Toys and Games area includes such a wide variety of materials and offers a range of experiences, children have many opportunities to explore the arts when playing here. There are puzzles with different images, game boards with imaginative designs, and building materials of all shapes, sizes, colors, and textures. As children use these materials, they can apply their knowledge of the arts to their play as well as take away ideas for further art explorations. Here are examples of how children's experiences in the Toys and Games area relate to *The Creative Curriculum® for Preschool* objectives for development and learning.

Examples of What a Child Might Do	Examples of Related Objectives for Development and Learning
Draw and layout a new board game.	33. Explores the visual arts
Play a game of musical carpet squares.	34. Explores musical concepts and expression
Add new finger play movements to a song.	35. Explores dance and movement concepts
Use a flannel board and props to tell a story.	36. Explores drama through actions and language

Materials for the Arts in the Toys and Games Area

Children's play in the Toys and Games area can be fairly open ended. They might use the toy house to dramatize a family event or arrange carpet squares and then sing a song as they hop from square to square. Children may also be inspired to create new visual art from the colorful and varied depictions found on puzzles and games. Adding a few art materials to the Toys and Games area helps children focus their learning and discover new ideas for their play.

Materials

- puzzles with a variety of examples of images, colors, and designs
- toys that encourage dramatic play (e.g., play house, fire station, airport, farm, etc.)
- boxes of various sizes
- writing and drawing materials
- board games with different designs, pieces, and layouts
- story sequence cards
- building materials of different textures and colors
- manipulatives of different shapes, patterns, and colors
- puppets and props for dramatic play
- materials for creating games and puzzles (e.g., paper, scissors, cardboard, markers, etc.)

Suggested Books

(Titles preceded by an asterisk are included in the *Teaching Strategies® Children's Book Collection.*)

Ben Draws Trouble (Matt Davies)

**A Birthday Basket for Tía* (Pat Mora)

Crabtree (Jon and Tucker Nichols)

Dancing Drum (Cohlene)

The Day the Crayons Came Home (Drew Daywalt)

Fiona's Lace (Patricia Polacco)

I Had a Favorite Dress (Boni Ashburn)

Just Behave, Pablo Picasso! (Jonah Winter)

Listen to My Trumpet! (Mo Willems)

Little Blue and Little Yellow (Leo Lionni)

Noisy Nora (Rosemary Wells)

Numbers on the Move (Teresa Benzwie)

Press Here (Hervé Tullet)

Squeaking of Art, The Mice Go to the Museum (Monica Wellington)

Why is Blue Dog Blue? (George Rodrigue)

Using Toys and Games to Teach the Arts

There are so many opportunities for interactions in the Toys and Games area that draw children's attention to details of the arts in their play. Ask questions that prompt children to notice, describe, and comment on the artistic elements of their play. For example, when playing a board game with a child, wonder aloud about how the pieces were made or how the board was designed. Encourage children to apply their own ideas when playing with toys and games. Here are some examples of what teachers might say and do as they interact with children in the Toys and Games area to promote learning of the arts:

Dance

This game gives us instructions each time we land on a square. Your space says to spin around three times.

I wonder how we can use these rain sticks to make up a new dance.

Let's use this song chart to add our own dances to the song.

Music

You made up a song about the family who lives in this house? Would you like to sing it for me?

I hear you making music with those toys. What sounds can you make with them?

It looks like you all are in a marching band! What are you using for instruments?

Drama

Can you tell me a story about the fire fighters at the fire station you're playing with?

What story can we tell with these puppets?

I see you're the train conductor running the train around the tracks.

Visual Arts

There are so many colors in this puzzle! Which colors do you see?

You're drawing a picture that looks like bouncing balls. They're bouncing high.

I wonder what pattern it will make on your paper when you dip that block in paint and paint with it.

These colored beads look like the kind used in the mosaic in this book.

Observing Children's Understanding

As you observe children engaged with toys and games, look for these indications that they are learning and applying art concepts:

- Working together to gather props for a play
- Describing the patterns seen on a game board
- Using building materials to make a colorful creation
- Talking about how to put a puzzle together by noticing details in the picture
- Wondering aloud about how to make music with toys
- Deciding on which manipulatives to use to make a mosaic
- Using building materials to make a new home for the toy family
- Looking at a puzzle and then drawing a similar picture

The Arts in the Cooking Area

Children's interactions and experiences in the Cooking area give them a chance to explore characteristics of food that may otherwise go unnoticed. Fruits and vegetables especially lend themselves well to discussions about colors, patterns, and designs found in food. For example, as you cut an apple in half, a child may notice the star pattern made by the seeds or you might lead a discussion about the colors of peppers and tomatoes and what the different colors indicate. Here are examples of how children's hands-on experiences in the Cooking area relate to *The Creative Curriculum® for Preschool* objectives for the arts.

Examples of What a Child Might Do	Examples of Related Objectives for Development and Learning
Create a chart showing the colors of the rainbow found in fruits and vegetables.	33. Explores the visual arts
Sing a song as part of a daily routine to prepare for mealtime.	34. Explores musical concepts and expression
Talk about how certain foods provide energy for moving our bodies.	35. Explores dance and movement concepts
Act out the process of eating during a *Mighty Minutes®* activity.	36. Explores drama through actions and language

Materials for the Arts in the Cooking Area

With preparing and eating food comes the chance to encourage children to really use their senses to explore what they are preparing and eating. You may even find that children are more willing to try new foods when they've engaged in a discussion about how it looks, smells, and feels. Providing healthy eating choices offers children examples of foods that inspire art around the world and may inspire them as well in their artistic creations and experiences.

Materials

- variety of fresh foods
- shape cutters
- writing and drawing materials
- song charts featuring songs to sing before and after mealtime
- examples of artwork related to cooking and food
- dress-up clothes for food workers (e.g., chefs, wait staff, etc.)
- photos of different types of colorful foods
- images of elaborate food dishes
- samples of local restaurant menus
- cookbooks with photos and illustrations

Suggested Books

Barnyard Dance (Sandra Boynton)

Big Red Lollipop (Rukhsana Kkan)

Cezanne and the Apple Boy (Laurence Anholt)

Chicken Soup With Rice (Maurice Sendak)

Fast Food (Saxton Freymann)

Green Eggs and Ham (Dr. Seuss)

Hot Potato: Mealtime Rhymes (Neil Philip)

How Do Dinosaurs Eat Their Food? (Jane Yolen)

I Really Like Slop! (Mo Willems)

In the Night Kitchen (Maurice Sendak)

It Looked Like Spilt Milk (Charles Shaw)

The Magic Porridge Pot (Rosie Dickens)

Mean Soup (Betsy Everitt)

Mix It Up (Hervé Tullet)

Pretend Soup and Other Real Recipes: A Cookbook for Preschoolers and Up (Mollie Katzen)

Touch the Art: Pop Warhol's Top (Julie Appel)

Using the Cooking Area to Teach the Arts

When incorporating the arts into cooking experiences, it is important to be mindful of children who are food-insecure. Because these children do not have reliable food sources, they will not benefit from art experiences that include food for anything other than eating. Seeing food used as disposable art materials may be upsetting for some children. Instead, focus classroom art experiences on art that can be incorporated while preparing and eating delicious food. For example, children can create menus, sing a song while setting the table, and use rich vocabulary to describe the taste, smell, and feel of the food they eat. Here are some examples of what teachers might say and do as they interact with children in the Cooking area to promote learning of the arts:

Dance

While our bread bakes, we can stretch our bodies and rise up like the bread!

I see you dancing while you're shaking that butter.

Music

I like to listen to music when I'm cooking. I wonder what music we should listen to.

Look at all of these kitchen tools. I wonder if we can use any of them to make music.

What does it sound like when you pour the rice into the bowl?

Drama

I see you're wearing your chef hat while you use the mixer.

I wonder why chefs sometimes wear hats like these.

You would like to pretend this is a restaurant? What will we need to serve our guests?

Visual Arts

This cookbook has beautiful photos. This photo shows us where the wheat is grown.

I see you're drawing what you had for breakfast today. Would you like to help me make a recipe for that?

I wonder how we can make our paint as purple as these grapes.

Observing Children's Understanding

As you work with and observe children in the Cooking area, look for indications such as these that demonstrate an understanding of the components of the arts:

- Illustrating a class cookbook
- Pretending to be a server in a cafeteria
- Acting out the changes in food (e.g., popcorn popping, dough rising, etc.)
- Choosing music to listen to while preparing food
- Noticing the similarities between colors in food and in artwork
- Trying to make a snack that looks like the picture in the cookbook
- Asking questions about how to make a menu
- Describing a dance by relating it to food
- Singing a song while transitioning to mealtime

The Arts in the Block Area

Playing in the Block area is not limited to simply building structures and knocking them down. Children in the Block area can use blocks to explore creative ideas, make comparisons between building materials, notice patterns and designs, and build props and sets for dramatic play. Consider the ways that you can scaffold children's learning in the Block area by supporting their understanding of the arts and guiding them to recognize similarities between their play and their everyday art experiences. Here are examples of how children's art experiences relate to *The Creative Curriculum® for Preschool* objectives for art.

Examples of What a Child Might Do	Examples of Related Objectives for Development and Learning
Look at photos of unusual architecture.	33. Explores the visual arts
Use blocks as percussion instruments.	34. Explores musical concepts and expression
Create a path for moving smoothly through the interest area.	35. Explores dance and movement concepts
Pretend to be a superhero flying over tall buildings.	36. Explores drama through actions and language

Materials for the Arts in the Block Area

Materials in the Block area should enhance children's play by sparking new ideas for creative construction. By exposing children to a variety of designs, encouraging dramatic play, and asking open-ended questions, you can support children to broaden the scope of their understanding of how the blocks can be used creatively.

Materials

- posters that include geometric designs and patterns
- props for dramatic play (e.g., toy people and animals)
- images of interesting architectural structures
- objects to be used as percussion instruments
- puppets
- writing and drawing materials
- displays of children's block creations

Suggested Books

Alphabet Movers (Teresa Benzwie)

Broadway Beat (John Jacobson)

Get Into Art Places (Susie Brooks)

Home (Carson Ellis)

If You Lived Here: Houses of the World (Giles Laroche)

The Land of Lines (Victor Hussenot)

The Museum (Susan Verde)

Not a Box (Antoinette Portis)

Perfect Square (Michael Hall)

Seen Art? (Jon Scieszka)

The Shape of My Heart (Mark Sperring)

When a Line Bends . . . A Shape Begins (Rhonda Gowler Greene)

Using the Block Area to Teach the Arts

As you talk with children about their creations, your comments and questions will extend their learning. Even though the Block area might not be the best place to dance, you can still include discussions and experiences that address music, visuals arts, and drama. Here are some examples of what teachers might say and do as they interact with children in the Block area to promote learning of the arts:

Music

It looks like you're making a music hall out of blocks like the one in this picture.

The blocks are loud when you clap them together. What musical instruments do we have that make a similar sound?

Drama

I wonder how we could use the blocks to put on a puppet show for our visitors.

How will you make the stage for your play?

Which blocks work best to represent the tall trees in the story?

Visual Arts

This poster has so many lines going in different directions. I wonder if we can make the blocks look like that.

What pattern can we make with the blocks? Would you like to draw that pattern?

Architects have to draw their constructions before they build. What will you draw to help you make your structure?

Observing Children's Understanding

As you observe children in the Block area, look for indications such as these that demonstrate an understanding of the components of the arts:

- Drawing a design and recreating it with blocks
- Asking questions about how an unusual building was constructed
- Comparing the sound of the blocks clapping together with other instruments
- Making props and sets for dramatic play
- Figuring out how to use the blocks for representational art
- Experimenting with making quiet and loud sounds with the blocks
- Building houses and other structures for toys
- Describing the process of making a building from previously drawn plans

The Arts in the Technology Area

As with all content areas, the arts can be easily and vastly explored using tablets, computers, digital cameras, and other technology tools. From using a finger to draw on a tablet to looking at vivid images of famous works of art on a computer screen, children have virtually limitless options for using their time and experiences in the Technology area to enhance their learning of the arts. Photography, sculpture, music, drama, dance, paintings – examples of all of these and more can be readily found online. Here are examples of how children's explorations in the Technology area relate to *The Creative Curriculum® for Preschool* objectives for the arts.

Examples of What a Child Might Do	Examples of Related Objectives for Development and Learning
Create a digital "painting."	33. Explores the visual arts
Use keyboard keys as piano keys in a music app.	34. Explores musical concepts and expression
Imitate a dance seen in a clip of dancers from another country.	35. Explores dance and movement concepts
Read an e-book of a story and then act it out.	36. Explores drama through actions and language

Materials for the Arts in the Technology Area

In addition to using the computer to research questions about different types of art, this interest area offers even more opportunities for learning beyond looking at images online. The tablet, smart board, digital camera, tablet, or a digital device for audio and video recordings can all be used as tools to express children's artistic ideas and share them with others. Be sure to provide writing and drawing materials in this area for children to use when inspiration strikes.

Using Technology to Teach the Arts

Children who enter your program with experience using technology tools may already have an understanding of how these tools can be used creatively. However, it's important to remember that technology should only be used to enhance learning. Your interactions with children as they use these tools is what they will benefit from the most. Here are examples of what you might say and ask to promote arts learning in this interest area:

Dance

Look at how quickly the dancers move their feet in the video. Can you move your feet that quickly?

Would you like to record your dance so that you can show your family later?

I wonder how we can find out why people do this traditional dance during a celebration.

Music

This app will help us write our own song. We can put the notes on the staff to make music.

I like the music you chose for the background of your recording. It's very soothing.

You're making music with the keys. What instrument does that sound like?

Drama

We can use the computer to write your script.

I wonder how we can find out what kind of materials are used to make those puppets.

This video shows actors rehearsing for their play. That means they're practicing.

Visual Arts

You're making a bold line with your finger. I see that you are making a shape inside of another shape.

This artist is an action painter. Watch how he moves when he paints. Would you like to try it?

We can zoom in on the tablet to see the tiny details of this painting. What do you notice?

Observing Children's Understanding

As children use a variety of technology devices to explore the arts, look for indications of their understanding, such as:

- Using the computer to research an artist
- Creating a painting using an app on the tablet
- Printing out a drawing made on the computer
- Taking pictures and displaying them around the classroom
- Demonstrating how to make music with the keyboard
- Recording music and playing it back for a classmate
- Working with a partner to design costumes for dramatic play
- Watching a video of dancers and then creating a new dance

The Arts in the Dramatic Play Area

Dramatic play is a great way for children to explore the arts and for you to observe their creativity. In addition to choosing a role and acting out a part, dramatic play can also mean creating props and sets or using toys to recreate familiar scenarios. Support children as they explore their creativity, and be mindful of children who are not inclined to perform for others. Help them contribute to dramatic play and offer their own ideas for drama. Here are examples of how children's explorations in the Dramatic Play area relate to *The Creative Curriculum® for Preschool* objectives for the arts.

Examples of What a Child Might Do	Examples of Related Objectives for Development and Learning
Paint a tree to hang on the wall to represent a forest.	33. Explores the visual arts
Ask other children to play in a band.	34. Explores musical concepts and expression
Move like an animal around the room.	35. Explores dance and movement concepts
Pretend to make pancakes using a toy stove.	36. Explores drama through actions and language

Materials for the Arts in the Dramatic Play Area

Dramatic play occurs when children spontaneously use the props to imitate adults and real-life situations. This interest area is a natural venue for creative exploration as children think of new ways to express ideas through drama, which can lead to more ideas about visual art, dance, and music. Take stock of this interest area regularly. You want to make sure that props are open ended and support the current dramatic play interests of children.

Materials

props based on children's ideas for dramatic play scenarios

writing and drawing materials

musical instruments

dance props (e.g., tap shoes, scarves, costumes, etc.)

images of actors on stage

digital device for audio/video recordings

mirrors

open-ended props (e.g., cardboard boxes, scarves, cardboard tubes, etc.)

props that represent different jobs in the community

Suggested Books

(Titles preceded by an asterisk are included in the *Teaching Strategies® Children's Book Collection*.)

Curious George and the Rocket (H. A. Rey)

The Farmyard Jamboree (Margaret Read McDonald)

Goldilocks and the Three Dinosaurs (Mo Willems)

Harold and the Purple Crayon (Crockett Johnson)

How to Draw a Dragon (Douglas Florian)

Klimt and His Cat (Berenice Capatti)

Matisse the King of Color (Laurence Anholt)

Mr. Wayne's Masterpiece (Patricia Polacco)

Picasso and the Girl With the Ponytail (Laurence Anholt)

Presto Change-o! (Edouard Manceau)

Snow White in New York (Fiona French)

Stompin' at the Savoy: The Story of Norma Miller (Alan Govenar)

Touch the Art: Brush Mona Lisa's Hair (Julie Appel)

Touch the Art: Make Van Gogh's Bed (Julie Appel and Amy Guglielmo)

The Usborne Book of Fairy Tales (Heather Amery and Stephen Cartwright)

**Who Wears What?* (Judith Bauer Stamper)

Using Dramatic Play to Teach the Arts

You may find that children work together to carry out their own dramatic play with little prompting. You might also observe children in this interest area looking for additional ideas. As you observe and interact with children, think about how you can ask open-ended questions and offer comments that encourage children to further explore their creative ideas. For example, if children decide they are on a rocket ship, encourage them to use their imaginations to explore the sights and sounds of the experience. Children can then enhance their play with additional props, sound effects, or artwork depicting their surroundings. Here are some examples of what teachers might say and do as they interact with children in the Dramatic Play area to promote children's learning of the arts:

Dance

Look at your colorful costume! It looks like what we saw the dancers wear on our site visit.

I see you're pretending to have a party. Are you going to dance at your party?

Music

It looks like you've made an instrument repair shop like the one we saw in the book. Can you please fix this instrument for me? Can you help me make a sound with it?

I wonder what we'll need for our marching band.

Drama

Hello there, teacher. May I sit at the table while you teach me?

How can we make this area look like the forest from the story we read earlier?

What do you need to wear to keep you safe when you go to put out the fire?

What would happen if the farmer didn't bring the fruits and vegetables to your store?

Observing Children's Understanding

As you observe and interact with children engaged in dramatic play, look for these indications that they are learning and applying art concepts:

- Creating props for retelling a story
- Staying in character as you ask questions
- Asking for help designing a backdrop for a show
- Explaining why the area is set up to look like a house
- Dressing up and talking about the clothes in the interest area
- Recalling details from a site visit and adding props to the interest area
- Working with others to act out a show
- Painting a sign to hang on the wall for the pretend shop

The Arts in the Sand and Water Area

The Sand and Water area is a great interest area for supporting children's curiosity about the properties of different materials. Children may pay attention to the sound the water makes when it is poured into an empty bowl or the way they can draw in wet sand but not in dry. Here are examples of how children's hands-on explorations in the Sand and Water area relate to *The Creative Curriculum® for Preschool* objectives for the arts.

Examples of What a Child Might Do	Examples of Related Objectives for Development and Learning
Look at photos of sand sculptures.	33. Explores the visual arts
Tap on cups of water filled to different levels.	34. Explores musical concepts and expression
Move side to side while pouring sand from one container to another.	35. Explores dance and movement concepts
Pretend to work at a construction site while scooping sand.	36. Explores drama through actions and language

Materials for the Arts in the Sand and Water Area

Using materials typically found in a preschool classroom provides plenty of opportunities for children to explore the arts in this interest area. You can also supplement those materials based on children's interests. For example, if you show children photos of sand sculptures, you may want to add additional carving and molding tools for wet sand. Or if you notice children pretending to work at a construction site, offer hard hats and work vests for them to wear as they play.

Materials

- costumes
- digital device to record the sounds made by the sand or water
- photos of sand sculptures
- rocks, shells, and other materials found in sand/water
- variety of containers for making sounds with water
- materials for making sand-filled shakers
- colored sand
- variety of small vehicles
- props for pretend play (e.g., cups and pitchers, plastic test tubes, toy animals, etc.)

Suggested Books

(Titles preceded by an asterisk are included in the *Teaching Strategies*® *Children's Book Collection*.)

**The Adventures of Gary & Harry: A Tale of Two Turtles* (Lisa Matsumoto)

Downpour (Emily Martin)

Fancy Nancy: Sand Castles and Sand Palaces (Jane O'Connor)

The First Drawing (Mordicai Gerstein)

Float (Daniel Miyares)

Flotsam (David Wiesner)

Harold and the Purple Crayon Under the Sea (Liza Baker)

I'm the Best Artist in the Ocean (Kevin Sherry)

Journey (Aaron Becker)

Mouse Paint (Ellen Stoll Walsh)

Pool (Jihyeon Lee)

Water Dance (Thomas Locker)

Using the Sand and Water Area to Teach the Arts

Think about all of the ways that children can creatively engage their senses at the sand and water table. Their experiences there may also inspire them to create new types of art such as sand sculpture or musical water. Encourage children to explore dramatic play ideas as well as you support their explorations of art experiences using sand and water. Here are some examples of what teachers might say and do as they interact with children in the Sand and Water area to promote understanding of the arts:

Dance

That water flows so smoothly. Can you move your body smoothly like that?

I wonder if we can make up a dance using the sand shakers that we made.

Music

Why do you think the sound changes when we pour more water into the bottle?

I like the rhythm you're making when you drip water out of the eye dropper.

What happens when we fill the bottle with sand instead of water? What sound does it make?

Drama

I see you're working very hard to build the castle for the princess.

What will you need to finish making your sand bricks?

You made a waterfall! And you're the mermaid swimming.

Visual Arts

I see you drawing in the wet sand. What does it feel like?

What can we do with water to make our picture?

How can we change the texture of our dough with sand? What can we make with it?

Observing Children's Understanding

As you observe children in the Sand and Water area, look for indications such as these that demonstrate an understanding of the components of the arts:

- Tapping on water pipes to make sound
- Describing how the water moves through the funnel
- Filling a container with colored sand and describing the process
- Drawing in wet sand
- Pretending to be a construction worker moving a bulldozer through the sand
- Asking questions about how sand sculptures are made
- Using tools to sculpt with sand
- Working with another child to create a scenario for the play animals in the water

The Arts in the Music and Movement Area

The Music and Movement area is a fantastic place for children to connect their music experiences to other artistic experiences that often coincide with music. As children play or move to music, they may add in more intentional dancing or make connections to visual art. Here are examples of how children's art experiences in this interest area relate to *The Creative Curriculum® for Preschool* objectives for art.

Examples of What a Child Might Do	Examples of Related Objectives for Development and Learning
Talk about the movement represented in a painting.	33. Explores the visual arts
Join in with other children playing instruments.	34. Explores musical concepts and expression
Create a dance to accompany a new song.	35. Explores dance and movement concepts
Participate in a song that includes movements to represent different ideas.	36. Explores drama through actions and language

Materials for the Arts in the Music and Movement Area

Think about how you can supplement the materials in this area in order to support children's further art explorations. For example, adding drawing materials can help children "see" the music they listen to. Introduce new and unusual musical instruments and recordings of music from around the world. Add props for creative expression through dancing and drama such as costumes and masks.

Materials

variety of costumes and masks

recordings of world music

photos of unusual instruments

audio or video recordings of instruments being played

a digital device to record children's experiences

photos of dancers

writing and drawing materials

images of a variety of works of art

Suggested Books

Action Jackson (Jan Greenberg)

Baby Danced the Polka (Karen Beaumont)

Boom Bah! (Phil Cummings)

Degas and the Dance (Jill DeVonyar)

Degas and the Little Dancer (Laurence Anholt)

Elephants Cannot Dance! (Mo Willems)

Giraffes Can't Dance (Giles Andreae)

Hilda Must Be Dancing (Karma Wilson)

How Can You Dance? (Rick Walton)

I Hope You Dance (Mark D. Sanders)

Kali's Song (Jeanette Winter)

Meet the Orchestra (Ann Hayes)

Olivia Forms a Band (Ian Falconer)

The Only Boy in Ballet Class (Denise Gruska)

Popsy in Ballet My Way (Tammy Laframboise)

Swing Sisters (Karen Deans)

Using the Music and Movement Area to Teach the Arts

When interacting with children in this interest area, make sure to observe first before entering their play. Although children will likely be eager to include you in their music and movement experiences, it is important to give them time to fully explore their artistic ideas. Encourage children to share their ideas with others and, if interested, collaborate to create new opportunities for exploring the arts. Here are some examples of what teachers might say and do as they interact with children to promote their understanding of the arts:

Dance

Your dance is very fluid. That means you're moving smoothly.

I wonder how we can make our shoes make a tapping sound like the shoes in the video.

What kind of dance do you think you would do if...?

Music

Your instruments sound great together! I'm going to close my eyes and try to name each instrument I hear.

How can we find out what makes the drum so loud?

I wonder if we can make our own instruments.

Drama

I see you're using your flashlight to dance like a firefly.

What costume will you wear as the orchestra conductor?

How can we make instruments like the ones in the story?

Visual Arts

How are the dancers moving in this painting? How can you tell they're moving?

What music does this painting make you think of?

I wonder if we can make a sculpture of someone dancing.

Observing Children's Understanding

As you observe and interact with children in the Music and Movement area, look for indications of their understanding of art concepts, such as:

- Playing musical instruments
- Talking about their roles as musicians and dancers
- Dancing along to a new song
- Comparing the sounds of different instruments
- Practicing singing in different pitches
- Asking questions about how certain dances are done
- Noticing the details of a performer's costume
- Explaining a plan for putting on a dance show

The Arts and the Outdoors

Children's art explorations outdoors are very different from those that take place in the classroom. Outside, children are free to move with big gestures, sing loudly, and use chalk to create artwork without worrying about a mess to clean up. Children's experiences outdoors may be an extension of their inside play (e.g., looking for leaves to add to their collage) or they may be creating all new experiences with the resources that are reserved for outside play. Here are examples of how children's explorations relate to *The Creative Curriculum® for Preschool* objectives for the arts.

Examples of What a Child Might Do	Examples of Related Objectives for Development and Learning
Use water to paint on the sidewalk.	33. Explores the visual arts
Hang a wind chime in a tree.	34. Explores musical concepts and expression
Dance on the playground with widespread arms.	35. Explores dance and movement concepts
Pretend to be the king of the castle while on a climbing structure.	36. Explores drama through actions and language

Materials for the Arts Outdoors

Children can usually find plenty of ways to explore their creative ideas outdoors. By adding a few materials and paying attention to the children's interests, you can scaffold their artistic experiences outside and encourage them to create freely – art, music, dance, and drama.

Materials

mirrors

large paper and paint for mural making

costumes that allow children to move freely

variety of classroom materials to be used as musical instruments

digital camera

props for dramatic play

recordings of lively music

writing and drawing materials

streamers and scarves

buckets and paintbrushes

Suggested Books

Art & Max (David Weisner)

Calling the Doves (Juan Felipe Herrera)

Can You Find It Outside? (Jessica Schulte)

The Cave Painting of Lascaux (Roberta Angeletti)

Chalk (Bill Thomson)

Cloud Dance (Thomas Locker)

Cuckoo (Lois Ehlert)

The Curious Garden (Peter Brown)

Duck! Rabbit! (Amy Krouse Rosenthal)

The Fantastic Jungles of Henri Rousseau (Michelle Markel)

Get Into Art Animals (Susie Brooks)

Harold's Trip to the Sky (Crockett Johnson)

King for a Day (Rukhsana Khan)

The Magical Garden of Claude Monet (Laurence Anholt)

Outstanding in the Rain (Frank Viva)

Rick & Rack and the Great Outdoors (Ethan Long)

Sidewalk Flowers (JonArno Lawson)

Sky Color (Peter H. Reynolds)

Van Gogh and the Sunflowers (Laurence Anholt)

Using the Outdoors to Teach the Arts

The time you spend outside with children is important because it gives everyone a chance to freely express themselves. Instead of being a spectator in children's outdoor play, take this time to join in the dramatic play or chalk drawing that occurs. As children play outdoors, extend their learning by asking questions that encourage them to think beyond their original idea and explore further. Here are examples of what you might say and ask:

Dance

How do we dance differently outside than inside?

What do you think we can use the balls for in our dance?

I wonder how we can move like the trees blowing in the wind.

Music

Listen to the outdoor sounds. What do you hear?

Can we use these natural materials to make instruments?

Why do you think that wind chime sounds different from this one?

Drama

I see that you're swinging high on your jungle vine!

What would happen if you step down into the sandbox? Does that mean you'll sink in the quicksand?

How can we use these cones to help us make the roads for bikes to ride on?

Visual Arts

I wonder what will happen when the chalk drawing gets wet.

Look at all of the beautiful colors in the sky. Do you think we could make colors like that with our paint?

Those trees look like the landscape painting we saw in our art book.

Observing Children's Understanding

As you observe and interact with children outdoors, notice when they demonstrate an understanding of art concepts, such as:

- Using natural materials to make collages
- Creating musical instruments from sticks and other items
- Choosing roles for dramatic play on the climbing equipment
- Making roads in the sandbox and pretending to drive the trucks along them
- Acting as a crossing guard while children ride their scooters
- Dancing using big movements
- Asking questions about how lines were painted on the playground
- Carrying a basket and pretending to be Little Red Riding Hood

9 Planning Your Arts Program

Guiding Children's Learning of the Arts 219

Creating an Environment for Learning the Arts 220

Integrating the Arts Throughout the Day 221

Guiding Children's Learning of the Arts

In preschool, many children are excited to try new creative experiences. They are typically confident artists, musicians, and actors. For children who are less outspoken, you may find that one-on-one interactions help a child feel more confident and will help you to better understand his or her interests and abilities. Pay attention to what children prefer to do and offer plenty of those experiences. Also look for opportunities to introduce new skills and creative ideas.

No matter what your current study topic or daily plan may be, the arts should always be a part of children's everyday learning. Not all components of the arts need to be included every day, but they should be considered when planning to decide how to incorporate them. Remember to follow children's lead as well as they come to school with their own songs, dances, and ideas for music making.

Keep the following questions in mind when planning for children's learning of the arts:

- What interest have children shown in the arts?
- How can I choose daily resources and enhance interest areas in order to support children's exploration of the arts?
- What are other ways I can include the arts in the preschool day?

Your Teaching Practice

Taking pride in the work that you and your children do does not mean that work samples and displays must look perfect. Look around your room at the displays of children's artwork. Do the examples look like they were created entirely by children? If so, then they may look messy and disorganized. Remember that children are proud to display their creative work, and where you might see a mess, they see a masterpiece. Think about how you feel about the displays in our room and how the displays reflect the work you do with children.

Creating an Environment for Learning the Arts

Because of children's natural interest and pleasure in creative activities, including the arts in your classroom doesn't require a great deal of planning time in addition to your other preparations. You can think of ways to add songs, dances, and drama to any part of the day. However, you can supplement these simple moments with intentionally planned individual, small-group, and large-group experiences that enhance children's creative experiences and knowledge.

Strategies for Creating Spaces for Arts Experiences

To create an environment for learning the arts, consider the basic principles that are presented in the following chart.

Strategies	Examples
Organize materials to encourage children's hands-on art explorations.	Include art materials around the room that invite exploration (e.g., streamers for movement, masks for dramatic play, musical instruments, etc.).
Display photos and examples of art, artists, musicians, dancers, and actors.	Throughout the room, look for opportunities to include examples of the arts for children to see at eye level and reference during their play, such as • prints and posters of famous works of art • photos of actors in costume • examples of a variety of musical instruments • images of dancers from around the world • examples of children's artwork signed by the artist
Include learning materials for the arts in all interest areas.	Think about how art enhancements to the interest areas will support children's current investigations. Look for ways to extend children's learning in a particular interest area by introducing art materials.

While offering art materials throughout the day and throughout the room goes a long way toward encouraging children's learning of the arts, it's the interactions you have with children that will support their deeper understanding and critical thinking of how art materials are used, how art can make them feel, and what their artistic contributions to the classroom community might be.

Integrating the Arts Throughout the Day

As previously mentioned, most children are eager to pick up a paintbrush or musical instrument and explore different ways to use it. That's why it is easy to provide a classroom environment that supports children's art learning. But, as the teacher, you have an opportunity to make the arts so much more than just a sheet of paper and a paintbrush or a familiar song to dance to. The arts can be an integral part of your daily experiences with children, independent of the time of day or study topic that you're currently focusing on. Consider the following ideas for incorporating the arts into daily experiences and reinforcing children's knowledge of the arts.

Arrival

Preparing the Environment

Choose a *Mighty Minutes®* activity that includes a song or dance to welcome children as they begin their day at school.

Display a print or poster of a work of art for children to see when they arrive.

Post lyrics to a new welcome song for children and families to see when they enter the class.

Display children's artwork from the previous day.

Interactions

Sing a welcome song that includes children's names as you welcome them.

Show children an example of a work of art and ask children to look at it and point out something they notice.

Invite children to enter the classroom by pretending to be a character or animal (e.g., *Let's pretend we're puppies like the puppies we saw yesterday at the animal shelter.)*.

Large-Group Time

Preparing the Environment

Display a work of art (either abstract or figurative) to discuss with children.

Post lyrics to the song you plan to share with children.

Set out any musical instruments or movement materials needed.

Review any story you plan to share for story retelling ideas and props needed.

Prepare any clips of recorded music to share with the group.

Interactions

Introduce musical instruments and demonstrate how to use them.

Ask questions that prompt children to observe a work of art and discuss it.

Encourage children to join in any songs or dances you share.

Introduce a new song or dance, and repeat it a few times so that children can learn it.

Refer to the lyrics of the song you share.

Build time in your large-group experience for children to be up and moving around the space.

Choice Time

Preparing the Environment

Set up materials in interest areas, such as musical instruments, props in Dramatic Play, audio and/or video recordings of musicians, dancers, and actors, etc.

Refer to the current study topic for ideas on enhancing interest areas for experiences related to the arts.

Display works of art around the room at children's eye level.

Prepare any art materials needed for chosen art projects.

Have ready a recording device for creating audio or video recordings.

Interactions

Interact with children by describing what you see them doing.

Notice aloud how children create different types of art.

Talk with children about examples of visual art displayed around the room.

If applicable, support children to further explore the current study topic through art investigations.

Join in children's dramatic play as a way to extend their learning and encourage new ideas.

Record children's music, dance, and dramatic play experiences to share with families later.

Remind children of any unfinished artwork from early in the week. Ask them if they want to continue that play or begin something new instead.

Small-Group Time

Preparing the Environment

Gather any art materials to be used for the experience.

Prepare print or other visual materials.

Provide writing and drawing materials.

Interactions

Include songs, dances, and drama in small-group experiences.

Encourage children to draw their ideas and/or illustrate the ideas generated by the group.

Work with children to create new songs and movement activities.

When possible, use song lyrics, drama, or movement to help children better understand the learning taking place during this time.

Snack and Mealtime

Preparing the Environment

Display examples of art related to food, such as still life paintings.

Post the lyrics to a simple song to sing as children come to the table.

Include a few examples of decorative serving pieces, such as a multicolored bowl or a plate with a design.

Interactions

Sing a song with children that signals them to join you at the table.

Talk with children about any visual art examples.

Invite children to make placemats using construction paper. When laminated, they can be used and cleaned easily. Point out what you notice about children's artwork on the placemats.

Allow children to take turns dramatizing roles such as chef or waiter.

Transitions

Preparing the Environment

Choose *Mighty Minutes*® and *Mega Minutos*® to introduce children to new songs.

Plan in advance for any appropriate activities that include singing, dancing, and other movements, such as:

Mighty Minutes 06, "This Is the Way"

Mighty Minutes 34, "The Wave"

Mighty Minutes 106, "Silly Dance"

Mighty Minutes 181, "Line Dancing"

Mighty Minutes 30 "Bounce, Bounce, Bounce"

Mighty Minutes 63, "Going on a Journey"

Mighty Minutes 137, "Cat & Cow Yoga"

Clear a space for children to move their bodies freely during transitions.

Interactions

Sing a familiar song with children that signals the next classroom experience.

Assign children different roles to play during transitions (e.g., *Let's move like monkeys on our way to the door.*).

Include children when selecting one of the *Mighty Minutes*®.

Outdoor Time

Preparing the Environment

Add musical instruments, scarves and streamers, and other music and movement materials to the outdoor space.

Hang a wind chime outdoors.

Include props for outdoor dramatic play (e.g., traffic signs, butterfly nets and binoculars, construction worker vests, etc.).

Provide materials for children to create their own wind chimes.

Include art materials for weaving, such as colorful ribbons, shiny string, etc.

Interactions

Encourage children to use the outdoor equipment for dramatic play (e.g., the climbing structure is a mountain or the sandbox is a pit in the jungle).

Form a marching band with children using a variety of materials.

Invite children to sing songs and vary the volume of their voices as they sing.

Call out a variety of movements for children to explore.

Rest Time

Preparing the Environment

Choose calming music to play.

Set up props for children to put baby dolls and stuffed animals to bed.

Interactions

Ask children to join you in a movement activity that gets progressively slower and quieter to help them prepare to rest.

Invite children to put their babies to bed before resting.

Sing a familiar song with children that signals rest time.

Departure

Preparing the Environment

Post lyrics to a song to share with families.

Make copies of a song that includes new words to a familiar tune.

Interactions

Share the take-home song with families when they arrive. Encourage families to sing the song at home together.

Invite children to sing with you as they prepare to leave.

Ask children to pretend to be different people or animals during their departure routine (e.g., *Can you howl like a wolf while you lift your head to put your sweater on*?).

End the day with a shared dance experience.

References

Ärlemalm-Hagsér, E. (2013). Respect for nature–A prescription for developing environmental awareness in preschool. *CEPS Journal, 3*(10), 25–44.

Bailey, M., & Blagojevic, B. (2015). Innovate, educate, and empower: New Opportunities with new technologies. In Chip Donahue (Ed.), *Technology and Digital Media in the Early Years: Tools for Teaching and Learning* (pp. 162–182). New York: Routledge; Washington, DC: NAEYC.

Bentley, D. (2013). *Everyday artists: Inquiry and creativity in the early childhood classroom*. New York: Teachers College Press.

Bentley, D., & Reppuci, A. (2013). "I think they all felt distressed! Talking about complex issues in early childhood. *Childhood Education, 89*(1), 9–14.

Berson, I. R., & Berson, M. J. (Eds.). (2010). *High-tech tots: Childhood in a digital world*. Charlote, NC: Information Age.

Blagojevic, B., & Thomes, K. (2014). Preschoolers take tech outdoors. *Teaching Young Children, 7*(2), 30–31.

Bond, V. L. (2015). Sounds to share: The state of music education in three Reggio-Emilia-inspired North American preschools. *Journal of Research in Music Education, 62*(4), 462–484.

Bradley, K., & Szegda, M. (2012). *The dance of learning handbook of research on the education of young children*. Abingdon: Routledge Handbooks Online.

Brenneman, K. (2014). The progress of education reform: Science in the early years. *Education Commission of the States, 15*(2).

Brillante, P., & Mankiw, S. (2015). A sense of place: Human geography in the early childhood classroom. *Social Studies: From a Sense of Self to a Sense of the World, 70*(3), 16–23.

Brown, V. (1990). Drama as an integral part of the early childhood curriculum. *Design for Arts in Education, 91*(6), 26–33.

Carraway-Stage, V., Henson, S. R., Dipper, A., Spangler, H., Ash, S. L., & Goodell, L. S. (2014). Understanding the state of nutrition education in the Head Start classroom: A qualitative approach. *American Journal of Health Education, 45*(1), 52–62.

Catterall, J. S., & Peppler, K. A. (2007). Learning in the visual arts and the worldviews of young children. *Cambridge Journal of Education, 37*(4), 542–560.

Center for Information Science Education at the Florida Museum of Natural History/ University of Florida. (2004, 2014). *Marvelous explorations through science and stories: Our natural world, teachers' guide*. U. S. Department of Health and Human Services, Administration for Children and Families, Office of Head Start.

Charlesworth, R. (2011). *Understanding child development* (8th ed.). New York: Thomson Delmar Learning.

Cicconi, M. (2014). Vygotsky meets technology: A reinvention of collaboration in the early childhood mathematics classroom. *Early Childhood Education Journal, 42*, 57–65.

Cohen, L. E., & Stupiansky, S. (2013). *Learning across the early childhood curriculum (advances in early education and day care, volume 17).* Emerald Group Publishin.

Conscious Discipline. (2014). The school family: The foundation for connections. http://consciousdiscipline.com/about/the_school_family.asp accessed 10/21/2015.

Couchenour, D., & Chrisman K. (2013). *Families, schools, and communities: Together for young children* (5th ed.). Belmont, CA: Wadsworth Cengage Learning.

Currenton, S. M., & Ryan, S. K. (2006). Oral storytelling: A cultural art that promotes school readiness. *Young Children, 61*(5), 78–89.

Derman-Sparks, L., & Olsen Edwards, J. (2010). *Anti-bias education for young children and ourselves.* Washington, DC: NAEYC.

Dodge, D. T., Colker, L. J., & Heroman, C. (2002). *The creative curriculum® for preschool* (4th ed.). Bethesda, MD: Teaching Strategies.

Dominguez, L., McDonald, J., Kalajian, K., & Stafford, K. (2013). Exploring the wild world of wiggly worms! *Science and Children, 51*(4), 44–49.

Donahue, C., & Schomburg, R. (2015). Teaching with technology: Preparing early childhood educators for the digital age. In Chip Donahue (Ed.)., *Technology and Digital Media in the Early Years: Tools for Teaching and Learning* (pp. 36–53). New York: Routledge; Washington, DC: NAEYC.

Dow, C. (2010). *Young children and movement: The power of creative dance.* Washington, DC: NAEYC.

Engdahl, I., & Rabusicová, M. (2011). Children's voices about the state of the earth. *International Journal of Early Childhood, 43*(2), 153–176.

Fantozzi, V. B., Cottino, E., & Gennarelli, C. (2013). Mapping their place: Preschoolers explore space, place, and literacy. *Social Studies and the Young Learner, 26*(1), 5–10.

Feeney, S., & Freeman, N. K. (2012). *Ethics and the early childhood educator: Using the NAEYC Code* (2nd ed.). Washington, DC: NAEYC.

Feeney, S., Moravcki, E., Nolte, S., & Christensen, D. (2010). Who am I in the lives of children? An introduction to early childhood education (8th ed.). New York: Pearson.

Fred Rogers Center. (2012). *A framework for quality in digital media for young children: Considerations for parents, educators, and media creators.* Author.

Gibson Warash, B., Day, J., Workman, M., Troilo, J., Law, K., & Devito, M. (2013). History invades the preschool classroom. *Journal of Modern Education Review, 3*(6), 478–483.

Guernsey, L., & Levine, M. H. (2015). Pioneering literacy in the digital age. In Chip Donahue (Ed.), *Technology and Digital Media in the Early Years: Tools for Teaching and Learning* (pp. 104–115). New York: Routledge; Washington, DC: NAEYC.

Hamlin, M., & Wisneski, D. B. (2012). Supporting the scientific thinking and inquiry of toddlers and preschoolers through play. *Young Children, 67*(3), 82–88.

Hawkins, K. (2014). Teaching for social justice, social responsibility, and social inclusion: A respectful pedagogy for twenty-first century early childhood education. *European Early Childhood Education Research Journal, 22*(5), 723–738.

Heffron, S., & Downs, R. (2012). *Geography for life* (2nd ed.). National Council for Geographic Education.

Honig, A. S., & Mennerich, M. (2013). What does "go green" mean to children? Early Development and Care, 183(2), 171–184.

Howell, J., & Reinhard, K. (2015). *Rituals and traditions: Fostering a sense of community in preschool.* Washington, DC: NAEYC.

Hsiao, C-Y., & Shih, P-Y. (2015). The impact of using picture books with preschool students on the teaching of environmental concepts. *International Education Studies, 8*(3), 14–23.

ISTE (International Society for Technology in Education). (2007). *ISTE standards, students.* ISTE.

Jackman, H. L., Beaver, N. H., & Skinner Wyatt, S. (2015). The child's world: Social studies and dramatic play. (pp. 183–226). *Early education curriculum* (6th ed.). Stamford, CT: Cengage Learning.

Kahriman-Öztürk, D. (2010). Preschool children's attitudes towards selected environmental issues. Yayinlanmamis yüsek lisans tezi. Orta dogu Teknik Üniversitesi, Sosyal Bilimler Enstitüsü, Ankara.

Kaldor, T. (2015). Technology as a tool to strengthen the home-school connection. In Chip Donahue (Ed.), *Technology and Digital Media in the Early Years: Tools for Teaching and Learning* (pp. 201–217). New York: Routledge; Washington, DC: NAEYC.

Kara, G. E., Aydoes, E. H., & Aydun, Ö. (2015). Changing preschool children's attitudes into behavior towards selected environmental issues: An action research study. *International Journal of Education in Mathematics, Science, and Technology, 3*(1), 46–63.

Klerfelt, A. (2011). Call for articles: Special edition of the International journal of Early Childhood on early childhood arts education. *International Journal of Early Childhood, 43*(2), 185–186.

Kneas, K., & Perry, B. (2011). Using technology in the early childhood classroom. *Teaching Resources, Children's Book Recommendations, and Student Activities. Scholastic.com.* Scholastic.

Kom-Bursztyn, C. (Ed.). (2012). *Young children and the arts: Nurturing imagination and creativity.* USA: Information Age Publishing.

Koster, J. (2012). *Growing artists: Teaching the arts to young children* (5th ed.). Belmont, CA: Wadsworth Cengage Learning.

McDonel, J. S. (2015). Exploring learning connections between music and mathematics in early childhood. *Bulletin of the Council for Research in Music Education, 203*, 45–62.

Mills, H. (2014). The importance of creative arts in early childhood classrooms. *Texas Child Care Quarterly, 38*(1).

Mindes, G. (2015). Pushing up the social studies from early childhood education to the world. *Social Studies: From a Sense of Self to a Sense of the World, 70*(3), 10–15.

Moomaw, S. (2012). STEM begins in the early years. *School Science & Mathematics, 112*(2), 57–58.

National Council for Social Studies. (2009). Powerful and purposeful teaching and learning in elementary school studies. Position Statement: National Council for Social Studies.

National Council for Social Studies. (2010). *National Curriculum Standards for Social Studies: A Framework for Teaching, Learning, and Assessment.* Silver Spring, MD: NCSS.

NAEYC (National Association for the Education of Young Children). (2013). All criteria document, 17–18. Retrieved from www.naeyc.org/files/academy/file/AllCriteriaDocument.pdf

NAEYC, & the Fred Rogers Center. (2012). Technology and interactive media as tools in early childhood programs serving children from birth through age 8. (Position Statement adopted January 2012).

National Research Council (NRC). (2012). *A framework for K–12 science education: Practices, crosscutting concepts, and core ideas.* Washington, DC: National Academies Press.

NSTA (National Science Teachers Association). (2014). *NSTA position statement: Early childhood science education.* National Science Teachers Association.

PBS Parents. (2015). Creating with media: Preschoolers. Retrieved from www.pbs.org/parents/childrenandmedia/creating-preschool.html

Pinciutti, P. (1993). Creative drama and young children: The dramatic learning connection. *Arts Education Policy Review, 94*(6), 24–28.

Ranck, E. R. (2012). Where in the world are our children? The child as emerging geographer. *Exchange* (19460406). (205), 28–32.

Robb, M. B., & Lauricella, A. R. (2015). Connecting child development and technology: What we know and what it means. In Chip Donahue (Ed.), *Technology and Digital Media in the Early Years: Tools for Teaching and Learning* (pp. 70–85). New York: Routledge; Washington, DC: NAEYC.

Robles de Meléndez, W., & Beck, V. (2013). *Teaching young children in multicultural classrooms: Issues, concepts, and strategies* (4th ed.). Belmont, CA: Wadsworth Cengage Learning.

Rogow, F. (2015). Media literacy in early childhood education: Inquiry-based technology integration. In Chip Donahue (Ed.), *Technology and Digital Media in the Early Years: Tools for Teaching and Learning* (pp. 91–103). New York: Routledge; Washington, DC: NAEYC.

Roy, D., Baker, B., & Hamilton, A. (2015). *Teaching the arts: Early childhood & primary education* (2nd ed.). Sydney: Cambridge University Press.

Samarapungavan, A., Patrick, H., & Mantazicopoulos, P. (2011). What kindergarten students learn in inquiry-based science classrooms. *Cognition and Instruction, 29*(4), 416–470.

Samuelsson, I. P., Carlsson, M. A., Olsson, B., Pramling, N., & Wallerstedt, D. (2009). The art of teaching children the arts: Music, dance, and poetry with children aged 2–8 years old. *International Journal of Early Years Education, 17*(2), 119–135.

Santoli, S., Vitualli, P., & Giles, R. (2015). Picturing equality: Exploring Civil Rights' marches through photographs. *The Social Studies, 106*(2), 72–76.

Saracho, O. (Ed.). (2012). *Contemporary perspectives on research in creativity in early childhood education.* USA: Cambridge University Press.

Sayers Adomat, D. (2012). Drama's potential for deepening young children's understandings of stories. *Early Childhood Education Journal, 40*, 343–350.

Sharapan, H. (2015). Technology as a tool for social–emotional development: What we can learn from Fred Rogers' approach. In Chip Donahue (Ed.)., *Technology and Digital Media in the Early Years: Tools for Teaching and Learning* (pp. 12–20). New York: Routledge; Washington, DC: NAEYC.

Sibley, A., & Kurz, T. (2014). Celebrating Earth Day with sustainability. *National Council of Teachers of Mathematics, 20*(8), 516–519.

Snow, C. E., Burns, M. S., & Griffin, P. (Eds.). (1998). *Preventing reading difficulties in young children*. Washington, DC: National Academy Press.

Suskind, D. (2015). *Thirty million words: Building a child's brain*. New York: Dutton.

Varelas, M., Pappas, C. C., Tucker-Raymond, E., Kane, J., Hankes, J., Ortix, I., & Keblawe-Shamah, N. (2010). Drama activities in ideational resources for primary-grade children in urban science classrooms. *Journal of Research in Science Teaching, 47*(3), 302–325.

Wright, C., Bacigalupa, C., Black, T., & Bourton, M. (2008). Windows into children's thinking: A guide to storytelling and dramatization. *Early Childhood Education Journal, 35*(4), 363–369.

Zan, B., & Geiken, R. (2010). Ramps and pathways: Developmentally appropriate, intellectually rigorous, and fun physical science. *Young Children, 65*(1), 12–17.

Index

A

Adaptive equipment, 34
Advanced learners, studies and projects for, 35, 116, 182
Afternoon activities. *See* Daily schedule
Animals, caring for, 11
Anti-bias education, 94
Arrival. *See* Daily schedule
Arts, 160–225
- benefits of, 161–162
- block play and, 201–203
- books for, 190
- classroom space for, 220
- components of, 163
- cooking and, 198–200
- culture and, 97
- daily schedule for, 221–225
- dance. *See* Dance
- Discovery area and, 192–194
- drama. *See* Dramatic play
- environment for, 220
- interacting with children, 190–191
- interest areas and, 185
- library and, 186–188
- materials for, 189
- music and movement. *See* Music and movement
- objectives, 80, 162
- observing and responding to children, 191
- outdoor play and, 213–216, 224
- program planning, 218–225
- sand and water play and, 208–210
- technology and, 203–205
- toys and games and, 195–197
- visual. *See* Visual arts

Audio materials, recordings of children's play, 18, 24
Awareness of technology
- observing and responding to children, 18–19
- research on, 17
- teacher's role in promoting, 18
- tips for families, 19

B

Bedding. *See* Rest time
Bentley, D., 161
Block play
- arts and, 201–203
- books for, 47, 126, 202
- interacting with children, 48–49, 126–127, 202
- materials for, 47, 126, 201
- observing and responding to children, 49, 127, 203
- science and, 46–49
- social studies and, 125–127
- technology and, 46–49

Books
- for arts, 190
- for block play, 47, 126, 202
- for cooking, 68, 141, 199
- for Discovery area, 39, 132, 193
- for dramatic play, 51, 129, 206
- for music and movement, 65, 146, 211
- for outdoor play, 75, 149, 214
- reading aloud and visual arts, 165
- for sand and water play, 62, 138, 209
- selecting for library, 59, 120, 187. *See also* Library
- story retelling, 174
- for toys and games area, 44, 123, 196
- for visual arts, 55, 135, 165

C

Center time. *See* Choice time
Child development and learning
- in advanced learners, 35, 116, 182
- in children with disabilities. *See* Children with disabilities
- cognitive. *See* Cognitive development
- language. *See* Language development
- physical. *See* Physical development
- social–emotional. *See* Social–emotional development

Children's work, displaying in classroom, 164
Children with disabilities
- adaptive devices for, 34
- studies and projects for, 34, 115, 182

Choice time
- arts and, 222
- science and technology and, 86–87
- social studies and, 156–157

Classroom space
- for arts, 220
- displaying children's work in, 164
- living things, inclusion of, 11
- for music and movement, 167, 170
- pets and plants in, 11
- for science programs, 82–84
- for social studies programs, 153–155
- storage of technology tools, 21
- technology in, 82–84

Climate, classroom discussions of weather, 15
Closing of day. *See* Departure
Cognitive development
- objectives of, 80
- visual arts and, 161, 162

Communication
- by children. *See* Language development
- with children. *See* Interacting with children

Computer play. *See* Technology
Content of curriculum. *See specific curriculum areas*
Cooking
- arts and, 198–200
- books for, 68, 141, 199
- interacting with children, 69, 141–142, 199–200
- materials for, 68, 140, 198
- observing and responding to children, 70, 142, 200
- science and, 67–70
- social studies and, 140–142
- technology and, 67–70

Coordination
- fine-motor skills, 24
- gross-motor skills, 161

The Creative Curriculum®
- arts, 160–225. *See also* Arts
- interest areas. *See* Interest areas
- science, 2–91. *See also* Science
- social studies, 92–159. *See also* Social studies
- technology, 2–91. *See also* Technology

Creativity and original thinking, 161, 162, 173
Critical thinking, 93
Culture
- arts and, 97
- family involvement and, 97
- music and movement and, 170
- social studies and, 93–94

D

Daily schedule
- for arts, 221–225
- for science and technology programs, 84–91
- for social studies programs, 155–159

Dance, 169–172. *See also* Music and movement
- arts and, 190
- benefits of, 169
- cooking and, 199
- Discovery area and, 193
- dramatic play and, 207
- library and, 187
- music and movement and, 212
- observing and responding to children, 171
- outdoor play and, 215
- research on, 169
- sand and water play and, 209
- teacher's role, 170
- technology and, 204
- tips for families, 172
- toys and games and, 196

Departure. *See* Daily schedule
Digital devices. *See* Technology
Disabled children. *See* Children with disabilities
Discovery area
- arts and, 192–194
- books for, 39, 132, 193
- interacting with children, 40–41, 133, 193–194
- materials for, 38–39, 132, 192
- observing and responding to children, 41, 134, 194
- social studies and, 131–134

Displays in classroom, children's work, 164
Diversity. *See* Culture
Dramatic play
- benefits of, 173, 205
- blocks and, 202
- books for, 51, 129, 206
- cooking and, 199
- Discovery area and, 194
- interacting with children, 52–53, 130, 207
- language development and, 173
- library and, 188
- literacy skills and, 173
- materials and props for. *See* Dramatic props
- music and movement and, 212
- observing and responding to children, 53, 131, 175, 207
- as outdoor activity, 215
- research on, 174
- sand and water play and, 209
- social–emotional development and, 173
- social studies and, 93, 97, 128–131
- teacher's role in, 174–175
- technology and, 204
- tips for families, 176
- toys and games for, 197
- visual arts and, 191, 205–207

Dramatic props
- arts and, 206
- science and technology and, 50–51
- selecting and displaying, 175
- social studies and, 129
- for story retelling, 174

E

Earth and the environment. *See also* Science
- block play and, 49
- cooking and, 69
- Discovery area and, 41
- dramatic play and, 52
- library and, 60
- music and movement and, 66
- observing and responding to children, 15–16
- outdoor play and, 76
- predictions regarding, 16
- research on, 14
- sand and water play and, 63
- study components, 14
- teacher's role, 15
- technology and, 72
- tips for families, 16
- toys and games and, 45
- visual arts and, 56

Emotional self-regulation. *See* Social–emotional development
End of day. *See* Departure
English-language learners (ELL)
- objectives for, 80
- studies and projects for, 33, 115, 181

Environment in classroom. *See* Classroom space
Equipment. *See* Materials and equipment
Ethnic diversity. *See* Culture
Eye level of children, classroom displays at, 164

F

Facial expressions, 175
Family partnerships
- culture and, 97
- music and movement and, 170
- tips for. *See* Tips for families

Fantasy play. *See* Dramatic play
Fathers, participation by. *See* Family partnerships
Feelings of children. *See* Social–emotional development
Fine-motor skills, 24. *See also* Physical development
Food. *See* Mealtimes
Friendships, 27

G

Games. *See* Toys and games
Geography and spaces
- block play and, 127
- cooking and, 142
- Discovery area and, 133
- dramatic play and, 130
- library and, 121
- music and movement and, 147
- observing and responding to children, 109
- outdoor play and, 150
- research on, 108
- sand and water play and, 139
- study components, 107
- teacher's role, 108–109
- technology and, 144
- tips for families, 110
- toys and games and, 124
- visual arts and, 136

Gifted children. *See* Advanced learners
Goals. *See* Objectives
Gross-motor skills, 161. *See also* Physical development

H

Health issues, learning about, 10, 12
Hearing impaired children. *See* Children with disabilities

I

Imagination, 161
Independence of thought, 163
Intellectual development. *See* Cognitive development
Intentional Teaching Cards™, 27
Interacting with children. *See also* Teacher's role
- arts, 190–191
- block play, 48–49, 126–127, 202
- cooking, 69, 141–142, 199–200
- Discovery area, 40–41, 133, 193–194
- dramatic play, 52–53, 130, 207
- library, 60, 121, 187–188
- music and movement, 66, 147, 212
- outdoor play, 76–77, 150, 215
- sand and water play, 63, 138–139, 209
- technology, 144, 204
- toys and games area, 44–45, 124, 196–197
- visual arts, 56–57, 136

Interest areas
- arts, 184–216. *See also* Arts
- block play. *See* Block play
- cooking. *See* Cooking
- Discovery area. *See* Discovery area
- dramatic play. *See* Dramatic play
- library. *See* Library
- literacy skills in. *See* Literacy skills
- music and movement. *See* Music and movement
- outdoors. *See* Outdoor play
- sand and water. *See* Sand and water play
- science in, 36–77. *See also* Science
- social studies in, 118–151. *See also* Social studies
- technology, 36–77. *See also* Technology
- toys and games. *See* Toys and games
- visual arts. *See* Visual arts

Investigations, tools for, 24

K

Kitchen area. *See* Cooking
Koster, J., 161–162

L

Language development
- dramatic play and, 173
- objectives of, 80
- visual arts and, 161, 162

Large groups
- arts for, 221–222
- science and technology for, 85–86
- social studies for, 156

Learning environment
- classroom space. *See* Classroom space
- daily structure. *See* Daily schedule

Letters. *See* Literacy skills
Library. *See also* Books
- arts and, 186–188
- book selection, 59, 120, 187
- interacting with children, 60, 121, 187–188
- materials for, 58–59, 120, 186
- observing and responding to children, 61, 122, 188
- science and, 57–61
- social studies and, 119–122
- technology and, 57–61

Life science. *See also* Science
- block play and, 48
- components of, 10
- cooking and, 69
- Discovery area and, 40
- dramatic play and, 52
- library and, 60
- music and movement and, 66
- observing and responding to children, 12–13
- outdoor play and, 76
- research on, 11
- sand and water play and, 63
- teacher's role, 11–12
- technology and, 72
- tips for families, 13
- toys and games and, 45
- visual arts and, 56

Literacy skills
books and. *See* Books
dramatic play and, 173
language development and. *See* Language development
objectives, 80
Living things
inclusion in classroom, 11
study of. *See* Life science

M

Machines, study of, 29–35
Make believe. *See* Dramatic play
Makerspaces, 7
Mapping, 108, 109
Materials and equipment
adaptive, 34
for arts, 189
for block play, 47, 126, 201
for cooking, 68, 140, 198
for Discovery area, 38–39, 132, 192
for dramatic play. *See* Dramatic props
for library, 120, 186. *See also* Books
for music and movement, 65, 146, 211
for outdoor play, 75, 149, 214
for sand and water play, 62, 138, 208
for science activities, 7, 12
technology, 23–25, 71, 143, 204
for toys and games, 43, 123, 195
for visual arts, 55, 135, 164
Mathematics, objectives, 80
Mealtimes
arts and, 223
science and technology and, 88
social studies for, 157
Mobile devices. *See* Technology
Morning activities. *See* Daily schedule
Motor skills
fine-motor skills, 24
gross-motor skills, 161
Movement. *See* Dance; Music and movement
Musical instruments, 167
Music and movement
benefits of, 166, 210
block play and, 202
books for, 65, 146, 211
classroom space for, 167, 170
cooking and, 199
culture and, 170
dance, 169–172. *See also* Dance
Discovery area and, 194
dramatic play and, 207
family participation in, 170
interacting with children, 66, 147, 212
library and, 188
materials for, 65, 146, 211
observing and responding to children, 67, 148, 168, 213
as outdoor activities, 215
research on, 167
sand and water play and, 209
science and, 64–67
singing, 167–168
social studies and, 145–148
study of music making, 177–182
teacher's role, 167–168
technology and, 64–67, 204
terminology, 167
tips for families, 168
toys and games and, 196
visual arts and, 191, 212

N

Naps. *See* Rest time
National Education Longitudinal Survey (NELS), 161
National Science Teachers Association (NSTA), 11

O

Objectives
arts, 80, 162
cognitive development, 80
English-language learners, 80
language development, 80
literacy skills, 80
mathematics, 80
physical development, 80
science, 4, 80
social–emotional development, 80
social studies, 80, 94
technology, 4, 80
Observing and responding to children
arts, 191
block play, 49, 127, 203
cooking, 70, 142, 200
dance, 171
Discovery area, 41, 134, 194
dramatic play, 53, 131, 175, 207
library, 61, 122, 188
music and movement, 67, 148, 168, 213
outdoor play, 77, 151, 216
sand and water play, 64, 139, 210
science, 8, 12–13, 15–16
social studies, 98, 102, 106, 109
technology, 18–19, 25, 27–28, 73, 145, 205
toys and games, 46, 125, 197
visual arts, 57, 137, 165
Obstacle courses, 109
Open-ended questions. *See also* Interacting with children
Discovery area and, 38
in physical science, 7
Operations. *See* Technology operations and concepts
Oral language development. *See* Language development
Outdoor play
arts and, 213–216, 224
books for, 75, 149, 214
interacting with children, 76–77, 150, 215
materials for, 75, 149, 214
observing and responding to children, 77, 151, 216
sand and water play. *See* Sand and water play
science and, 74–77, 89–90
social studies and, 148–151, 158
technology and, 74–77, 89–90

P

Parents. *See* Family partnerships
Peer relationships, 27
People and how they live. *See also* Social studies
block play and, 127
cooking and, 141
Discovery area and, 133
dramatic play and, 130
library and, 121
music and movement and, 147
observing and responding to children, 98
outdoor play and, 150
research on, 96
sand and water play and, 138
study components, 95
teacher's role, 97
technology and, 144
tips for families, 99
toys and games and, 124
visual arts and, 136
People and technology. *See also* Technology
observing and responding to children, 27–28
research on, 26
teacher's role, 27
tips for families, 28
People and the environment. *See also* Social studies
block play and, 127
cooking and, 142
Discovery area and, 133
dramatic play and, 130
library and, 121
music and movement and, 147
observing and responding to children, 102
outdoor play and, 150
research on, 100
sand and water play and, 139
study components, 99
teacher's role, 101
technology and, 144
tips for families, 103
toys and games and, 124
visual arts and, 136
People and the past. *See also* Social studies
block play and, 127
cooking and, 142
Discovery area and, 133
dramatic play and, 130
library and, 121
music and movement and, 147
observing and responding to children, 106
outdoor play and, 150
research on, 104
sand and water play and, 139
study components, 103
teacher's role, 105
technology and, 144
tips for families, 107
toys and games and, 124
visual arts and, 136
Pets, caring for, 11
Physical development
objectives of, 80
visual arts and, 161

Physical science. *See also* Science
block play and, 48
components of, 5
cooking and, 69
Discovery area and, 40
dramatic play and, 52
library and, 60
music and movement and, 66
observing and responding to children, 8
outdoor play and, 76
research on, 6
sand and water play and, 63
teacher's role, 7
technology and, 72
tips for families, 9
toys and games and, 45
visual arts and, 56
Pictures drawn by children. *See* Visual arts
Planning, daily schedule. *See* Daily schedule
Plants in classroom, 11
Play
audio and video recordings of, 18, 24
block play. *See* Block play
dramatic play. *See* Dramatic play
outdoor. *See* Outdoor play
recyclable materials for, 101
sand and water. *See* Sand and water play
Predictions on Earth and the environment, 16
Pretend play. *See* Dramatic play
Problem solving
arts and, 163
dramatic play and, 173
Process skills for social studies, 93
Project approach. *See* Studies and projects
Props. *See* Dramatic props; Materials and equipment
Puzzles. *See* Toys and games

Q

Questioning. *See* Interacting with children; Open-ended questions

R

Reading aloud and visual arts, 165
Recycling, 101, 111–116
Reduce, Reuse, Recycle study, 111–116
Relationships in classroom, 27
Research. *See* Theory and research
Respect for cultural differences. *See* Culture
Responding to children. *See* Interacting with children; Observing and responding to children
Rest time
arts and, 225
science and technology and, 90
social studies and, 159
Retelling stories, props for, 174
Rules
for cooperation and fairness, 97
for technology, 27

S

Sand and water play
arts and, 208–210
books for, 62, 138, 209
interacting with children, 63, 138–139, 209
materials for, 62, 138, 208
observing and responding to children in, 64, 139, 210
science and, 61–64
social studies and, 137–139
technology and, 61–64
Scheduling. *See* Daily schedule
Science, 2–91
block play and, 46–49
components of, 5
cooking and, 67–70
Discovery area and, 38–41
Earth and environment. *See* Earth and the environment
interest areas and, 37
library and, 57–61
life science. *See* Life science
materials and equipment for, 7, 12
music and movement and, 64–67
objectives, 4, 80
observing and responding to children, 8, 12–13, 15–16
outdoor play and, 74–77, 89–90
physical science. *See* Physical science
program planning. *See* Science programs
research on, 4, 6, 11, 14
sand and water play and, 61–64
teacher's role in, 3, 5, 7, 11–12, 15
technology and, 71–73
tips for families, 9, 13, 16
toys and games and, 42–46
visual arts and, 54–57
Science programs, 78–91
daily schedule for, 84–91
environment for, 82–84
objectives for, 80
overview, 79
planning considerations, 81
Singing, 167–168. *See also* Music and movement
Site visits, 97
Sleep. *See* Rest time
Small groups
arts for, 223
science and technology for, 87
social studies for, 157
Snack time
arts and, 223
science and technology and, 88
social studies for, 157
Social–emotional development
dramatic play and, 173
library and, 119–122
objectives of, 80
social studies and, 93
visual arts and, 161, 162
Social studies, 92–159
block play and, 125–127
components of, 95
cooking and, 140–142
culture and, 93–94
daily schedule for, 155–159
Discovery area and, 131–134
dramatic play and, 93, 97, 128–131
environment for, 153–155
geography and spaces. *See* Geography and spaces
interest areas and, 119
music and movement and, 145–148
objectives, 80, 94
observing and responding to children, 98, 102, 106, 109
outdoor play and, 148–151, 158
people and environment. *See* People and the environment
people and how they live. *See* People and how they live
people and the past. *See* People and the past
process skills and, 93
program planning, 152–159
research on, 96, 100, 104, 108
sand and water play and, 137–139
social–emotional development and, 93
teacher's role in, 97, 101, 105, 108–109
technology and, 143–145
tips for families, 99, 103, 107, 110
toys and games and, 122–125
visual arts and, 134–137
Sociodramatic play. *See* Dramatic play
Songs, 167–168. *See also* Music and movement
Spaces. *See* Geography and spaces
Speaking skills. *See* Language development
Special needs children. *See* Advanced learners; Children with disabilities
Start of day. *See* Arrival; Daily schedule
Storage of technology tools, 21
Storybooks. *See* Books
Story retelling, props for, 174
Story time. *See* Library
Structure for day. *See* Daily schedule
Studies and projects
for advanced learners, 35, 116, 182
arts (study of music making), 177–182
for children with disabilities, 34, 115, 182
for English-language learners, 33, 115, 181
inclusion of all children in, 33–35, 115–116
social studies (Reduce, Reuse, Recycle study), 111–116
technology (study of simple machines), 29–35

T

Tablets. *See* Technology
Teacher–family relationships. *See* Family partnerships
Teacher's role
- dance, 170
- dramatic play, 174–175
- interacting with children. *See* Interacting with children
- music and movement, 167–168
- observing. *See* Observing and responding to children
- science, 3, 5, 7, 11–12, 15
- social studies, 97, 101, 105, 108–109
- technology, 18, 21, 27
- tools and equipment, 24
- visual arts, 164–165

Technology, 2–91
- arts and, 203–205
- awareness of. *See* Awareness of technology
- basic operations and concepts. *See* Technology operations and concepts
- block play and, 46–49
- classroom space for, 82–84
- components of, 5
- cooking and, 67–70
- Discovery area and, 38–41
- interacting with children, 144, 204
- interest areas and, 37
- library and, 57–61
- materials, 23–25, 71, 143, 204
- music and movement and, 64–67
- objectives, 4, 80
- observing and responding to children, 18–19, 25, 27–28, 73, 145, 205
- outdoor play and, 74–77, 89–90
- people and. *See* People and technology
- program planning. *See* Technology programs
- research on, 17, 20, 26
- rules for, 27
- sand and water play and, 61–64
- science and, 71–73
- social studies and, 143–145
- standards for, 3
- storage and handling procedures, 21
- study of simple machines, 29–35
- teacher's role in, 18, 21, 27
- terminology for, 21
- tips for families, 19, 22, 28
- toys and games and, 42–46
- visual arts and, 54–57

Technology operations and concepts
- observing and responding to children, 22
- research on, 20
- teacher's role, 21
- tips for families, 22

Technology programs, 78–91
- daily schedule for, 84–91
- environment for, 82–84
- objectives for, 80
- overview, 79
- planning considerations, 81

Theory and research
- dance, 169
- dramatic play, 174
- music and movement, 167
- science, 4, 6, 11, 14
- social studies, 96, 100, 104, 108
- technology, 17, 20, 26
- tools and equipment, 23
- visual arts, 164

Thinking. *See* Cognitive development
Time concepts, 105
Time during day. *See* Daily schedule
Tips for families
- dance, 172
- dramatic play, 176
- music and movement, 168
- science, 9, 13, 16
- social studies, 99, 103, 107, 110
- technology, 19, 22, 28
- tools and equipment, 25
- visual arts, 166

Tools. *See* Materials and equipment
Toys and games
- arts and, 195–197
- books for, 44, 123, 196
- interacting with children, 44–45, 124, 196–197
- materials for, 43, 123, 195
- observing and responding to children, 46, 125, 197
- science and, 42–46
- social studies and, 122–125
- technology and, 42–46

Transition times
- arts and, 224
- science and technology and, 89
- social studies for, 158

Typing, 24

U

Utensils. *See* Materials and equipment

V

Videoclips of children's play, 18
Vision impairment. *See* Children with disabilities
Visual arts
- benefits of, 163
- block play and, 202
- books for, 55, 135, 165
- cognitive development and, 161, 162
- cooking and, 200
- Discovery area and, 194
- dramatic play and, 191, 205–207
- interacting with children, 56–57, 136
- language development and, 161, 162
- library and, 188
- materials for, 55, 135, 164
- music and movement and, 191, 212
- observing and responding to children, 57, 137, 165
- outdoor activities and, 215
- physical development and, 161
- research on, 164
- sand and water play and, 209
- science and, 54–57
- social–emotional development and, 161, 162
- social studies and, 134–137
- teacher's role, 164–165
- technology and, 54–57, 204
- tips for families, 166
- toys and games for, 197

W

Water play. *See* Sand and water play
Weather, classroom discussions of, 15
Words. *See* Literacy skills
Work time. *See* Choice time